In Babel's

Shadow

In Babel's Shadow

Multilingual Literatures, Monolingual States

Brian Lennon

UNIVERSITY OF MINNESOTA PRESS

MINNEAPOLIS • LONDON

Passages from the Introduction and chapter 5 appeared in modified form in "The Antinomy of Multilingual U.S. Literature," *Comparative American Studies 6*, no. 3 (September 2008). A portion of chapter 3 was published as "Two Novels by Arno Schmidt," *The Iowa Review* 29, no. 1 (Spring 1999).

Selections of quotations in chapter 2 are reprinted from William N. Locke and A. Donald Booth, *Machine Translation of Languages: Fourteen Essays* (Cambridge, Mass.: MIT Press, 1955); reprinted courtesy of MIT Press.

Published by the University of Minnesota Press
111 Third Avenue South, Suite 290
Minneapolis, MN 55401-2520
http://www.upress.umn.edu

Library of Congress Cataloging-in-Publication Data
Lennon, Brian.
    In Babel's shadow : multilingual literatures, monolingual states / Brian Lennon.
        p.   cm.
    Includes bibliographical references and index.
    ISBN 978-0-8166-6501-3 (hc : alk. paper) — ISBN 978-0-8166-6502-0
(pb : alk. paper)
    1. American literature—20th century—History and criticism—Theory, etc.
2. Multilingualism and literature. 3. Literature publishing—United States. I. Title.
    PS225.L46 2010
    809.'.9334—dc22

                                                              2009016600

Printed in the United States of America on acid-free paper

The University of Minnesota is an equal-opportunity educator and employer.

17 16 15 14 13 12 11 10   10 9 8 7 6 5 4 3 2 1

Nergis'e . . .

Contents

Preface

This book is not an archivally or forensically exhaustive study of its research object, multilingual literature. Rather, it is a critical essay on that object's conditions of possibility—an approach I believe is requested by its *liminal* character. This declaration entails a consequence best recognized straightaway.

Following as it did precisely a decade of post–Cold War New Economic euphoria—a senescence that saw the decline of the bitter postmodernism debates and a new, broad consensus on globalization—September 2001, we can now say, was a moment of both material and symbolic trauma for United States–based literary humanists. Powerless to influence either the subsequent terms of public debate (such as it was) or the policy of the U.S. state they serve as educators, both liberal centrist and left-leaning humanists revived world-scaled discourses of interconnection in crisis, even conspiracy, that stood all along in the shadow of spontaneous and inevitable globalization. This anachronistically more sinister (and realistic) sense of contraction is, we could say, partly natural—as persons, intellectuals feel as literally vulnerable as anyone else—and partly performed, in conscious or not entirely conscious self-adjustment within the power grid of higher education on a war footing. For reasons at once beyond and not beyond suspicion, perhaps, literary humanism in the wake of what is called "9/11" was newly receptive to synoptic models of its domain, culture, as a world-system—models reactivating the scientism of both the structuralist literary criticism preceding what is in the United States now called "high" theory *and* the neo-Marxist cultural critique that through the twentieth century fought both structuralist formalism and its poststructuralist "textualist" phenomenalization.

There are two things to be said about this from the start. On the one hand, the return to system—if I am right to call it that—can be understood as a tactic (or reflection) of interdisciplinary competition: in this case, an opportunity for long-standing new historicist or resurgent neo-Marxist projects to ensure that antisystemic (poststructuralist) "high" theory in its pure form is (and remains), so to speak, "dead." On the other hand, it was surely, and equally, and classically an *extra*disciplinary effort to restore—or to project—the power of intellectual critique to intervene in the world (the world here, in a canonical and dubious distinction, meaning the world quite outside the academy). Without doubt, we can agree that the second gesture here is more salutary, both for the profession itself and for the world in which we would have liked it to intervene. Yet it is surely not beyond reproach to point to the mode of control invoked by and in both gestures, and to wonder if the reassertion of control, in a response to its loss, is the best or the only progressive mode of active mediation of the social by the intellectual class. Each of these two interwoven strands of discourse, I am saying, sounds a distinctive and distinctively wobbly note of resistance to, even paranoia about, what we might term aesthetic madness: conceived in the interdisciplinary arena as hyperintellectualized textualism divorced from the real world, and in that real world, at the social border of the institution itself, as the techno-theocratic unreason of a new global, perpetual war.

To the extent that this itself is nothing short of an imperial dilemma, to speak of what Paul Gilroy has called "postcolonial melancholia" as the ground of U.S. literary humanism today is of course *not* to assert the permeation of its faculties by anything so simple as recognition—of either the crisis or the maintenance of what we call "globalization." Rather, it is to speak of the object of aversion, in the sense that connotes movement and fixation at the very same time, and which throws into relief the operational history, within literary humanism, of Euro-Atlantic modernity's historic struggle with itself—a struggle by which much of this study, by habit if not desire, certainly remains enclosed. That such enclosure is not, in itself, to be taken as a fait accompli, as the systemist perspective demands, but rather as a mode of regeneration, does not release it from imperatives either categorical or motivated; but it does, I think, demand *thought.*

In the preface common to both the French and English editions of *Mélancolie et opposition: Les débuts du modernisme en France,* Ross Chambers reflects with some melancholy on the modes of opposition his book is likely to arouse in its implied readers.[1] Born in the seminar, not in the archive, *Mélancolie et opposition / The Writing of Melancholy* "can pass as a study in literary history," Chambers observes, "but it is not the work of a historian":[2] a feint suggesting a noncasual working difference between the process of scholarship and its product arrested at stages on life's way. The historian's work from which Chambers excuses himself, we can only assume—for he is apologetic, here, not polemical—is perhaps best imagined as a kind of antiquarianism, what Nietzsche called *Sammelwut,* or "collecting mania,"[3] than historiographic labor or historical understanding tout court: a distinction whose subtlety turns on the relationship of the historical understanding to the print materials of its transmission.[4] That relationship, of course, has a long and perhaps necessarily vexed history of its own, understood not as a positive object but as a limit or horizon that binds our thinking of history; Chambers invokes it—in confession, perhaps, as much as prescription—in an attempt to clear ethical space for contemporary criticism, in the consensually bureaucratic matrix in which it must live. To suppose in history, Chambers argues, a primary framework ("cadre") within which one situates, as secondary objects, works of literature produced in and by it, is to impoverish *each* space. Neither, by consequence, can—must—a literary work's historical context itself be taken as an object independent of, and therefore independently determining, the literary work. Historical context, Chambers suggests instead, is a "product of reading" ("effet de lecture")—enacted (banally) by a critical agent, yet just as proximately by the "self-situating devices" of literary texts themselves.

Taken at slant, this gambit implies a negative verdict on historiography as a *reflex,* rather than as a method for literary studies.[5] By implication, it is by making use of what Chambers calls the "critical genre of 'readings'" ("la 'lecture'") that one *reads* works of literature—whatever other genres and modes may be brought to manipulate them in other, justifiable or unjustifiable, ways. And as readers employing that genre, critics producing "readings" do certain things that historians do not or cannot always do. This is not without its sacrifices (though one may justifiably choose instead to think of the—equitable—division of intellectual labor): in critical readings, Chambers admits, "remarks of the most specific and pertinent nature are at times found side by side with generalizations that, for lack of elaboration, may appear tenuous."[6] But such structural dissonance is unavoidable, as well, insofar as readings are "meant to be suggestive and to serve as working hypotheses," and will unavoidably provoke discontent in a reader who feels that real work is yet to be done. The anxiety disclosed by Chambers's charming riposte—that such a reader "will have my full approval"[7]—is in fact quite close to the surface; and it is perhaps not without meaning, then, that in this same sentence Chambers moves from calling *Mélancolie et opposition / The Writing of Melancholy* "this book" (in the English) or "l'ouvrage" (in the French) to calling it "my essay" ("mon essai").

Of course, apologetics for what we might here call critical essayism—for a *literary*-critical mode of writing about literature, with compensatory stress placed on the first term—have both left and right versions (as well as their conflation, in Lukács's "left ethics with right epistemology").[8] Chambers invokes, without explicitly thematizing, a distinction between normative literary criticism and historiographic literary scholarship that is lost today in conversion to our abused productivity designator, "research"— a term of capitulation about which Heidegger, in his 1938 essay "Die Zeit des Weltbildes" ("The Age of the World Picture" or "The Time of the World Image"), already said everything that has to be said.[9] Reversing that conversion, Chambers's book (or his essay) is written not only "on" its topic, but also *through* it, exploring melancholy's mediation, and indeed also negation, of literary-critical cognition itself. This reflexivity is most vivid in the preface Chambers wrote for the English edition, reflecting on "the chain of writing" in "collective textuality"—an intimacy between critical writing and its literary objects—set in play in the original composition and publication of *Mélancolie et opposition* in French: an undertaking in which the privacy of a discrete language-world is linked to the primary productivity of literary composition.[10] One might recall, here, the distinction drawn by Elizabeth Bruss between criterial and evidential grounds for argument in the literary humanities, and her insight (or suggestion) that rather than merely documenting contemporary literature ex post facto, literary criticism might influence or even join its production— a consensual imbrication of investigation with its objects, Bruss notes, that does not broadly obtain in the working methods of the sciences, even when those methods presume such liaison.[11] Reading Chambers closely, one sees that the proximity forced by composition in French is itself a figure for "the lacunary, even arbitrary nature" of the seminar "manner of working" and its discontents, which include conflict between the demand for evidence and the demand for inspiration.[12] The anticipation of discipline at the hands of a reader unhappy at finding one of these criteria unaccompanied by the other is, we could say, one of the contradicting conditions of the genre of the preface itself, insofar as it requires one to precede, and to account for, what is always already, and fatally, done as one had to do it.

The largely unself-conscious, and so even more pernicious ways in which we scholars discipline each other, today, even as we row the lifeboat of inter- and transdisciplinarity into the next storm, reflect this struggle with the temporality of our own knowledge. As literary studies in the United States reverts to magical positivism, in a vulgar form of the historiography for which none of us are properly trained in the first place, one is tempted to see in the hand-wringing over its impending death a kind of vengeful satisfaction—the satisfaction one obtains in fantasizing one's own funeral, the shock of mortality freezing the strife of faculties in studious repose. Or that of the captain, perhaps, going down with his ship, in the cathartically pure heroism suppressed by a long life of administration. With disciplinary self-reflexivity impaired by proletarianization, aging of the managerial professoriate from the top, and the intellectual timidity of terrified job (and job security) seekers, the extorted reconciliations of a synoptic left historiography may be all that remind us, today, that literary studies might be or become something more than itself.

But if you are a good reader, you have already sensed that my book, too, will consist less of historiographic synopses than of essays *at* critical "readings," in what one might consider cross-sections of the contemporary moment—and that with Chambers, I am invested in literary works' own accounts of their contexts of production: contexts that are never strictly evidentiary.[13] In the frangible class of fungible objects with which I am concerned, here—literary works all but stillborn, and palpably haunted by what they are not and cannot be, in the object-universe of archival posterity—that account is principally, if not merely externally, oppositional: a stance against the matter of the book itself, as a vehicular container, the editorial custody of which imposes rules of circulation at some odds with the specific form of "literarity" it carries. Legible in such works' opposition to their own contexts of production, I will suggest, is an idiosyncratic, if entirely and unstartlingly inevitable commentary on the globalizing and globalist impulses of the new century. For the work of contemporary literature composed and printed in multiple, alternating national languages, *rather* than translated (however inventively) from one language into another, can be read—and can be understood to read itself—only monumentally, as a mark of the literary-historiographic print archive's limit *as* archive.[14] That archive expires, I will suggest, in the public or private discourse of immigrants, migrants, and exiles whose cosmopolitan multilingual experience, and actual use, of language (in code-switching behavior, for example), which, while indisputably bound by its own rules, can be neither represented nor expressed by the material apparatus of U.S. trade book publication and distribution—which marks, instead, the verge of what, in contemporary literature, it is possible to *write and have read* (in other words, to have published, and remarked and commented on, in books such as the one you hold in your hands).[15] In addition to posing the problem of such representation in its very structure, such a work often reflects on it volubly, generating a running discourse on form's intimacy with content and its inflection of posterity in the archive. It is that discourse, in its generation from a specific conjuncture, to which I have tried to tune my receiver.

My own sense of opposition, of course, comes with the required measure of critical distance, including the forms of hesitation documented in Chambers's self-study. And with good reason: I am far from an expert in reading capital (and I do respect my elders). Still, from a perspective attentive to the uninterruptedly sanctioned ignorance of academic literary humanists now as then, nothing seems more fundamentally innocent than post-1968 transavantgardist and other determinedly First Worldist left *and* centrist figurations of encirclement or enworlding, which, read for their covert or overt polemics, informed us that opposition was now simply enclosed.[16] If it is not decisive that the weight of this worldliness moves from left totality to liberal "globe," it is beyond question that I am as constrained by my own formation as anyone else. Working in a context very much bound by the resource allocations and modes of discipline in U.S. academic culture, I am aware that the implications of my argument here are bound by the nonpossible project of transnationalizing the study of imperial U.S. literature and culture—a topic I do take up explicitly in more than one place.

To take seriously, on the other hand, comparative literature's having "won its battles" in dissemination through the nationalized formation of U.S. literary studies is to acknowledge that the primary context for this book is in some ways a long-standing, in other ways a new (or newly vigorous) argument over what is "world" literature—and what was or is comparative, ever or anymore, in comparative literature.[17] We may as well call this argument "the world literature debates," situating it in the wake of other, related debates—the postmodernism debates of the 1970s to 1990s, the cosmopolitanism debates beginning in the 1980s—some of whose terms it might seem to have taken over.

Some of these positions emerge from recent exchanges in the journal *New Left Review,* as well as in books either born in or living an afterlife in that journal's pages, including Franco Moretti's *Graphs, Maps, Trees: Abstract Models for a Literary History,* Christopher Prendergast's collection *Debating World Literature,* and Pascale Casanova's *La république mondiale des lettres* in its North American travels.[18] Others may be found in the 2004 report of the American Comparative Literature Association entitled *Comparative Literature in an Age of Globalization* and in recent special issues of *Comparative Literature,* the journal of the American Comparative Literature Association, and *Comparative Literature Studies,* devoted to the topics "Death of a Discipline" and "Globalization and World Literature," respectively.[19] Influential recent monographs include David Damrosch's *What Is World Literature?,* Emily Apter's *The Translation Zone: A New Comparative Literature,* Rey Chow's *The Age of the World Target: Self-Referentiality in War, Theory, and Comparative Work,* Wai Chee Dimock's *Through Other*

Continents: American Literature across Deep Time, and Martin Puchner's *Poetry of the Revolution: Marx, Manifestos, and the Avant-Gardes,* among others.[20] One might also cite the continuing influence exerted by Gayatri Chakravorty Spivak's *Death of a Discipline* and *Imperatives to Re-Imagine the Planet*—toward or away from which a great deal of the work just mentioned explicitly or implicitly charts its course.[21]

One might say that positions in the world literature debates are attracted at changing distances, like iron filings around a magnet, to the antipodes of two mutually exclusive points of assertion. One is the idea that literature lives in *systems*—and where world literature is concerned, in a cultural world-system: a notion we might say is qualified heavily at times, and at other times hardly qualified at all. The other is the idea that literature is, or has, a way of life that might not always thrive in such a world-system. To the extent that "system" here refers to a complex, bounded unity, and implies our discovery, rather than creation, of its schema of organization, my own position, in this book, is the (latter) skeptical one. It's the position of someone who has always tried to practice and to produce literature, while simultaneously—or at least alternately—also analyzing and interpreting it. As a working writer of literature, as well as of literary criticism—wares with meaningfully distinct markets—I have gained a certain insight at first hand into the process by which specific systems of publication construct specific systems of literary history, and so *structure*—one might even say rig—the past for the scholar's research. It also seems to me that this structuring of literary history is not always and in every case (or even often) schematic or systematic: rather, it is in some ways quite literally mad, and as such, partly illegible.

I remain mindful, however, of one of Franco Moretti's macro-methodological points: that it remains easier, in the scholarly culture of the humanities, to demolish a working hypothesis than it is to propose one.[22] The emphasis on the generative and the collaborative, in the "scientific" method Moretti borrows for literary historiography, is one aspect of his project that appeals to me deeply, because it cuts against the competitive skeptical individualism of professional critique. We might return, in this context, to Chambers's invocation of the hypothetical and suggestive seminar manner, and to his self-consciously melancholic anticipation of what Stanley Cavell elsewhere called the Socratic reader, who only reacts to others' assertions, himself (the masculine pronoun is diagnostic) venturing none.[23] For at bottom, my own arguments here, too, are hypothetical, making a promise of conversation, not of the (first or) last word.

This book carries or implies, without necessarily propounding, three arguments. The first is that world literature is less a system, suggesting a set of relationships exposed by research, than it is a *scene*—a focus of new or renewed attention by writers, critics, scholars, and other professional readers—that *generates* such relationships as much as (or more than) it discovers them. In my view, this generative or creative quality of the culture industry is not necessarily and automatically complicit with ideological projects designed to camouflage economic predation in the name of globalization, as a polemic always ready to hand suggests. For it also functions as a counterforce against the positivism elevating research over writing in the production of humanistic knowledge, the creation of new objects continually rewritten as their discovery, in competitive, end-oriented regimes of institutional surveillance and quantification.

The second argument is that world literature is best defined by *antinomies*—insoluble, and precisely in their insolubility, *useful* paradoxes and problems. World literature, I will suggest, is not a body of works or a class of objects, but an act of and an encounter with worlding contradiction: of privacy by publicity, silence by speech, locality by globality (or transnationality, or transregionality); of poetry, the idiolectic refinement of discrete languages, by prose, their translative generalization; of "practice" by what "theory" stands for, when they stand (as they often do) under the signs of poetry and philosophy.

This mixed quality, and the contradiction it embodies, suggests that we might think of world literature, in something of a thickly descriptive and "pessoptimistically" affirmative sense, as *kitsch*. This is the third argument of this book. "Kitsch," here, signals not the exhaustive translatability or iterability of elements in an interconnected system—in other words, perfect transparency—but rather something like public nonrelation, in the partial opacity or illegibility of the kitsch object. In the visible–invisible kitsch of writing in multiple languages, I will suggest, we find figures for parallel—that is to say, multiple and simultaneous—national identity, a kind of globalism categorically inverted or virtualized. Among other places, I have found models for this antinomy in Juliana Spahr's antisyncretic readings of multilingual Pacific literatures, and in a Euro-Atlantic context, in Emily Apter's work on comparison and "nontranslation."[24] In the world literature debates, which so often turn on imputing progressive or regressive value to something we might call "literarity," kitsch itself embodies a highly productive *antinomy*, or constitutive obverse, of literature.

It may surprise some to read that this book has its origin in new media studies. Certainly, I have parted ways with the gadget lovers, in an area in which complacently energy-dependent boosterism, in the equation of what is new with what needs attention, is in some ways still a critical norm. Still, in formulating a *limit* for contemporary literary book publication, and so for the criticism dependent on it, I have tried to describe a need for electronic literature, as an archive and engine of forms of textual culture that book culture today really does block—from visibility, and in that, from both critical and archival presence. This has meant backing up from the "new" in new media, on the one hand, and stepping up to the end of printed books, on the other—working a fold in the disciplinary temporality of new media studies, at the very limit of the literary-capitalist print culture through which academic literary *and* new media studies still reproduce themselves, today. To negotiate, or, in academese, to "problematize" the very idea of a class of critical objects, rather than taking it for granted, is really nothing less than an ethical imperative (though the question of whether an imperative is a cause or a mood is an important one). Those who object to this as pointlessly self-conscious have, I venture, already killed something in themselves.

If this in turn means that the implied object of this book lies over its own horizon, and that what I have written is and is about something more than it seems—and that this itself is necessary, and unremarkable—that, in these ever-heady days, is just one way of saying that one way we scholars might save ourselves is by coming to know again, in our own work, the rhetoricity of discipline: to arrogate to ourselves, as an entitlement of *writing*, all the complexity of the cultural objects we seek and defend. Is it too much to say that this matters?

Acknowledgments

The transitional object you hold in your hands would not exist if not for the perspicacities of Susan Squier, N. Katherine Hayles, Douglas Armato, and Steven G. Kellman. To them, I owe my profoundest thanks.

Ursula Heise has been a sponsor, interlocutor, and friend from the start. David Damrosch pointed me to critical objects, suggested approaches, and furnished me with many hints and sparks, while acting as a general advocate. Bruce Robbins has been an ally and protagonist. Their support for this project—and indulgence of its fancy—has been extensive.

The responsibility for its infelicities is, of course, mine alone.

Djelal Kadir suggested a productive shift of mode, as well as some negotiations of my critical idiom. I despair of ever matching his erudition, but I hope I may relay his professional and personal generosity when my time comes. His and Juana Celia Djelal's hospitality (part of a general art of doing things right, and well) has been both a comfort to and a model for me.

Franz Peter Hugdahl provided more useful ideas, references, and clarifications than I can count. Ben Conisbee Baer, Nergis Ertürk, David Golumbia, Grant Farred, and Eric Hayot read and commented on versions of these essays, as did Rosalind Morris and Michael Golston at a much earlier stage. Alisa Braun, Linda Ivanits, and Aaron Rubin helped me with translation gags in languages out of my range.

I count myself lucky to have had the editorial and production staff of the University of Minnesota Press and its partners as my collaborators.

Doug Armato advocated for my manuscript with commitment. Laura Westlund, Daniel Ochsner, and Mike Stoffel (along with Neil West at BN Typographics West) supervised the book's final configuration, design, and production, in each case with both aptitude and economy. Sue Breckenridge copyedited it with respect for the deliberation of every phrase in my final draft. All along the way, Davu Seru and Danielle Kasprzak ensured fluent communications.

Among my many supportive current and former colleagues at Penn State, I owe special thanks to Robert Caserio, Robin Schulze, Mark Morrisson, and Carey Eckhardt, as well as to Susan Squier, Jeff Nealon, Janet Lyon, Michael Bérubé, Aldon Nielsen, Jonathan Eburne, Hester Blum, Jim West, Jane Juffer, Cheryl Glenn, Rachel Teukolsky, Xiaoye You, Tom Beebee, Eric Hayot, Paul Youngquist, Cecil Giscombe, and Julia Spicher Kasdorf.

Michael Lennon and Linda Cantagallo gave me my first books; Nejat and Feza Ertürk, the person I read them with, today. To *live work* together, in what is still never definitively alienated labor, is providential.

As for the many others, my life and conversation with whom marks this book more or less obliquely, they are too many—or too singular—to list here.

Where not otherwise noted, translations are my own.

In Babel's
Shadow

Introduction

Antinomies of Literature

Ich ekelte mich oft vor den Menschen, die fließend ihre Muttersprache sprachen. Sie machten den Eindruck, daß sie nichts anderes denken und spüren konnten als das, was ihre Sprache ihnen so schnell und bereitwillig anbietet.
[I was often disgusted by people who spoke their mother tongues fluently. They gave the impression that they couldn't think and feel anything but what their language so quickly and readily offered them.]

—YOKO TAWADA, "Das Fremde aus der Dose"

Translation is a victory and a threat, a necessity and a violation, a fundamental or given of all discourse and an intractable problem for it. Translation links such antipodes in a paradox animating our notions of what literature is and can be—and no less so in an age when literature seems less plainly relevant than ever.

This book took shape at a time when failures of understanding—at every level—seemed to loom everywhere; indeed, *did* loom everywhere (a situation that hasn't improved). Since then, among other effects that may or may not have been foreseen, the new direction of U.S. national political imperatives has revived support for foreign language learning as a component of human or cultural intelligence—in both the humanistic and the military strategic or technocratic senses of "intelligence."[1] Across the political spectrum, lack of competence in languages other than English is now acknowledged as a serious deficit of educational, economic, and military resources in the United States—though the conclusions drawn from this premise vary widely, both practically and politically. Against the background of realignments precipitated by the events of 2001, including

waves of performative nativism and contempt for humanism and the push-
back of demands for immigrants' rights, the struggle for a new plurilingual
American intelligence devolves on the politics of plurilingualism in everyday *and* literary life. Gloria Anzaldúa's challenge to North American Anglos
to "meet her halfway" in Spanish is, it seems, finally being taken seriously[2]—
at least to the extent that interregnal vogues for translation studies and
global English studies are being imperiled by a drive toward what we might
call "nontranslation studies" and a renewed emphasis (from both right and
left) on idiolectic incommensurability.[3]

   This book joins that shift in focus already underway. At the same time,
it attempts to reflect on this shift critically. One might say that in the critical study of contemporary literature, the plurilingual spirit of this new
emphasis collides with the monolingual letter of the publication industry
that produces books, our professional research objects. On the one hand,
the reimagination of comparative literature as emanating from Istanbul
rather than Marburg,[4] and of an "American literature" originally and anarchically multilingual,[5] reflects a premium placed on language acquisition
and its stakes in a contemporary critical politics of global culture. And
this is, straightforwardly, a displacement of value reflecting increased self-
consciousness about the cultural *and* linguistic Anglocentrism of professional literary-critical discourse itself.[6] On the other hand, the commercial
publication of books, dominated by transnational media conglomerates
with Anglophone resource bases and deep investments in export translation, works in various ways to undermine that interest.[7] In the production of research objects for scholars of contemporary literature, language
difference, the condition of multiple language acquisition, is displaced by
translative *representation* of language difference. To the extent that scholars
understand themselves as analysts of already given objects, regarding intervention in the *process* of literary production as beyond their practical or
desired ability, the premium placed here on language difference is, I will
suggest, insufficiently theorized.

New initiatives galvanized by "9/11" notwithstanding, we might say that
a great deal of critical discourse in both English/U.S. and comparative
literary studies in U.S. institutions retains marks—or bears scars—of the
apparently complacent era preceding the crisis of 2001. Flourishing in

an Anglophone gap, as it were, between the vanishing of the old Russian-speaking adversary and the emergence of a new, Arabic-speaking one—a gap defined by the euphoric rhetoric of global political, economic, and cultural interconnection—that discourse is marked by immense interest in translation and its operations and contexts. Even when, as in a great deal of work in literary studies, the routine complications, outright failures, and at times utter impossibility of translation are articles of common sense (or faith!), this immense industry of translation commentary is no less bound to the concept of the (translated) product: a perfectly natural thing, after all, for a discourse conducted in, and about, printed books.[8]

On the one hand, there is a genuine urgency to questions of translation today, in an era marked by the return (after an all too brief hiatus, perhaps) to narratives of both spontaneous and organized cultural incommensurability on a world scale. On the other hand, urgent questions do tend to flatten in the repetitions of discursive recirculation: a currency in which translation and its metaphorics appear almost virally affluent, since they are all (incipiently, at least) global in scale, squaring happily—too happily, perhaps—with the official story of globalization. It seems to me that the effects of that affluence are reproduced even at the minimal level of publication, where the texts that we ourselves produce, discoursing on it, are managed. And this is, then, a determination—or a fate—in which the composition, publication, and dissemination of literature, and the composition, publication, and dissemination of literary criticism itself find themselves nontrivially enmeshed, in a kind of print-cultural codependence that exerts on that criticism, in turn, a certain demand for recognition.

It is in trying to frame this book with that recognition that from the start, I want to emphasize two grounds of my work here. The first is that the typographic conventions of the authorial–editorial translation of foreign words, in books published in U.S. English today, are effects of editorial discipline keyed to that determination, and thus constructions of reader "markets" implied *in* that discipline by a very concretely stratified U.S.-Anglo-global publishing industry. As such, it is my argument here, they are important and substantively supplemental, rather than merely incidental features of the lives of the literary objects we call books. While the analytic power of the sociology of taste in the now broadly sedimented North American critical legacy of Pierre Bourdieu, for example, declines, in my view, as it becomes synoptic, a fundamental insight of the history and sociology of the book, as a material consumer product and archival object, is vitally important here. That is the idea that "writing a book"—more than the writing of a "text," which it is also—is an imagination, an anticipation, and a pursuit of publication in an imagined world, which serves as a line of demarcation for a literary work's composition and indeed, in its forms of life. This activity, in turn, comprises an array of micronegotiations of matters of social position and status, labor, work, career choice (or lack thereof), imaginations of time and value, and desire, in a matrix linking the formal question of style to that of content presented to reader–consumers who purchase books produced and marketed by brokering agents in pursuit of quantifiable profit and growth, who must serve (sometimes against their will) its minimal exclusive criteria for *publishability*.

To reorient ourselves around this (entirely banal) *limit* of contemporary literature-in-publication is, I will suggest, to restore a usefully nonfrivolous legibility to several ostensibly peripheral areas of writing and publication. One consists of such oft-discounted epiphenomena of book reading (titles, title pages, dedications, and epigraphs, for example, but also *choice and format of type and page layout*) as are catalogued by Gérard Genette under the rubric "le péritexte éditoriale."[9] Another is the relationship of the publisher's public "epitext," the marketing and promotional documents that support the book as a consumer product, to the *private* epitext—documents such as diaries, letters, and "avant-textes" preserving incomplete, unfinished, or otherwise nonpublished, nonvisible writing—that precede or follow publication.[10] Still another, of course, is that unpublished writing itself.

The second ground of my argument is that the work of literary critics and scholars who work with published books (of course, not all do!), and especially those who, as in my own fields—twentieth-century and contemporary North American and world literature—work with published works of contemporary literature, is bound to and by the book-publishing industry, an industry that has seen significant change since the 1990s, with new consequences for the material availability of contemporary and future literature. To the extent that editorial pressure to write nondifficult English prose,[11] for example, for a "general reader," shapes a seduction discourse of availability to reader–consumers,[12] I will suggest that it touches the question of incommensurability materialized on the page by literary plurilingual "code-switching." Among U.S. students—the last such non-specialized (if very much captive) readers, perhaps—undergraduate complaints about "difficult" reading in their de jure native tongue might be understood to be something of a piece with graduate student resistance to foreign-language requirements, itself reflecting the status quo of the conglomerated Anglophone publishing industry's excessive trade surplus. In U.S. university literature courses, the teaching mandate of availability necessarily overlaps with the teaching ideal of translatability, the availability of published books for purchase with the availability of the text to a collectively and contractually (if seldom actually and individually) monolingual readership. (We can hear this in the plaintive tone of many descriptions for cross-listed courses in U.S. comparative literature programs, for example, which promise that notwithstanding their languages of original publication, all texts will be available and discussed in English.) This collision of the effacement of language, in the teaching ideal of exhaustive and universal translatability, with the national language reality, so to speak, of the university (in the United States, at least), is the paradox of the institution in which many of us, in the readership for *this* book, do our work. It is also a key to the "white economy" (in Paul Mann's sense of that term) of critical debate over the existing and possible relations of aesthetics to politics—a debate that for so many of us, these days, at once sustains and frustrates that work.[13] In the end I suspect, following Derrida on this point, that the university can incorporate revolutionary ideological *content* more readily than it can bear serious challenge to national language and all the "juridico-political contracts" it guarantees.[14]

In this book, I attempt to develop an answer to one principally *disciplinary,* and as such, obtusely impractical question. That question, put deliberately nonliterally, is this: Why do we speak of, or in, translation when we might also, or *instead,* speak of, or in, multiple languages? That is to ask: in an "increasingly globalized" world,[15] in which both overprivileged and underprivileged individual monolingual and plurilingual speakers of different languages come into closer and more frequent public and private discursive contact—a contact the reflection of which the professional study of culture prides itself on detecting in the emergent—do the production, the study, and the reproduction of the study of literature remain procedurally *translatively* monolingual?[16] Immense intellectual industry is focused today on translation, its problems, its contexts, and its theories: a perfectly fine and natural thing, after all, in such an increasingly economically and culturally globalized world. The increasing importance of translation, in that increasingly globalized world, would seem to demand, or at least to legitimate, translation's elevation to the status of a discipline in itself. In the territories of Anglo-American literary studies, the transformation of Translation Studies from a secondary *practice* akin to "creative writing" into a primary scholarly discipline was achieved through "a rediscovery of the work of the Russian Formalist Circle," as Susan Bassnett put it in her foundational *Translation Studies* (1980), and its embrace of literature as an object of rigorously pseudo-scientific study.[17] Among other things—a point on which Bassnett is quite clear—this means the competitive disciplinary reimagination of the difference of Benjamin Lee Whorf's "language-worlds" in terms of modelable systemic or polysystemic difference, difference that is always already "really" relation.[18] Whorf as "strong determinist" is integrated in this way into a science of culture that rewrites incommensurability as contact, just as Roman Jakobson's fundamentally taxonomic approach to poetic language integrates it into literary science as an eccentric category of (non)translation called "transposition."[19]

My intention here is not to disvalue ground-breaking work by Bassnett, André Lefevere, and other major figures foundational to the discipline of Translation Studies, work from which I have learned a great deal[20]—but merely to remind my reader that Translation Studies conceived itself initially, at least, and in Lefevere's and Bassnett's own earliest modes of advocacy, as a semiotic discipline. Until the work of Lawrence Venuti turned Anglo-American Translation Studies in a new direction, it appeared little interested in the insights produced by poststructuralist critiques of structuralism's problematic scientism, its reincorporation of difference into relation, and the coding model of translation that accompanied the taxonomy of systems. In my own view, this was a significant loss. Among other things, in transforming translation from a secondary (re)writing practice into a primary scholarly discipline, Translation Studies erased precisely the theoretical advantage of that practice: its deixis with respect to theories of literary theory itself as something other than (or in addition to, or more than) descriptive science.

This doubling down on discipline is a mode of bureaucratic leverage with benefits, and costs, that are plain. One legacy of Translation Studies understood as (poly)system science is a model of translation-as-process-as-product, with the first conjunction, "translation as process," more or less fatally underwritten by the second. Where it operates in translation studies today, this model is manifest in focus on the activity or process of translation as means, or on the product of translation as end—for example, in self-sustaining debate of the translatability and untranslatability of literary language and/or (or and thus) cultural difference, where translation as a center of reference, be it positive or negative, goes unquestioned. Thus taken for granted, translation serves to generate metaphors for perpetual motion and transfer—between languages, cultures, and particular forms of knowledge—easily conflated with globalization as the play of free or autonomous, nonsocial or inhuman market forces. Alternately, it generates metaphors for stasis, immobility, and resistance to those forces that in no way question the primacy of their structures of representation.

This complicity of critique in sustaining what it seeks to destroy (or conserving what it wishes to reform) should force us to examine more closely the role that institutionally driven careerism plays in publication, and how the disciplinary strictures of professional academic life, in an effect that none of us can ever fully escape, essentially *coerce* innovation. Again, my intention here is not to disvalue anything in the work of scholars in my own or in related fields of interest, in whose steps this book can after all, and at best, only follow. Yet it is through the practice of writing that we scholars *create* new subgenres (of literature, as of literary and cultural theory) and establish new fields to contain them, writing up our creations in a scientized idiom of discovery. My own view is that methodological self-reflexivity on this issue should be nonnegotiable for any of us, and that its integration into critical methodology can only strengthen its method, in ways that the conventional institutional gloss of that term still merely hints at.

Globalization, as Djelal Kadir reminds us in just such a self-reflexive gesture, is not a phenomenon, but an act, with an agent—an act of "worlding" or circumscription, of tracing a circle that includes *and* excludes.[21] Plainly, then, scholars, to the extent that they function as agents and not merely subjects of globalization, are agents of this circumscription as well.

Or, to put it somewhat less bleakly, which is to point to what can be done: when scholars understand themselves strictly as (at worst) collectors or (at best) analysts of empirically presumed objects, rejecting intervention in literary production itself as beyond their professional range—or failing to imagine it in the first place—the distinction between the *existing* or *emergent* and the *possible*—between the past and present and the future— goes missing.[22]

Globalization, to put it plainly, is not only, or not always, a form of translation, which is always and everywhere *systemic*, a figure of difference in (always already given) relation. Rather, it is a happy or unhappy figure for that which escapes understanding—flows, simultaneities, networks, deterritorialization, annihilations of the space and time of representation—and so also, even often, a mode of incommensurability, of the incommensurable difference of languages, cultures, and forms of knowledge. Though as Timothy Brennan argues (and as I follow his argument here, in the essay composing chapter 4), we can, and indeed *must* understand this incommensurability in terms of collision—that is to say as contact, not as complete autonomy—I think it is worth differentiating weak from strong contact, including the strong contact of Brennan's own model of secular "conversion." That distinction might be understood to turn on the mercantilized computational concept of "optimization" I discuss in the essay composing chapter 2, and to enable us meaningfully to distinguish *language acquisition as a practice* from translation as (only) one of its practical applications. It is this, we might say, that gives us the difference between speaking of, or in, translation, when we might also, or instead, speak of, or in, multiple languages.

Plurilingualism in Translation

Book publishing in the United States today can be divided into three distinct sectors: trade publishing, based for the most part in New York City and integrated during the 1990s into multinational media conglomerates; scholarly publishing, consisting mainly of domestic university presses (few of which are as strongly supported as they once were by their host institutions); and "independent" publishing, encompassing everything from high-visibility regional publishers competing with the trades but not yet integrated into the New York system (Graywolf Press in Minnesota, for example) to very small presses tied to specific regional or local literary, intellectual, political, or independent scholarly communities. For almost anyone working in, working for, or working with publishing (which is to say anyone who produces books), and for any reasonably discerning reader, the distinction between trade publishing, on the one hand, and scholarly and independent publishing, on the other, is plain.[23] In most cases, it is a distinction between radically different levels of (and levels of access to) economic resources, and thus of particular "classes"—admittedly an abusive term here—of literary writers marked by specific dispositions of time and work: sometimes, and most plainly, those who can hope to earn a living from writing alone versus those who cannot. This distinction also marks a point of transition in an individual literary or academic writer's career, with the jump to trade publishing (which either reflects or produces, depending on how one sees it, a broader readership) serving as a symbolic form of upward mobility.

Virtually all books published for distribution in the United States by U.S. trade publishers are published in English, for a readership that by market mandate is presumed monolingual in English.[24] But as the work of Lawrence Venuti, among others, has consistently emphasized, a large portion of the market for books published in the United States is extranational: that is to say, a market for books published in translation *from* English.[25] Regarded as a market, this "global" literary readership—a presumed monolingual Anglophone readership at home, plus a presumed monolingual non-Anglophone readership abroad—represents two sources of pressure for editorial standardization: one directed toward readability for the largest possible Anglophone home readership, and the other toward translatability for the largest possible multinational readership abroad.[26] In books published in the United States, words and phrases in languages other than English are obstacles, therefore, not only for the monolingual Anglophone reader, but also for the translator, whose principal task is resolving the source English into the target language of a foreign market. What we might call strong plurilingualism—the interpolation into English of significant quantities of a language or languages other than English—is today found exclusively in books published by "independent" publishing houses not oriented in this way to translation.

One consequence of this is that editorial conventions for managing foreign languages can best be observed in an emerging canon of contemporary

U.S. multiethnic literary memoir and fiction published by the trade division of the publishing industry (a development discussed in the essays
composing chapters 4 and 5). And here we can see something of the functional paradox at work in contemporary notions of transnational literature:
a paradox for which I prefer the term *antinomy,* to emphasize the constitutive or permanent character of contradiction at the *ground of publication
itself* over its research character as an object of interest in an always already
given field. For the narratives of language acquisition and bi- or plurilingual experience of which so many such multiethnic U.S. literary works
consist must make frequent reference, from within the original English
in which they are published—this, after all, is the story they tell—to a non-
English language or languages: to the language(s) the story they tell has
taken them *from.* And yet to "speak" in that language or languages—to
interpolate it in significant quantities into their original English—would
be to violate the market mandate of transmission, including transmission
as foreign (re)translation. This is where the editorial apparatus of a trade
publisher exerts itself visibly, and where academic criticism and scholarship of contemporary literature—often and oddly less perceptive, on this
issue, than some book criticism in the popular media—can find itself circumscribed: "worlded."[27]

We might say there are three main conventions for managing languages
other than English in U.S. trade-published books. First, they are *contained*—
confined to single words, phrases, or brief exchanges of spoken dialogue,
as touches of cultural verisimilitude (or its simulation) that "season" the
text ever so lightly with the foreign without dulling its domestic flavor.
Second, they are tagged (by convention, with italic type) to mark them as
voiced (as breaks in a continuum of subvocalized prose) and to mark them
as "foreign" language. Third, they are translated—usually in direct apposition, as in "The Mexican said *Hola,* or hello." Languages other than English
are administered, so to speak, in an ethnographic or pedagogic mode pre-
suming the lowest common denominator, Anglophone monolingualism.[28]

Notwithstanding, however, the plurilingual intercultural initiatives of
the Common European Framework for Language Learning and Teaching
and the presence in its midst of a constitutionally plurilingual nation-state
(Switzerland), such domesticating conventions can be observed in literature published in continental Western Europe, too—even (or especially)

in a work widely celebrated for its mixture of languages (such as Turkish German author Emine Sevgi Özdamar's *Mutterzunge,* discussed in the essay composing chapter 5). This, then—and here is the broader frame of my argument—is hardly an effect of Anglophone (or Anglophile) cultural barbarism, as some might see it. Rather, it is a structural function of the *nationalized languages of book publishing* generally. The national and international book publication of literature requires, indeed *enforces,* national linguistic standardization. Furthermore: it is in no way upset by moderate challenge to the national standard (in the low-/high-culture erudition of dialect mimicry, appropriation of argot or specialized jargon, and so on). Such challenge, often enough, is recoded as innovation—hybridization or syncretism of the national language—and thus serves to reassert the standard while expanding its flexibility and powers of incorporation as a *literary* standard.[29] What the nationalized languages of book publishing cannot tolerate, on the other hand—and where the line dividing trade from scholarly and independent presses is drawn—is departure from the national standard: moving inward, in one direction, toward idiolectic private or invented language, and outward in the other, toward extranational, public plurilingualism.

To clarify this distinction, I want now to contrast two examples of plurilingualism in literature, or more to the point, of *plurilingualism in translation,* the antinomy for which I will subsequently attempt to define some use. One example, we might say, dramatizes the either/or of bilingualism in the United States; the other, what we might call the "all but" of plurilingualism in continental Europe.

"No publisher in his right mind"

The first comes from Ilan Stavans's "language memoir" *On Borrowed Words: A Memoir of Language.* Published in the original English by Viking in 2001, this narrative traces its narrator's crossing from Mexico (and Spanish) to the United States (and English) by way of Israel (and both Yiddish and Hebrew). In a scene in the book's last chapter, a coda, Stavans's narrator is sharing breakfast with Richard Rodriguez, the author of *Hunger of Memory,* another English language memoir of plurilingualism, while the two discuss writing, identity, and language in their lives and work. "What does the switch from one language to another really entail?" asks "Rodriguez" at one point, referring to the narrator's four primary languages. Here is the narrator's answer (partly, as you will see, reported in direct quotation, and partly narrated):

> "My English-language persona is the one that superimposes itself on all previous others. In it are the seeds of Yiddish and Hebrew, but mostly Spanish." I invoke the Yiddish translation of Shakespeare's *King Lear*, which, in its title page, read *"fartunkeld und farveserd"*—translated and improved. . . . "You know, sometimes I have the feeling I'm not one but two, three, four people. Is there an *original* person? An essence? I'm not altogether sure, for without language I am nobody. Language makes us able to fit into a context. And what is there to be found in the interstices between contexts? Not silence, Richard—oh, no. Something far less compelling: pure kitsch."[30]

Within this sentence, a phrase in Yiddish, "fartunkeld und farveserd," is "translated" by an appositive in English, "translated and improved," in apparent obedience to the editorial conventions I described above. Though it violates these conventions at times, *On Borrowed Words* for the most part follows them, minimizing the quantity of Spanish and Yiddish inserted into the English text, invariably italicizing it, and frequently translating it (accurately), as in this typical example: "Until my mother said, *'Shoyn genug,'* enough is enough, *ya es suficiente.*"[31] In the sentence invoking a Yiddish translation of *Lear*, however, the English appositive is a paratranslation, encoding a tropism or a solecism that must remain opaque to the reader with no knowledge of Yiddish.[32] Here the editorial convention is used against itself, as it were, its very resistance to the act of imagination forced to demand it.

On Borrowed Words is a fascinating text in part for this doubling, which at once submits to the artifactual monolingualism demanded of it as a (trade) *book*—though not without analyzing that submission at some length—and subverts it with a "secret" resistance splitting its readership, as here. An early chapter, "México Lindo," works through the contrast between books as objects, or as commodities *containing* writing, and books as texts, or sites of writing's dissemination. One form of the narrator's self-conscious experience of books, he tells us, consists (naturally enough) of reading them; the other—which at times seems more urgent, or is more absorbing—of collecting, transporting, packing or unpacking, arranging, or (in a scene of the anxiety of influence, focused on Borges) destroying them. The conflict between these two modes of interaction with books, which turns on the narrator's reading of Walter Benjamin's essay "Ich packe meine Bibliothek aus" ("Unpacking My Library"),[33] is a conflict between private and public forms of experience—the distinction between which the literary capital of New York, when the narrator finally arrives there, totally obscures. Abandoning the "portable home" of his library, the narrator immerses himself in the city's quotidian—for which he then finds only analogies for *reading* suffice (New York, for example, is a "huge book" of "multilingual poetry"[34]). In this city, people read books in public: a habit producing memories of privately imagined (read) experience anchored to public and vividly real space. To collect books without reading them is, as Benjamin hinted, to return them to the radical privacy of writing as lived time—that is to say, as an index to mortality. This subversion of exchange finds its analogue in reading books in public (in the hypostasized public of the city), where it reintroduces privacy into the public sphere. Against this more radical confusion, the narrator concludes, the "local color" of literary detail—the tourist's (or nationalist's) emblematic camel, as signifier for authentic cultural difference—can never be anything more than *representation*.[35]

As memoir, *On Borrowed Words* is in fact the story of a second memoir represented within it—a private or "countermemoir" composed by Bobbe Bela, the narrator's grandmother, when she learns that he plans to write a memoir as such (a memoir for publication: by more or less clear implication, *On Borrowed Words* itself). Not least in the illegibility of its representation within another text, *this* memoir also confuses the distinction between public and private writing. Though "private" (not intended for publication), Bobbe Bela's countermemoir is, like *On Borrowed Words*, composed in an acquired, rather than in a native language (here, Spanish rather than Yiddish), in purposeful manipulation of the registers of symbolic power and the boundary dividing the domestic from the public sphere. This publicity within privacy, addressing itself to the narrator—and, through him, to his readership as a published author—forces him to the question of plurilingual verisimilitude, within which there lies a kind of abyss. To publish a memoir, the narrator reflects, is to transform oneself into a fictional character: here, a monoglot. "Shouldn't *[On Borrowed Words]* be written in at least three or four languages? . . . But no publisher in his right mind would endorse such an endeavor."[36]

This "memoir of language" cannot capture the silent and private art of a divided, multiple, plurilingual self; it can only express it, in vulgar and public form, as kitsch. In the interstices of multiple language-worlds, we find not the sacred poetic autonomy of literariness, but the collective and prosaic equivalence of plurilingualism *in translation*. The specularity of the breakfast scene with "Richard Rodriguez" itself—its reanimation of two author-functions in a species of allegorical dialogue, as between talking heads or figurines—seems a conscious forcing of generic bad taste over the high-metafictional mode of the narrator's Oedipal father, Borges. Though finally, *On Borrowed Words* is a concession to the publisher "in his right mind" (meaning, motivated by profit) rather than a serious challenge to what that sanity represents, the narrator's choice of kitsch over silence here is significant—and meaningfully counterweights that concession.

Rodriguez's own *Hunger of Memory,* by contrast, famously constructed public plurilingualism (understood as both the presumption and the goal of bilingual education policies) as "sentimentality"—a key term of derision for the failure or refusal to recognize the border marking the domestic sphere of family (and the private language of home, with its hierarchies of tradition and authority) and the public sphere of school (and the leveling language of modern democratic citizenship). In its resistance to the "middle-class pastoral" of 1980s identarian multiculturalism, *Hunger of Memory* shares with *On Borrowed Words* a fascination with the "public privacy" of writing and its defacements: just as the writer writes not to give others "voice," but to distinguish (and obscure) himself against them, the political representation of "cultural rights" is designed to deny the ethnic immigrant access to power, by enclosing her in her own cultural idiom. If, all things considered, and for all its intellectual ferocity, *Hunger of Memory* remains unpersuasive (and now clearly mistaken) on one point,[37] it is in regarding the realpolitik of English as the public language of the United States *now and in future* (if that were the case, the U.S. Senate would not have felt the need again to exercise, as it did most recently in March 2008, a national language resolution).[38] Here, the kitsch excess of the gaps between Stavans's narrator's language-worlds is the object, not the subject

of instruction—a distinction that *Hunger of Memory*'s subtitle, *The Education of Richard Rodriguez,* signals clearly. Cloaked in respect for cultural
rights, the pastoral sentimentality that Rodriguez diagnoses (entirely correctly) as a convenient way of denying the immigrant citizenship finds perfect expression in the weak plurilingualism of political figures like New
York City mayor Michael R. Bloomberg and President George W. Bush,
addressing in public the "Latino vote"—yet witness how quickly Bush's
debatable Spanish proficiency turned controversial during the massive
immigrants' rights marches of 2006, and had to be denied by the voice
of the White House: one indication that "speaking Spanish in public" is
not the innocence Rodriguez's narrator makes it out to be.[39] Rodriguez's
narrative's antinomian "scholarship boy," at the same time a good student
and a bad student, serves to instruct us in the conflict between private and
public authority; yet the gaze of the silent, "alien" Mexican laborers, in
the scene where he acts as their Spanish–English interpreter,[40] is nothing
if not an exteriorization of that conflict, in a way that fundamentally under-
cuts the narrator's central argument: that intimacy is not a function of
language, which is rooted (or takes root) and cannot be exchanged, but a
function of "community," which can.[41] The ethnic confusion that engulfs
the family—the mother's "inexplicably" Irish surname, the siblings' in-
consistency of complexion, the identifications way off the mark that, the
narrator says, "people" keep making[42]—serves less to illustrate the narrator's point, which is that anyone willing to distinguish civic from ethnic
life has already, in a sense, become a U.S. American, than to point to the
language (rooted or no) through which they can exist *as* a communal
group at all.

"JUST VITAL MYSTERIES LOST"

My second example of plurilingualism in translation comes from Swiss
British writer–scholar Christine Brooke-Rose's 1968 novel *Between*, published by Carcanet Press in Manchester, United Kingdom (and like many
of the author's books, intermittently out of print).[43] Unlike *On Borrowed
Words* (and *Hunger of Memory*), *Between* follows few of the standard editorial conventions for writing in multiple languages; in fact, it goes well out of
its way to resist them. In the following passage, the narrator, a simultaneous interpreter working the academic and diplomatic circuits of postwar

Europe, is having her hair dressed during a stay in Istanbul. Glancing at a
shop sign lettered in the Arabo-Persian alphabet abandoned by the Turkish republic in 1928, the narrator asks the Turkish hairdresser in English:
"What does that mean?" The ensuing exchange, which turns on the in-
comprehensibility of the sign to *both* parties, alternates between or mixes
English, French, Turkish, and German:[44]

> Madame? Up there. Ah. Arabe. Je ne sais pas madame. Just vital mysteries
> lost, euphemized into proverbs for the day. I wouldn't mind if they'd got
> stuck in the eighteenth century or the seventeenth but the nineteenth ugh.
> Ça va comme ça madame? Oui, merci, teşekkür ederim. Lutfen madame.
> Allaha ısmarladık. Güle güle! So go the thankyous the goodbyes the welgo-
> home in the smattering of the mouthpiece at twentynine or fortyfive even
> and the baby-face stares out of lather under the letters Müjde! . . . Hayranım.
> Turkish ladies surely. Hayranım lutfen. Hayranım. Er—la toilette s'il vous
> plaît. . . . Merci. Tuvalet. ERKEK. KADIN. Of course KADIN. Ka-dın ka-dın
> ka-dın. Not hayranım which looked up in the pocket-dictionary says haylaz
> *faul,* hayli *viel,* hayran *verwundert* where when and to whose heart did one
> do that?[45]

Written in English, with digression in German and French and dialogue in Italian, the pages of *Between* are liberally seasoned with words or
phrasing in Bulgarian, Czech, Danish, Dutch, Greek, Polish, Portuguese,
Provençal, Romanian, Serbo-Croatian,[46] Slovene, Spanish, and Turkish, in
a field of interlinguistic vertigo lending itself readily to established critical
models of postmodern, postmediated experience. Claire Kramsch has
written recently, for example, of the novel's "echoic, circular style, where
voices mesh and float into one another without any particular attribution or sense of ownership," raising "the crucial question of the identity
and loyalty of the multilingual protagonist."[47] As this assessment (along
with the quotation I offer above) more or less correctly suggests, many
of *Between*'s pages are radically plurilingual, seeming in some ways to
demand reading fluency in, at the very least, three primary languages. And
indeed, a great deal of the aggressively metonymic (national) language play
of Brooke-Rose's text would be lost on an Anglophone reader, say, with no
or little usable reading knowledge of French and German.

It is important, however, to qualify this assessment, for a close consideration of the text of *Between* as a *book* demonstrates that such triple fluency is not truly required. To start with, a significant majority of *Between
is* written in English—enough of it, in any case, to console a monolingual
Anglophone reader of sufficient negative capability. Secondly, and perhaps more significantly for any such claim: the pseudoequality of English,
German, and French forms a core to which other languages are clearly
peripheral. Literally emanating from the north and west of Europe, this
plurilingualism is also *virtuosic*—a display of the traditional literary comparatist's most traditionally mastered skill.

This is not to reject Kramsch's reading of the novel, which is sensitive
elsewhere to precisely this nuance. It is, however, to remind us that, as I
show in a closer reading of *Between* in the essay composing chapter 2, *no*
published text (thus, no *book*) can fail to declare *some* "particular attribution," however complexly qualified or refracted. It is important, as well, not
to understate the essential volatility of compliance with editorial convention, or to overstate the case for disobedience. Still, it is worth noting the
very robust challenge posed by *Between,* published in 1968, to the conflation of reader with consumer now routine in the era of corporate media
conglomeration—as well as its raising of the bar for pragmatism in language politics as in book publishing. The difference between *Between* and
On Borrowed Words is, we might say, a difference of imagination with
respect to the "publisher in his right mind," and to the reader's relationship
with that publisher. If, as might be argued on any number of grounds, this
difference cannot be definitive, neither then, it seems to me, can it be made
entirely negligible. It seems to me that we can trace a critical fissure here in
the paradigm forming around what Kramsch, following Alice Kaplan, and
followed by others, calls the "language learning" or "language" memoir: a
new genre of twentieth century (and especially contemporary) autobiography, as examples of which both Stavans's memoir and Brooke-Rose's
essayistic novel have been identified.[48]

To mark this fissure, this book proposes a distinction between "strong"
and "weak" plurilingualism in published literature. This is not, I want to be
clear, the *qualitative* distinction it may seem. Rather, in order to set aside
the unresolvable debate over subversion in "devolved" or decolonized

English, this is strictly and necessarily a quantitative distinction keyed to the economic and material limits of contemporary print (book) media, in two principal ways. First, because the appositive or *serial* translation of foreign words in a text literally doubles them—when performed in obedience to the editorial conventions discussed above, a redundancy designed to contain the foreign language by matching and subordinating it to its English equivalents. Second, because the less such redundancy—the more a literary work's plurilingualism becomes effectively *parallel*, rather than serial—the more compacted a *text*'s potential circulation as a *book* (as Stavans's narrator's "publisher in his right mind" always already knows).[49]

This distinction has a certain limited use. Let me stress its limits. I am not primarily concerned, in *In Babel's Shadow: Multilingual Literatures, Monolingual States*, with plurilingualism in the practice of everyday life, or in the civic life of officially plurilingual nation-states. Neither am I concerned with plurilingualism in literature predating the formation of nation-states, national languages, and markets for book products written in, or translated into, national languages. Nor, finally, is multinational plurilingualism, as I discuss it here, to be conflated with the vernacular origin or the vernacularization of national languages. My concern in this book, rather, is primarily with literature *as* and *in* print, and in the book publication, in national and international book markets, of writing in multiple national languages.

This book also proposes a distinction between the idea of a literary "system" and that of a literary *scene*. The paradox of strong plurilingualism—of a literary work so *public* it vanishes—says something, I think, about the optics within which we construct research fields. Functionally speaking, literature in a world-system, as figured in the work of Franco Moretti, or a "world structure," in the work of Pascale Casanova, equates literature with *publication*.[50] The virtue of such models, I want to be clear, is considerable: not least in their honorable commitment to what Moretti, following Margaret Cohen, calls the "great unread" of extant, that is, *surviving* literature. Among other options, this permits us escape from the revolving binary of incorporation and resistance, of "inside" and "outside," within which a position can be maintained only through exhaustingly unrelenting surveillance. But the vice of such models, I will suggest here, lies in their attachment to the optic of the field: a failure to distinguish, or a lack of interest in distinguishing, *writing* literature from getting it published. *Everyone is inside* in what Casanova, naturalizing market competition, calls—though perhaps with irony—"the long and merciless war of literature."[51]

While such models are useful, in other words, in the contexts to which those who offer them tend to confine them—that is to say, in the literary *past*—they do not help us to imagine *potential* literature, whose publication is undecided. This matters to those of us who specialize, as I do, in *contemporary* literature and literary culture. Every new trend we signal with the buzzword "emergent," we might say, is conditioned by the not yet or the never-to-be published—and indeed, by the *unpublishable,* that invisible shadow on the scene of literature. A *scene* is only what happens, at any given moment, to be *seen.*

Christopher Prendergast saw this early on when, reviewing Casanova's work following its original publication in French, he complained that in the new world republic of literature she imagines, literature seldom gets credit for being anything but a printed book—that is to say, a historically extant material object.[52] The problem for the literary *present,* as Prendergast signaled clearly in his criticism, is that publication archives a winners' history of what is today sharply accelerating exclusivity. I will set aside, for the moment, the scholarly industry of research and recovery that this generates and justifies, since I am not myself a historian by training. I will venture the obvious point, however, that our imagination of the future is often limited by our knowledge of the past, and that by structuring literary history, models of world literature for the present exclude unfielded, unrecorded emergence: an exteriority that Immanuel Wallerstein, from whom the world-system model is adopted, readily grants to annihilated "antisystemic movements," and by which he means principally antistatist movements suppressed by their statist analogues.[53] As Wai Chee Dimock puts it in a recent attempt to address this problem without abandoning the project entirely: "[T]he literary field is still incomplete, its kinship network only partly actualized, with many new members still to be added."[54]

To think literature as circulation is to think it as *scene:* as publication, that necessary step onto (or into) a scene. But to think literature as scene, to "see" it in the optic of circulation, is also to imagine, to form an image of, literature that isn't yet there. There is a space here, I am saying, for nonrelation. Not the private nonrelation of avant-garde autonomy, moving from idiom to nonsense to silence, seeking escape from appropriation. Rather, a *public* nonrelation: something like kitsch, as Stavans's narrator suggests.[55] By the same token, the problem here is not to account for, or to apostrophize, diamantine nodes of the local; the problem, rather, is how to think strong plurilingualism *within* our models of the world, the globe, the planet. Strong plurilingualism, strong as it is, is not "babble," but plurilingualism in translation, plurilingualism in a public sphere.

In Babel's Shadow

The narrator of Yoko Tawada's story-essay "Das Fremde aus der Dose" is a Japanese migrant to Hamburg who, although able to read and to speak German, enjoys the company of people who cannot yet read or speak that language—young children, tourists, migrant workers—and especially enjoys the company of those who "choose," as she puts it, not to learn to read and write.[56] Her illiterate friend Sascha, met by chance at a bus stop, seems to the narrator to accept "jede Art Unlesbarkeit" ("every form of unreadability"): this is why, presumably, she never asks the narrator the "othering" questions that curious Germans ask, questions that displace and irritate the narrator in their request for native information, in forms both distancing and assimilating: "Stimmt es, daß die Japaner . . . ?" and "Ist es in Japan auch so, daß . . . ?"

Tawada, who writes in, publishes in, and is translated from both German and Japanese, is, like others in her position in Germany and elsewhere in the Euro-Atlantic global literary metropolis,[57] acutely aware of the tokenism lurking in her reception as a "migrant writer," of the desire to assimilate the foreign that coexists with genuine native curiosity, of the privilege that makes *her* an acceptable Other, and of the economics of book publishing, which preserves only a tiny fraction of textual culture in the form of literature, but whose transnational and translational dynamics also require "canned" foreign literature, literature "aus der Dose." The narrator of "Das Fremde aus der Dose" valorizes neither her own cultural hybridization—for this serves mainly to position her as a representative of Japan on a German public stage—nor the cultural purity of illiteracy as "alternative," to be embraced in symbolic rebellion by those already possessing its privilege. She prizes her friendship with someone who chooses not to read her, who is uninterested in reading her, who is comfortable with a face that is not also a text—or a book. Her own position as a nonnative speaker of German makes her profoundly, physically wary of fluency in *any* language, of the exclusionary exuberance of monolingualism, its inherent self-celebration; her emphasis, we might say, is on fluency as a kind of ethical weakness, rather than on nonfluency as ethical strength.

Tawada's narrator's rejection of fluency, which refuses to positivize *non-fluency*, is something of an analogue for my working method in this book. One of my premises here is that the literary avant-garde marks the sensible limit of literary studies as such (that is, insofar as it does not become something else), and so, in a way, its defining historical problem. This is not, however, to say that I accept the law of enclosure that makes of the avant-garde's historicity its permanent obsolescence.[58] For the problem with that history is that the agonistic drive of the avant-garde, its hostility toward (which coexists with a desire for) distinction, itself ensures that part of that history cannot be retrieved, that it is gone forever—not ahistorical in the sense that it was not lived, in particular lives lived at particular times, but ahistorical in the sense that history as what is preserved, what remains visible in the recorded and the researched past, excludes it. The agon of the avant-garde dramatizes the *circumscription* of literary research, faced with the unrecorded passing of so much (indeed, most) life, in a world most of which has perhaps never yet been—and may not want to become—literarily modern. So that while the avant-garde is, as Casanova puts it, "la seule histoire réele de la littérature,"[59] providing the resistance illuminating literary authority and tradition in its historicity, it is by its very nature a history of secession, of disappearance and self-erasure from that history, as schematized by literary authority—and thus a discontinuous history, a history riven with gaps. It is not the autonomy of art of which we scholars speak when we speak of the avant-garde, but the discursive assertion of that autonomy, in a critical argument that cannot be won (or lost), since it stands on the unverifiable. The *actual* autonomy of art is its radical privacy, its nonpublication, which makes it invisible, unknowable—the conditions of possibility of which Paul Mann has analyzed in his brilliant, and brilliantly tortured, *The Theory-Death of the Avant-Garde*.[60] While this autonomy is not, I think, impossible or unreal in the lived present, it seems crucial to recognize the fundamental understanding driving Mann's *book*, as a material embodiment of his critical thought. This is that the actual autonomy of art is unavailable to scholarship, and that in undertaking scholarship one has already, in a sense, made one's choice.

It is the choice that avant-garde discourse marks as "mainstream," or in the vocabulary of rock-and-roll purism, "selling out"—crude terms, perhaps, but not for that reason meaningless ones, for the compromises of professional specialization in an institution dedicated to research and conservation. The avant-garde, this book presumes, is not historical in the sense that it is dead, over, impossible; it is historical, rather, in the sense that its history is all that the scholar can *see* (and precisely, of course, what the avant-garde itself often *cannot* see). What avant-gardists call "the underground," that subsurface range from which one at once wants, and does not want, to be dug out—and through which one may speak of a "ground" by positioning oneself beneath it—captures the paradoxical codependence of literary language and translation. Translation is an antinomy of literature, which cannot "live" at all without translation—yet cannot live entirely *in* it, either. What we call literature lives, if it lives at all, only in Babel's shadow.

Translucinación

Both foreign language learners and translating machines founder on idiom, that crucial integrant of native-level fluency. In a way, this book had its start in that insight. In U.S. literary culture, at least, the space of the avant-garde has been claimed for a long time, now, by a gradually homogenizing advocacy network for the postmodernist countertradition of what was once called the New American Poetry (and its historically diverse descendants). By the time I began the composition of these essays, the preoccupation with manipulations of English syntax and register in the autocriticism of such U.S. poetic avant-gardes, with which I had had a brief but fruitful set of associations, had come to seem to me more and more *idiolectic:* radically modernist in its reversal of transcendence from the signified onto the signifier, and so paradoxically if not unexpectedly logocentrist, deeply enmeshed in a writing practice whose most sophisticated terms all but excluded nonnative speakers of English, reliant as it was for its effects on violations of culturally specific language registers (which have to be recognized in the first place, in order for their violation to be recognized). In this First Worldist insurgent universe, poets and poet-critics mobilized the vanguardism of "material language" against a domestic opponent (Anglophone lyric formalism) in an intrasystemic and autotelic conflict that, for all its symbolic cosmopolitanism, struck me finally as insistently and somewhat insidiously ethnocentrist, an intellectual counterculture every bit as dedicated to its own visibility as its enemies. This is to say that if both demotic and technical language are to be understood, as such critical projects wish it to be, as literary foreign elements in a native (national) language culture of everyday communication, it nevertheless follows that literary English, even (or perhaps especially) avant-garde experimental literary or self-consciously antiliterary English, *belongs* to English, is less a stranger to English, than French or Turkish or Japanese (or most any subnational language), for example, is or ever can be. David Damrosch has analyzed the paradox by which *Finnegans Wake,* by any right a stupendous example of cultural and linguistic cosmopolitanism, becomes a national or regional curiosity in its resistance to translation, to amplified circulation—while *Dubliners,* on the face of it far less ambitious in its range of reference, "gains" in translation, and so opens itself to amplification as world literature.[61] Building on this insight, and inflecting it, one of my most general ambitions in this book—again, an ambition that is carried or implied, rather than fulfilled—is to put the contemporary legacies of both Joycean "fascicular" Anglophone literary modernism *and* its denigrated or valorized rival, the rhizomorphic Anglophone literary modernism of Gertrude Stein, to the test *of* world literature at its Euro-Atlantic limit.[62]

Let me give as a second example two editorial projects, one in the autocurating tradition of the avant-garde and focused on the present and the future, the other scholarly and looking to the past, using historical archives to challenge the founding myth of an Anglophone United States. Like Marc Shell and Werner Sollors's *The Multilingual Anthology of American Literature,* the tenth issue of *Chain,* an annual edited by U.S. poet-scholars Jena Osman and Juliana Spahr, mixes examples of plurilingual and monolingual literature written in languages other than English, by visitors to, exiles from, and onlookers to the United States, with commissioned English translations of each work.[63] In a gesture of which both teams of editors are fully cognizant, and that they recognize as problematic, the ambitiously elastic linguistic horizon of each project is simultaneously stretched and then snapped back, reconstituted. In both projects—one revising the monolingual foundations of the federal United States of America, the other recognizing and problematizing the monolingualism of Anglophone avant-garde syntactic radicalism—the editors' discomfort with what they are doing is clear. "Translucinación," Osman and Spahr write in their introduction, defining the neologism that gives the issue its title, "is . . . a cross-cultural encounter loaded with hope and yet always in danger of going wrong."[64] And Shell observes: "The editors of this multilingual anthology, with its pervasive 'English Plus,' facing-page, bilingual format, do not enter the fray in a political vacuum insofar as the very notion of common language is always fraught with political difficulty. . . . *The Multilingual Anthology of American Literature* attempts to recuperate forgotten American languages and literatures and to indicate how much remains to be done. At the same time, it inevitably recuperates the same movement toward 'anglicization' that led to the need for recuperation in the first place."[65] Of course, publication isn't publication without reading, and in the structurally monolingual literary culture of the United States, one makes the choice to write in English or else possibly not to write (or if writing, not to be read) at all. This is simple editorial (and social) convention, which none of us can ever fully escape. And yet each of these editorial projects paradoxically requires precisely the monolingualism that it has the potential, but never the full potency, to overturn, insofar as it must serve it in a way, in order to challenge it. This is not inconsequential, either. There are, and have been, alternatives—including *policies of nontranslation*.[66] And there are alternatives in authorship as well as in editorial policy, examples of which are suggested (though examples are perhaps ultimately of less than decisive utility) in the closing essay of this book.

Some *antinomies* of literature, then. Despite its inversion of avant-garde autonomy, strong plurilingual literature shares its material fate: publication only by smaller publishing houses, without the resources to publicize books or even to keep them in print. If those of us who seek out such works want to teach them, for example, we will face the problem of how to teach them only after we have faced the problem of obtaining them, which is also the problem of "seeing" them, of knowing they are out there at all. Strong plurilingualism, this book argues, presents the maddening figure of an avant-garde that eludes scholarship, not because it lives in a subculture that can, with sufficient industry, be disclosed—that is, in a secret idiom—but because it whirls in orbit out there, in a public space so public it escapes notice.

Literature is *published writing*—that's the first antinomy. In the words of Alice Kaplan, which serve as both subtext and super-text of the essay composing chapter 4, the "language memoir," a memoir of second- (or third- or fourth-) language acquisition, is the *Bildungsroman* of a *second* (or third, or fourth) self in language. And as Peter Cowley has observed, this marks the language memoir's interest in language learning, *rather* than, and in important contradistinction from, translation.[67] Yet in order to be published, to move from the process of life writing to the genre "language memoir," the memoirist must choose *one* language among her others. Unavoidably, literature is *plurilingualism in translation*—that's a second antinomy.

To the extent that such structural contradictions define a zone of "systemic" thought designed precisely to avoid confronting the present as a historical problem—and that indeed, makes of the very notion of "literariness" that problem's deflection—they certainly deserve opposition by a systemic thought radically open, by contrast, in its heuristic totality. But the extent to which both such models, in their application to the archives of textual culture, have always been forced to rely on extant literature whose both archival and canonical positivity in literary-critical and literary-historical disciplinary space is guaranteed in advance—and which is always already, and autocritically, a survivor of whatever opposition its author and its author's alienation have posed through and to it—might force us to pause, perhaps now more than ever, at a time when rival imperial formations are imagined at once as fragments of a "globe," translative analogues for each other, *and* as incommensurate alternate worlds. It is less pathognomic than epistemic, perhaps, that the most exotic interlude of Brooke-Rose's *Between* is set in Turkey, at the last conceivable border of a cosmopolitical Europe, where every other language used in this work more or less comfortably dwells. Approaching the Izmir Archaeological Museum, the bus carrying the narrator of Brooke-Rose's novel passes, over and over, a place called *Yavaş*. Or is it a road sign meaning *Slow*? Here, as elsewhere, in scenes of interpellation that fail because the subject is being hailed in the wrong language, translation, and its positional reconstitution of the narrator as a self *in* language, is meaningfully deferred. The opacity of Turkish is a running joke here, an othering, symbolically marking the border of Euro-Atlantic modernity, beyond which its community of imperial *and* subjugated languages breaks down. At the same time, in marking that border, it recognizes what lies beyond it as distant, differential, and real, and it is more in these small gestures of *deferring* translation, perhaps, than in its larger modal shifts that *Between* looks (and asks us to look) elsewhere. That substitutive, insufficient, and "masocritically" vulnerable gesture is also, and certainly fatally, this book's own.[68]

1

Language as Capital

I'll give them back their English language. I'm not destroying it for good!
—JAMES JOYCE, qtd. in Max Eastman, *The Literary Mind:*
Its Place in an Age of Science

Bilingual, trilingual, multilingual, plurilingual, polyglot: these terms commonly indicate not only verbal facility in more than one distinct language, but a high degree of embodied or spontaneous social fluency, as well. When we use the terms "bilingual" or "plurilingual," or any of these other variations, we often mean to signal that two or more languages in some sense divide the person possessed of them, that she or he "thinks" or even (or consequently) "exists" in more than one *world* of language, and that the common distinction between native or mother tongue and foreign or acquired language is less strict, or less important than it might otherwise be. Plurilingual speakers are those who speak two or more distinct languages acquired through migration, displacement, education, travel, passive or active experiences of economic and/or cultural domination, or by birth into social settings marked by these dynamics; plurilingual societies are both composed by, and reproduce such speakers. Some nation-states are constitutionally plurilingual, in that they recognize more than one language (or even many distinct languages) as official languages of the state; others are constitutionally or federally monolingual, or de facto and structurally monolingual, despite sizable bilingual or plurilingual minority populations.[1]

In his work on language policy and global English, Alastair Pennycook has suggested that we think of the English language, and the plurilingualism (either native or as acquired) in which English is a component, as forms of cultural or nonmaterial (symbolic) capital, as Pierre Bourdieu defined it.[2] This critical gesture is useful for theorizing the language politics of the book market and of plurilingualism in published books, and I want to pause here, before I go any further, to consider its advantages and disadvantages.

For Pennycook, learning English is an "act of desire" for language as capital, understood as "embodied" in Bourdieu's sense, or accumulated through learning and integrated into a "habitus" that cannot be transmitted instantaneously, like money or property rights: "As Bourdieu suggests, the type of language, the particular accent and form are closely linked to questions of standardization and power. The standard language, or various forms of the standard language have always been linked to the maintenance of power and status, and indeed it is the teaching of a particular version of the standard language in schools that is one of the cornerstones of the transmission of cultural capital. Children who already have access to the standard come bestowed with cultural capital."[3]

With some of the modifications proposed by Pascale Casanova—expanding Bourdieu's concept of the "literary field" beyond the nation-state paradigm, and bringing it into contact with elements of world-system theory[4]—Bourdieu's analyses seem to provide a useful framework for understanding plurilingual literature in national and transnational book markets defined by official national languages and mediated by translation from and to the dominant standardized language of book publishing, English.[5] For nonnative speakers of English, in this schema, what is desired is native-level fluency in English, while native speakers of English desire (less urgently, perhaps, and with more overt temporization) fluency in languages *other* than English. Language as capital can help, for example, to explain the premium placed on language *possession* (if not necessarily language *acquisition*) even in a transnational business culture apparently secure in its domination. We can see that plurilingualism is valued in U.S. business culture, for example, as both a real asset, useful in negotiation with speakers of other languages, and as a symbolic asset displaying powers of appropriation or waste with respect to foreign languages[6]—and that these functional and performative justifications are not always clearly distinguishable. As Leonard Forster noted in 1970:

These terms ["bilingual" and "polyglot"] turn out to be rather loose in application, and linguists, who have been devoting a good deal of attention to these problems in recent years, now have a rather different set of terms which is gradually coming into use among laymen too. This last became apparent to me when I saw in Montreal, a bilingual city which is very much aware of problems of sociolinguistics, an advertisement reading: "Make yourself bilingual, trilingual! Berlitz School." I do not think the Berlitz School would seriously suggest that anyone is likely to become bilingual in the traditionally accepted sense by its good offices alone.[7]

There are other gains to be had from understanding language as capital. As Pennycook observes, Bourdieu's model permits us release from abstract binary formations of opposition—high to low, or elite to popular culture—which stand or fall on what Bourdieu socialized as "distinction."[8] The dominance of U.S. English in the world today can be understood as a function of the power wielded by U.S. English as cultural capital, not by the natural genius, or any other genetic quality, of English (or one of its variants) as a language among others.[9] English is the language *happening* to possess powers of legitimation and consecration—a form of inherited wealth for native speakers, an object of desire for nonnative speakers, where English accreditation confers "institutionalized" cultural capital: a certificate guaranteeing access to power.

Other consequences depend from adopting Bourdieu's schema. It provides a rejoinder, for example, to euphoric figures of rhizomorphic or tactical proliferation or dissemination, which counter the understanding of power as a systemic integration of the "field" with antisystemic emphasis on an equally powerful heterogeneity always already established.[10] Though to be sure, we must be careful to resist the assumption that English is the same everywhere across space and time, in its European history as well as in its colonial, imperial, and post- or neocolonial histories—that there is, in other words, any *necessary* transnational connection between given speakers and writers of English—we should also acknowledge that celebrations of the impurity and heterogeneity of English have long served the rhetoric of Anglophone cultural imperialism itself. Emerson, to take an example from U.S. literary history, celebrated the English national character as "many-headed" and "many-nationed," writing that English "colonization . . .

annexes archipelagoes and continents, and their speech seems destined to be the universal language of men."[11] Variegation—the proliferation of difference—in Emerson's rhetoric, here, is not a quality of culture or language that subverts power, but on the contrary, one that intensifies it: "Everything English . . . is a fusion of distant and antagonistic elements. The language is mixed; the names of men are of different nations,—three languages, three or four nations."[12] Though in many of his writings Emerson demonstrates a strong desire to resist English cultural domination, he seems finally to decide it is irrepressible: "Those who resist it do not feel it or obey it less. The Russian in his snows is aiming to be English. The Turk and Chinese also are making awkward efforts to be English."[13] The singular variegation and incorporative powers of the English language justify a policy of *only* translation:

> I do not hesitate to read all the books I have named, and all good books, in translations. What is really best in any book is translatable,—any real insight or broad human sentiment. . . . The Italians have a fling at translators, *i traditori traduttori,* but I thank them. I rarely read any Latin, Greek, German, Italian, sometimes not a French book in the original, which I can procure in a good version. I like to be beholden to the great metropolitan English speech, the sea which receives tributaries from every region under heaven. I should as soon think of swimming across Charles River, when I wish to go to Boston, as of reading all my books in originals, when I have them rendered for me in my mother tongue.[14]

Well-situated literary writers and their brokers today enjoy a substantial transnational market for books written in or translated into a more or less standardized English, as well as a much larger market for books translated *from* a more or less standardized English. This transnational market links national markets for books in English in wealthy countries (in Western Europe as well as in North America, the United Kingdom, and Australia and New Zealand) to submarkets for books in English in other countries where English was introduced by colonialism, to submarkets for books in English in countries where English is a commonly learned second (or third, or fourth) language. This transnational market for books in English is supplemented by individual national markets for books translated *from*

English into other languages. Any work written in standard English, or capable of being translated into standard English, as well as works written in nonstandard Englishes that do not deviate *too greatly* from standard English (and do not incorporate languages *other* than English), can potentially gain access to this material distribution network.[15]

It is important not to overlook weaknesses in this model, which might be said to gloss too quickly over the substance of deviation. Lawrence Venuti has pointed to the paradoxical dependence of linguistic hegemony on the activity of translation—that is to say, on the activity of plurilingual agents or agencies. Insofar as any translator must, in the common sense, be at minimum bilingual, Venuti reasons, it follows that any ostensibly global language can only become and remain maximally worldly, as such, precisely through the plurilingualism of those who administer it: a plurilingualism that symbolically, at least, complicates its global hegemony. Venuti reads this in terms and frames adapted from the work of Deleuze and Guattari, as the "indigenization" or minoritization of global U.S. English. It is in its very dissemination (its imperial "success") that global U.S. English must submit to "local differentiation," in Venuti's words, in "the heterogeneity of a minor position."[16] In precisely its asymmetry and inequality, then—in precisely, that is to say, its exploitative and domesticating dynamics—translation offers the possibility of a translation ethics understood as respect for the "irreducible heterogeneity of linguistic and cultural situations."[17] Because it is fundamentally ethnocentric, translation "can never simply be communication between equals": it *demystifies,* rather than mystifying domination.

Is there anything unpersuasive in this position? Not necessarily. Still, while granting the immanent heterogeneity of a dominant language, we might notice that granting it still always affirms the decision to write in it—in Pennycook's terms, to desire language as capital. What Venuti's position tends to obscure, meanwhile, is a desire or entitlement *not* to write in the dominant language, *not* to desire its cultural capital, or to desire but not to obtain it. This, we might say, is where the systemic integration of the "field" and the antisystemic idiom of proliferation (or its "open" versus closed systems approach) converge in a common oversight. If the "field" *optic* does integrate existing or emergent variation, and thus forecloses on and obscures possible variation, we might say that the idiom of proliferation permits us too easily to conflate the immanent (vernacular) hybridity of a national language with the more radical difference, *in national book market terms,* between one national language and another. This is the conflation at work, we could say, in Forster's image of the gradient:

> We are in fact all of us more polyglot than we think. Any normally educated person uses his native tongue on a variety of different levels for different purposes. These levels should be conceived of as forming not steps but a rather irregularly inclined plane like the slope of a hill. They merge into one another, so gradually that we often do not realize which level we are operating on. The levels at or near the bottom, which we use for, perhaps, vulgar abuse, are so different from those near the top, which we use for solemn occasions or technical discussion, that they are practically different languages. . . . Inconsistency in maintaining stylistic levels makes a painful impression on the reader or hearer similar to that made by mistakes in gender or in the use of irregular verbs in a foreign language.[18]

Obviously, this cannot compare with the *incomprehension* of a foreign language, which is an experience (if it is total incomprehension) of the incommensurable, not of the inconsistent. To put it in Venuti's terms: in retrieving the translator from "invisibility"—in recognizing her powers of agency, here—we ought not, perhaps, to condemn *to* invisibility those who *decline* to be translated.

Devolution

On the one hand, native speakers of English living in structurally monolingual Anglophone nation-states, such as the United States and Australia, or in states united by Anglophone hegemony, such as the United Kingdom, are today the native speakers of a world language the monolingual indigenous base of which corresponds to recent historic centers of global economic and military power. Even if one foregoes the (mistaken) assumption that nonnative speakers learn English in order to "get to" the center, to interact with native speakers or to Westernize themselves generally,[19] the relative neutrality of Latin, for example, as a common language outliving the Roman imperium is still a long way off for English today. Monolingual native speakers of English are today the active or passive beneficiaries of

Anglo-American national cultural projects including a particular vision of a particular form of economic and cultural capitalism and a specific history of economic and cultural colonialism, imperialism and neocolonialism; even if, as some would argue, they are forgiven that coincidence by those who realize, wisely and well, that the English language is not intrinsically *anything,* to claim it is not to make it so, and it is an open question whether the claim serves precisely to naturalize an imbalance of power by declaring its analysis passé. Though there are more nonnative than native speakers of English in the world today (by some estimates, the ratio is as much as four to one), standardized instruction in English conforms to one of two models, Standard American English and Standard British English, and the United States and the United Kingdom compete with each other in the global market for instruction and instructional training in English as a Second Language (ESL) and English as a Foreign Language (EFL). The industry publishing books written in English, and reaping income from sales of translation rights for books written in English, is dominated by conglomerates whose operations are physically and financially secured in the United States and the United Kingdom. At the very least, the system that governs *the publication of literature* in English, the resources of which are concentrated disproportionately in native-speaking Anglophone countries, and in which nonnative writers in the language must be vetted by native speakers to gain access at all, is not so easy to subsume under claims for an already completely decentered "world English." Perhaps no one but a monolingual native speaker can write in English without calculating the advantages and disadvantages of publication in English, or without being aware of the actual geographic and geopolitical locations of transnational brokers who can make (or not make) that happen.

Thus as Robert Crawford reminds us in his study of marginal Scottish and U.S. Englishes, writing is always local, never inscription into a pure medium, and "crude, unitary" constructions of English lump Smollett, Carlyle, Eliot, and Joyce into "English literature," placing their non-Englishness under erasure. Yet writing is never *only* local; Babel, the proper name, becomes "confusion" as soon as it is uttered, or written, and if to write in a "minority" language is at one level already to be translated, then to write in English is to be translated again—to enter into the transnational circuit of English without being able to limit its appropriations or to refuse either the power *or* the disempowerment it confers. When he confronts this circuit—a loop including his own work here, along with that of his resistant research objects—Crawford pits writing itself against its theoretical double, deconstructive "translation":

> If post-structuralist thought deconstructs ideologies of authority, then, since it does this for *all* ideologies, its practical effect is often to maintain the status quo rather than to support any counter-movement. Often what small or vulnerable cultural groups need is not simply a deconstruction of rhetorics of authority, but a construction or reconstruction of a "usable past," an awareness of a cultural tradition which will allow them to preserve or develop a sense of their own distinctive identity, their constituting difference.[20]

Redressing this oversight, Crawford chooses to focus on "devolved" English, as an English always already stripped of its centralized power. Despite his particularizing rejection of Derrida and of poststructuralism more generally, however, Crawford is forced to extrude the historical or theoretical distinction between a category of "Gaelic" writing, for example (or a Scots moving away from, rather than into anglicization), and that of writing in such a "minoritized" English. Crawford's focus on *what can be published and read in English,* to the exclusion of what one would need (in varying depth, to be sure) other "languages" in order to read, is a self-limitation to what is visible, sensible, schematizable, and appropriable on behalf of an Anglophone reader—and so a "worlding" or division and circumscription of those "small or vulnerable cultural groups" on whose behalf he speaks. That Crawford feels the need to insist, again and again, that "Reading [Hugh MacDiarmid's] *A Drunk Man [Looks at the Thistle],* we should not forget that we are reading a Scottish text; just as reading *Ulysses* is an experience of Irish literature, and reading the *Cantos* and *The Waste Land* is a particularly American experience"[21] speaks to the leveling effect of a common language, and masks the *choice* made to write in (publishable) English. Crawford wants to see linguistic devolution—a word made to bear more weight than it should here, perhaps—where by his own admission, challenges to the status quo of one Anglophone center of power come mainly from another, rival center of power, in the form of mergers and acquisitions:

[T]here is a widespread wish in recent poetry to be seen as in some manner barbarian, as operating outside the boundaries of standard English and outside the identity that is seen as going with it. Such a wish unites post-colonial writers such as [Les] Murray and [Derek] Walcott with writers working within the "Anglo-Celtic archipelago." It joins the post-colonial and the provincial. Indeed, though the continuing strength of London metro-politan publishing houses and journals and of Anglocentric literary history may distort the picture, it is surely true that, for most creative users of the English language today, one of the fundamental questions is how to inhabit that language without sacrificing one's own distinctive, "barbarian" identity. . . . All these writers operate in a climate where the power of the English cultural center is under increasing challenge—not just from the rival center of New York, which is coming to dominate English publishing through the takeover of such houses as Chatto, Cape, the Bodley Head, and Hutchinson, but also from the "provinces" and barbarian regions, home of such innovative houses as Bloodaxe Books.[22]

That "continuing strength" distorts the *potential* picture of literature, to be sure, but not its present reality: what is obscured, here, is that what is published *is* "the picture." Literary scholars write by and large about books in print; what we notice—necessarily belatedly, since our pro-fession is to review, not to generate—as "increasing challenge" is often only the appearance on our own, attenuated horizon of a vanguard party already being hounded, in realms invisible to us, as an establishment unto itself.[23]

System and Scene

It would seem a mistake, on the other hand, to take any *system*—here, the systemic *image* of a "world" in publication—for the world itself. This is a risk inherent in the transposition of sociological world-system and "world structure" approaches into literary studies—despite the great value and the many nuances of influential recent work in this area by Franco Moretti and Pascale Casanova, for example. What these approaches share, one might say, is a tendency to subordinate to extant or "surviving" literature's patterns of circulation not merely its modes, but also its grounds or con-ditions of production.[24]

A basic assumption of world-system theorists such as Immanuel Wallerstein and Giovanni Arrighi (as well as for some of their critics in third-wave modernization theory, such as Anthony Giddens),[25] is that capitalism is inherently globalizing, establishing a world economy that exceeds the nation-state and reduces it to an entrepreneur operating competitively within that economy. Like Bourdieu's notions of "cultural capital" and the "field," the image of a unitary, yet dynamic world-system helps us imagine the nationalized languages of book publishing as a complete set of complexly interrelated markets. Within such a schema, the work of André Lefevere suggests, the language of the world-economy will presumably be that of its most successful "entrepreneur," in this sense; translation, in its commercial and military applications as much as its humanist practice, is unavoidably devoted at the same time to domesticating foreign languages *and* to what Lefevere called the "ideological projection" of an imperial language into foreign target cultures.[26]

When Casanova adapts features of world-system theory to describe the circulation of literature through a "république mondiale des lettres," the dominance of a world language (Latin, then French, then English) becomes central, since it sets the standard for *visibility* on the literary world scene. A literary work, in Casanova's republic of letters, adopts a stance toward translation, and thus toward its own possibilities for circulation, by modulating and configuring those factors according to perceived distributions of power in a system composed of cores and peripheral areas, or a matrix of structural relations linking the realm of the dominant to that of the dominated. In a world literary space defined by national literatures, then—Casanova's basic schema—writing in multiple languages can aim to maximize circulation, either through formal choices or choices of representation, or it can aim to minimize circulation, through formal choices aimed at blocking translation. This, too, is illuminating for any analysis of the international book market.

Literary historians such as Casanova stress the *temporality* of this relation between a cultural "core" and a cultural "periphery"—an important nuance that underscores the dynamism of the cultural world-system, reminding us that central and peripheral positions are positions in motion, not fixed elements. For Harald Weinrich, linguistic thresholds—the boundaries of national languages—become such temporal thresholds, as well, once we factor in the lived time it takes to acquire a second language, then again to write literature in it—as with what he calls "Chamisso authors."[27] Global English, for Weinrich, is a structure of class division in world literature:

> All writers who lack the good fortune of having grown up in a genuinely anglophone or a postcolonially anglophone land . . . will have a hard time with world literature. If, for instance, they have been driven from central or eastern Europe to Germany, they must come to terms with German as a "subglobal" language, which of course drastically curtails their prospects for entry into world literature . . . all non-anglophone authors pay this price, in the hard currency of lived time, for the label *world literature,* and so too do all Chamisso authors.[28]

And yet, while the linguistic cosmopolitanism of Weinrich's "Chamisso author" is a hardship on the one hand, clearly it is an opportunity on the other. As a product of globalization, the polyglot is an ambiguous figure in monolingual national cultures, exempt (for better or worse) from the responsibilities of national attachment and able to pass, happily or unhappily, for a native where she is not one. Social class, among other factors, determines whether a Chamisso author's mobility is voluntary or involuntary, voyeuristic travel or exilic migrancy, a cosmopolitanism "from above" or from below. Casanova suggests that a language's "literary capital" can be measured by the number of plurilingual speakers it has, cosmopolitans and polyglots linking languages of the periphery to a language at the center, in a floral figure:

> [O]n pourra mesurer la littérarité (la puissance, le prestige, le volume de capital linguistico-littéraire) d'une langue, non pas au nombre d'écrivains ou de lecteurs dans cette langue, mais au nombre de polyglottes littéraires (ou protagonistes de l'espace littéraire, éditeurs, intermédiares cosmopolites, découvreurs cultivés . . .) qui la pratiquent et au nombre de traducteurs littéraires . . . qui font circuler les textes depuis ou vers cette langue littéraire.[29]

> [I]t becomes possible to measure the literariness (the power, prestige, and volume of linguistic and literary capital) of a language, not in terms of the number of readers and writers it has, but in terms of the number of

cosmopolitan intermediaries—publishers, editors, critics, and especially translators—who assure the circulation of texts into the language or out of it.[30]

This figure describes a *structure*, Casanova argues, in which the objective relations of a literary "field" (in Bourdieu's sense of the term) can be reproduced outside the interconnected totality of positions implied by "system"—and which in breaking the flow of dissemination from core to periphery marks the violent struggle for domination that constitutes literary space.[31] Literary space is not a reflection of material conditions, then, but rather a circuit through which material conditions run—economic centers serving to *produce* beliefs about literary centrality, which then recreate and reinforce material conditions, neither wholly determined by, nor wholly determining them. While world-system theory can therefore be adapted to the specific conditions of literary study as a remedy for its myopias, it cannot itself account for the double existence of literary space, "once in things and once in thought."[32]

Casanova's refinement of her model, in response to the critical challenges of Christopher Prendergast and others, is effective. The "double life of literary space" does indeed allow us to avoid the reductions inherent in identifying *all* writing in the English language, for example, with acknowledged or unacknowledged capitulation to access conditions set by the material center of the English-language publishing industry—without either pretending that inequalities do not exist, or that gatekeepers do not *desire* to be resisted, precisely so they can re-market resistance as the pluralist dynamism and heterogeneity of the center. The idea that material conditions and beliefs about material conditions are interdependent and mutually constitutive, rather than unilaterally determining and determined, also allows us to conceive a role for literary criticism and scholarship as symbolic intervention in the complex of beliefs formed by, and forming, the commercial market for literature. That is, in fact, what research does—albeit often too late—when it retrieves writers whose literary productions were regarded as uninteresting and thus unworthy of publication.

Yet to invoke the power of imagination over material conditions in this way is to remind us that not all that is thought, or indeed, all that is *written*, is also *published.* The release provided by "structure" from the totality of "system" here is only partial: while it makes visible *more* of the resistance of the dominated (this is the wholly admirable political impulse in Casanova's work), it can only accomplish its goal through another, more comprehensive *structuration,* a broader or more expansive circumscription. Precisely in *structuring* that resistance and integrating it, this gesture only pushes "unfielded," invisible, or annihilated and unrecorded struggle further into the periphery—into the radical exteriority of Wallerstein's own "anti-systemic movements."[33]

The main article of Casanova's own "literary belief"—the one to which she herself most fully subscribes—is that fundamentally projective certainty of the vanguard, that new trends and movements *are* emerging, and that in emerging, they are automatically reconfiguring existing knowledge, in ways that require adjustment and—more to the point—demand it. This is precisely what drives the marketing of new writers, particularly writers from "new" (newly independent) countries, as well as the self-marketing of the criticism and scholarship of contemporary literature, where so much rests on one's ability to see over the horizon: to mark and remark new movements and trends, to report on what is "emerging." We could say that globalization studies itself, as a recently emerging scholarly "trend," displays this logic prominently. Introducing a special issue of *PMLA,* "Globalizing Literary Studies," Weinrich observed that contestation of "world English" is itself almost entirely *contained by* (conducted in) English:

> The contributions assembled in this issue of *PMLA* [119, no. 5, 2004] . . . argue—fairly, to be sure—for and against globalization, but it seems beyond question for all authors, both "hyperglobalists" and their opponents, that the entire discourse of globalization is to be conducted in English. One need only inspect the bibliographic references cited in the contributions to this collection. Of a total of 687 titles cited, seven are in Spanish, five in French, two in Italian, and one each in Russian and German. All the remaining 671 titles are cited in English, including . . . the Goethe quotation on world literature. Hence, even among authors who remain comparatively skeptical about globalization, multilingualism has been for all intents and purposes abolished, and English appears as the quintessential language of globality.[34]

To write in English means to expose oneself both to the transnational (English-based) book market and to the transnational (English-based) community of critics and scholars, who retranslate the work in English into various non-English language markets and specialized discursive communities in accordance with this logic of emergence. If the difficulty of distinguishing resistance to English from "capitulation" to English in writing in English means that broad generalizations are themselves little more than a basic component of this logic of emergence, it is nevertheless obvious that the "distinction" Casanova describes is available only in certain languages and not in others, whether an individual writer elects to use them—and to accrue their advantages—or not.

The task, then, may be neither to integrate world literature more tightly into a world-system, through strenuous qualifications or modifications of the systemic or structural relation itself, nor to sacrifice comparative relations entirely to a global destructuration always already and automatically in effect. In fact, if we wanted to turn Casanova's model against itself here, we might observe that the conflict between these two tropes—the statist and anarchist receptions, as it were, of literariness—is itself a structuring principle of literary criticism.

We can observe it, for example, in the introduction Anthony Burgess wrote for a 1970 reprint of G. V. Desani's successively celebrated, neglected, and revived (or reappropriated) plurilingual novel *All about H. Hatterr,* originally published in 1948. Openly sparring with F. W. Bateson, who wrote with condescending benevolence of the unique creative license enjoyed by "métèque" writers in English, Burgess (with his own form of condescending benevolence) celebrates linguistic mongrelization as the very ground of literature and literariness itself. Intrinsically, Burgess argues, the English language "is plastic, and as ready to yield to the *métèque* as to Mr. Bateson. Indeed, if we are to regard Poles and Irishmen as *métèques,* there are grounds for supposing that the *métèques* have done more for English in the twentieth century (meaning that they have shown what the language is capable of, or demonstrated what English is really *like*) than any of the pure-blooded men of letters who stick to the finer rules."[35] But look at that "the *métèques*" again. An English article combined with a French noun, typeset in italics to mark it as a word in a foreign language.

A hybrid collocation, the English article marking the plural form of the noun as English, though in another context it might be French (as in "Les métèques sont des étrangers habitant Athènes"). Why, then, is it italicized? For this is presumably just the sort of irreverent mixing that Burgess means to celebrate in his defense of "the *métèques*": a defense relocating them, as Casanova might see it, to the imperial center, in a paradoxically truer-to-English-than-the-English form of double fidelity. If Bateson appears to have used the French term "métèque" (where the English "metic" was just as available) disingenuously, to mystify the reference and distance himself from any straightforward pejorative, Burgess finesses the issue incompletely here, retaining the term in the orientalist mode of the foreign as *produced,* an object of desire that he knows better than to desire. We can read this in the complex double voicing of Burgess's belletristic style. "This term *métèque* is pejorative," he concludes after two short paragraphs in which the word appears five times, "like 'wop' or 'dago,' and I am happy now to drop it. It is especially unpleasant to use it in connection with a writer like G. V. Desani."[36]

"Wop" and "dago," here, are addressed to the reader in the United States, where Farrar, Straus and Giroux issued the 1970 edition of *All about H. Hatterr* and where the Nairobi-born Desani had just accepted a position at the University of Texas after periods spent in England and India during the 1930s, '40s, and '50s. The message, of course, is that Desani is so far from the invading unwashed as to have joined that elite of the greater Commonwealth, who can teach the English, once more, what it means to be English. Not to worry! Burgess tells his U.S. American, by way of his British, audience: "Desani came to England, in fact, to demonstrate in live speech the vitality of the British rhetorical tradition—brilliant in Burke and Macaulay, decadent in Churchill, now dead. . . . Desani had to be praised not as a dweller on a cultural fringe who did remarkably well when one considered his disadvantages, but as a man squarely set in the great linguistic mainstream."[37] Burgess wants his readers to know that the Joycean English of *Hatterr* is a purposeful contrivance, rather than a contingent effect, and that when Desani chose—as in *Hali,* his only other major work—he could write in grammatically perfect and idiomatic, if rarely "sober" English.[38]

But Burgess's real purpose in this brief essay is to retrieve *Hatterr* from the underground into which it descended by 1951, three years after its initial publication, and where it remained for the following nineteen years, an out-of-print cult classic. "Inexplicably," he writes, "unless the difficulty of classifying the book be a sufficient explanation . . . *All About H. Hatterr* went underground and became a coterie pleasure."[39] Burgess writes in the canonizing mode of the critic of taste, reviving an unjustly neglected unique modern classic for an audience with fresh eyes: an endeavor that valorizes both the obscurity of the author and the self-sacrificing perspicacity of the critic in drawing him out again. Tactically conflating "Language" with "English" here, Burgess counterposes the text's capaciously worldly idiom to the published book's failure to maintain more than a self-selecting audience. Desani's English, Burgess is careful to emphasize, is impure—but gloriously so. The pedantic condescension of a Bateson, which reasserts the privilege of the native speaker, refuses the clinamen or bounded deviation in language producing high literature: "It is what might be called Whole Language, in which philosophical terms, the colloquialisms of Calcutta and London, Shakespearian archaisms, bazaar whinings, quack spiels, references to the Hindu pantheon, the jargon of Indian litigation, and shrill babu irritability seethe together. It is not pure English; it is, like the English of Shakespeare, Joyce, and Kipling, gloriously impure."[40]

Shakespeare, Joyce, and Kipling (then Desani) are innovators in the English language, deliberate abusers of the cultural-linguistic conventions of their time, who through gradual recognition of their merits are naturalized into literary greatness. Variation here is the caretaking of English, that which exercises it, extending its range as it moves toward "whole" language.[41] It need not be merely irritable to point out that Burgess's well-intentioned critical gesture, of rescuing an underread author from oblivion, is also a way of assimilating Desani's novel's generic and linguistic variation, within the English language and within British literature, to precisely those places once again. For Burgess, Desani's novel is proof of the vitality, flexibility, and incorporative powers of English as both a language of literature and a language of global culture, and as such deserves restoration to that intranational and international circulation that can only take place in English.

Bemused irritation colors Burgess's conclusion, as he considers the implications of Desani's voluntary withdrawal from global literary circulation: "I mean that, having produced a masterpiece . . . he seemed content to give his time to journalism and to be tied down to a weekly *feuilleton* for one of the magazines of the *Times of India* group." The invocation of the *feuilleton*, in all its untranslatably specific cultural and generic positioning and its connotations of enlightened frivolity, is telling: again, we must have recourse to italicized French, so as best both to condemn and to affirm *Hatterr's* unbearable lightness. "But," Burgess concludes, resolving the issue by fiat in the act of willing audience into being, "it is the public that counts."

Twelve years later, with *All about H. Hatterr* out of print again, another British novelist revived G. V. Desani. In "The Empire Writes Back with a Vengeance," published in the *Times of London* on July 3, 1982, Salman Rushdie placed Desani at the head of a long line of decolonizers of English, from Flann O'Brien, Beckett, Joyce, Richard Wright, Ralph Ellison, James Baldwin, and Toni Morrison to Chinua Achebe, Ngũgĩ wa Thiong'o, Nadine Gordimer, André Brink, Derek Walcott, V. S. Naipaul, and R. K. Narayan. Where for the comparatively patrician Burgess Desani's obscurity represented a crisis of curatorial justice or legacy for British literature, for Rushdie it was a blind spot concealing a whole new politics of writing in English. Desani's "Whole Language" need not be justified as the syncretism always already intrinsic to English, even (or especially) that of the master signifier, Shakespeare: what it did, rather, was transvalue the idiom of the colonized, turning it against itself. "It was," Rushdie famously wrote of Desani's "authentically Indian voice," "the first great stroke of the decolonizing pen."[42]

For Rushdie, Desani's was a new internationalism possible only in English, the language of the Empire—over which the Empire, in its very "success" as such, can no longer maintain control.[43] H. Hatterr, the novel's protagonist (the "H" stands for Hindustaniwallah) is, in Burgess's words, "a grotesque autodidact who has built up a remarkable vocabulary with the aid of an English dictionary and a French and a Latin primer. His vernacular sounds like Higher Babu."[44] In truth, of course, as Rushdie makes clear, Hatterr is and knows more than that. Arguably, in Rushdie's way of reading it, the novel's English is "decolonized" twice: once, in the introduction of words and phrasing in languages other than English (Latin, Italian, French, Spanish, German, Dutch, Scottish, Welsh, Hungarian, Japanese,

Sanskrit, Hindi, Urdu, Kannada); again, perhaps, in mixing dialect and speech pattern, register, and slang from Cockney to Anglo-Indian and U.S. American (and including Shakespearean English and medical and legal jargon as well).

Intralinguistically, Hatterr makes use of what Braj Kachru calls "deviation simulating mistake," recreating Indian English variations (e.g., Burgess's "Higher Babu") commonly stigmatized as subcompetent (Indo-Anglian Babu English) or affected (Anglo-Indian Chee-Chee English).[45] *Inter*linguistically, meanwhile, he engages in complex and nested forms of code mixing. In this interlinguistic mode, *Hatterr* is virtuosic in Kachru's "loan shifts" and "lexis-bound translations"—especially, the literal translations of proper names and vernacular idiom.[46] It is this virtuosity, in fact, that calls into question some of the claims Rushdie makes *through* Desani. For we might say that the literal translation of vernacular idiom into English registers, in English, a cultural difference turning on forms of object combination or physiological tropism unfamiliar to the monolingual and monocultural Anglophone reader; its defamiliarizing (and/or comic) potential *depends* on that unfamiliarity.[47] This is translation as grotesque, a comic inversion of the hierarchy of cultural knowledge that is quickly domesticated and neutralized for the monolingual reader of English—whose own language is appealingly literarily deformed, becoming (entirely to its *own* credit) more capacious in the process. (This, perhaps, is why Burgess, invoking the great divide between mass culture and art, calls it *Higher* Babu.)

Another such "containing" device is the diminutive or primitivizing literal translation of proper names and the fabrication of grotesque proper names signifying extreme phonic difficulty from the standpoint of English: thus Sadanand, in *All about H. Hatterr,* is reduced to "Always-Happy" and Hiramanek to "Diamonds and Rubies," while we are treated to the comic-exotic unpronounceability of "Nighanteesrimahalingam" and "Anoopamsrimaharathanam Chety-Chety." If we look, furthermore, at the interpolation of words and phrases in languages other than English, a similar "containing" pattern emerges. Editions of *Hatterr* almost invariably italicize and appositively translate those interpolated words and phrases in South Asian languages (or the other languages of a demarcated hemispheric "East"). Hemispherically "Western" languages other than English, meanwhile, are treated somewhat less consistently; quite often, however, words in French, Spanish, Italian and German are let stand, without either the italics marking the word as foreign, or appositive translation. Thus we have "His entire revelation, apropos the mein kampf against my sex-mania, sounded like a super-horsepower De Quincey autobiographical!"[48] but "a *chhaya,* an evil shadow," "an *ojha,* an exorcist,"[49] "a *sanyasi,* a fakir,"[50] "*Jaldi!* Hurry!"[51] and "they were pukka (full, ripe)."[52] When they are not appositively translated into English, italicized words and phrases in South Asian languages are repeated at high frequency, in varying contexts, in the course of a passage spanning several pages, so that a reader unfamiliar with the language in question but willing to extrapolate from context is offered the chance. At times even hemispherically Western languages other than English are "domesticated" in this way, through translation by parallelism and interlinguistic puns that quite carefully privilege English: "After acknowledging my 'Good Evening' with a '*Boner Nochy!*' he thumped me on the back heartily."[53]

It is important to neither overread, or overlook the exceptions to, nor underread, or exaggerate the exceptions to, this pattern. There are South Asian language words and phrases in *Hatterr* that are italicized yet go untranslated—though some of these, such as *nirvana* (or *kismet*), have long since acquired a place in English. There are untranslated, half-italicized hybrid collocations. There are circuitous or ambiguous foreignizations, such as *todii,* presumably from the English "toddy" (itself from the Hindi *tāṛī*), and other disruptions of the conventions of italics, such as the lexically hybrid phrase "last sahana."[54] There are deliberate mistranslations: "Good, Sam," for "Nala, samy" (Kannada: "Nothing, sir"), "sugar" for the Sanskrit *sukarah* (hog).[55] And there are in all likelihood entirely invented words.

Yet in *Hatterr,* the interlinguistic leads insistently back to the intralinguistic, balancing the interpolation of foreign words and phrases, particularly in hemispherically "Eastern" languages, with a wealth of intricate attractions for the hemispherically "Western," and in particular the Anglophone ear. Hatterr tells us that his "autobiographical" is composed in "a language deliberately designed to mystify the majority, tempt 'em to start guessing, and interpreting our real drift, and allegory, what the hell we mean: pursue our meaning on their *sthula* (gross), the *sukshma* (subtle) and *para* (supreme) planes and levels, and still miss the issue and dash their heads against the crazy-paved rock of confusion."[56] The "majority" here is to experience Hatterr's discourse as mystifying, and yet for its sake, "foreign" words are both marked with italics (to forestall any confusion with English) and translated in apposition. This is the defining paradox of *Hatterr*, whose author considered it untranslatable, yet whose narrator—within whom the fictional verbal agent of a novel as *text* cannot be entirely distinguished from the editorial agent of the apparatus producing a *book*—carefully tends the novel's garden of language, allowing weeds to sprout but never to spread.[57] *Hatterr* is a plurilingual novel in English that is untranslatable not because of the presence of languages other than English within it, but *despite* their presence, contained not only by the disproportionate ratio of English to languages other than English, but by the intense intralingual variation of English itself, which imagines a not merely competent Anglophone reader, but a positively *literary* one. Nonexhaustively, this includes variation of modes of address ("Mr. Marlowe"; "Dr. John Keats"), conscious archaism ("O equal to the first-born of my wife"; "may thy ancestors grow winding beards and be dragged by their toe-nails to the dark pits"; "list" as a verb; "avaunt"), Anglophone solecism of word, phrase, and idiom, in the mode of deviation simulating mistake ("A true office and gentleman and a great blue-stocking of Latin"), Anglophone portmanteau words ("sinfant," "sexaltation") and neologisms ("honeyfall," "mapomania"), Latinized diction ("I treated the ebony optic"), picturesque nicknames ("Kisscurl," "Loganberry-face"), and puns turning on Euro-Atlantic metrocentrist cultural knowledge ("eaten" for "Eton") and etymology ("talking French frankly"), as well as Joycean English-primary interlingual puns (French: "mud'ham" [Madame]; German: "min'hair" [mein Herr]).[58]

WRITING AND "WRITING BACK"

In *The Empire Writes Back,* the seminal early work of consolidation in postcolonial literary studies that took its title from Rushdie's *Times* essay consecrating *Hatterr,* Bill Ashcroft, Gareth Griffiths, and Helen Tiffin presented a rereading of postcoloniality as linked to a fundamental shift in the experience of language. Postcoloniality, for Ashcroft, Griffiths, and Tiffin, was as a condition defined by the historical impossibility of return to any authentic, precolonial vernacular culture—a prohibition extended to cover the presumably "colonial" concept of language as the transparent, direct, unmediated, representation of essence:

> A characteristic of dominated literatures is an inevitable tendency towards subversion, and a study of the subversive strategies employed by post-colonial writers would reveal both the configurations of domination and the imaginative and creative responses to this condition. Directly and indirectly, in Salman Rushdie's phrase, the "Empire writes back" to the imperial "centre," not only through nationalist assertion, proclaiming itself central and self-determining, but even more radically by questioning the bases of European and British metaphysics, challenging the world-view that can polarize centre and periphery in the first place.[59]

One important methodological consequence of this move, as critics like Monika Fludernik have observed, was a lifting of the "ban" on colonial mimicry in English—enabling readings of actual literary (and paraliterary) practice more sensitive to the complexities of that practice than the laws of colonial cultural domination permit.[60] But when writing in English is no longer understood as betrayal or capitulation to colonial power, then writing in the vernacular can no longer be understood (automatically, at least) as "resistance," and resistance, if we are to seek it at all, must be sought elsewhere. The idea of the postcolonial is thus, in more ways than one, a turn from the anticolonialism of a national language politics of self-determination to the politics of style and "resistance" refactored in stylistic subversion.

In some ways, the critical reception of "Indian writing in English" under the sign of world literature turns (then, as now) on this shift from language politics to the politics of style. For the monolingual Anglophone reader, at least, the varieties of stylistic "subversion" can be said to have two distinct, yet simultaneous effects. One, plainly, is the alienating effect of references to, and representations of, an unfamiliar culture in a familiar language. The other is the *refamiliarizing* effect of syntactic creativity, which in "breaking the rules" of communication draws attention from the signified world to the signifier, or from the object of representation to its means. If, in a published book, this means is never an abstract "Language" in general, but an arbitrary (specific) *national* language, then it follows that syntactic creativity in English *draws attention to English*, asserting by demonstration English's capaciousness as a *literary* language—and it is in this sense that to speak of the "Joycean idiom" of Desani's novel is not to commit a new category mistake (subsuming H. Hatterr's English under Joyce's, to which it is not identical, or suggesting anxieties of influence) so much as to acknowledge, by repeating its inversion, that anticolonial language politics remains latent in the postcolonial politics of style. Retrieving *Hatterr* for "English literature"—what both Burgess and Rushdie attempt, in different ways and for different reasons—is only possible once *Hatterr* has been written in English: a decision made, as the decision *not* to write in English might also have been.

Plainly, a familiar language (English, for the monolingual Anglophone reader of an Anglophone Indian novel) compensates for defamiliarizing representations, just as familiar representation (in firsthand knowledge of the topography of Dublin, for a reader of *Ulysses*) compensates for "defamiliarized" language. Both language *and* representation bear on a given text's range of cross-border circulation *as a book*—either in the original language, or in translation, or both. Yet one might note the nonnegligible difference between "marking" a text as foreign—which can be done without reducing its intelligibility to a reader of the text's major ("native") language—and rendering it unintelligible through structural variation, a function of, among other elements, the proportion of different languages combined in a text.[61] Just as dialect variation functions at once to challenge the norm of a standardized national language and to reaffirm it, by requiring a reader sensitive to this variation (in native or native-level fluency in the language), the representative suspension of one language within another allows a monolingual reader a form of experience of the foreign, as Yoko Tawada has put it, "aus der Dose," out of the can.[62]

Casanova shows how world literary criticism eagerly welcomes such linguistic subversion, as "young" or "developing" African English, for example, is assimilated to the stores of a global literary idiom. The international reception (and continuing celebrity) of Amos Tutuola's primitivized "African English," to take one example, is a story of ostensibly foreign variation recoded as innovation in the domestic sphere,[63] the ability of standard English to tolerate the naïve or knowing "abuse" of its decolonized speakers advanced in demonstration of its uncanny flexibility and powers of recombination as a literary language. The publication of *The Palm-Wine Drinkard* by Faber and Faber in 1952 was orchestrated in part by T. S. Eliot (who, like Burgess advocating for Desani, embraced the role of "metic" for himself, as well), and its international success—at least in one version of the story—by the Welsh poet Dylan Thomas, who praised the novel's fresh "young English" in an early review.[64] It should be emphasized, furthermore, that these are points of debate in the literary history of national literary cultures (however they be configured), not merely in the putative centers of what Casanova calls "literary capital," themselves. Debates around Anglophone Nigerian writing in the 1950s and 1960s, for example, distinguished between English programmatically or "naïvely" Africanized by contact with ethnic languages (Yoruba in Tutuola and Wole Soyinka; Ijaw in Gabriel Okara's *The Voice*), on the one hand, and a "standard" English (e.g., in Achebe), on the other—the *choice* of which emphasized the politics of literary structure over that of style.[65] The decision of Ngũgĩ wa Thiong'o to turn from writing in English to writing entirely in a subnational language, Kikuyu—going straight from global to local without even stopping at the continental option, Swahili—is among other things a refocusing of the frame in which translation as retrieval, and retrieval as translation, are conventionally understood (though to be sure, as a decision made in public, it ensures continuing interest, *in translation*).

RE-JOYCEING

In the era of "Commonwealth literature," Desani's critical champions, such as Syd Harrex, sometimes resorted to a less than adequately theorized distinction between Desani's (or Hatterr's) parodic virtuosity and the ostensibly naïve primitivism of canonically decolonized writing, implicitly valorizing the former over the latter in a gesture recalling Burgess's well-intentioned "Higher Babu."[66] Harrex noted disapprovingly that both Amos Tutuola and Raja Rao, simulators of orality in writing, had been widely celebrated for the creativity of their linguistic "eccentricities," while Desani, whose technique was an equally inventive, but determinedly textual and intertextual pastiche, had suffered neglect. Harrex read in Desani's parodic style a dialogue with the dilemma of linguistic resistance and incorporation missing, by implication, in Tutuola's and Rao's work: a level of complexity that, Harrex implied, had too deeply "puzzled," and in puzzling, repelled readers. (Hence the "neglect," which Harrex, like any good critic or fellow writer of conscience, desired to remedy.) In the attempt to retrieve Desani from obscurity, the critical drive here (shared by Harrex with Burgess and Rushdie alike) seems as unwilling to honor Desani's nihilism as to accept that there might be good progressive reasons to block appropriation by a "global" readership, to *refuse to be read* by the world. Desani's novel is "untranslatable," "a cult favorite," "sui generis," in a class of its own, unlike anything else in Indo-Anglian writing of the time—all of which is supposed to justify increased critical scrutiny and more intensive penetrations and schematizations of it as a literary object. It is an "early, largely underrated (post)colonial text which makes full use of the literary strategies of postmodernism in order to come to terms with the colonial condition."[67] It defies critical classification (exhorting the critic to more strenuous acts of classification), "creatively grappling with several languages and re*joyce*ingly playing with and between the english 'lingos' and 'vernaculars.'"[68]

Through the *Hatterr* persona he sometimes used in his commentary, meanwhile, Desani signaled a clear (if clearly ironic) ambivalence regarding the work's afterlife, and seemed to share little of Burgess's and Rushdie's (differently) appropriative confidence in the decolonizing pen. "The book has intrigued several translators," he wrote in a retrospective essay, "[b]ut the difficulties of style, and the personal syntax—rather than my man H. Hatterr as a personality—have made them give up. A highly spoken of Italian translator, not knowing its significance, let stand untranslated my *'Hail Kerlumby!'*—New York campus slang for *'Hail Columbia!'*—and, unable to identify Shakespeare's diction . . . dared to translate Shakespeare . . . in modern Italian of the *mezzo-signori* . . . It is pathetic. I cannot see my book in any language other than the English language."[69] Where Burgess retrieved Desani for Empire as the *métèque* always already subverting it from within, Rushdie placed him at the head of a *métèque tradition* poised to invert it.[70] To be sure, this is a wholly admirable attempt, on Rushdie's part, to force a context for the ahistorical reception of his own *Midnight's Children*, then being read all over the world (so to speak) as an eccentric work of genius like any other (a problem Rushdie revisited in a later and more notorious essay drawing its title from *Hatterr*).[71] From here the only intractable problem, perhaps, lies in the manner in which Rushdie repeated the gestures of his own advocates, displacing onto Desani the foundational act of invention *he* had been credited for. One might ask if such *taxonomic* models of the dynamics of subversion and inversion do not ultimately disavow precisely that "mad" illegibility whose detectable traces they pursue with such vigor.[72]

"A NOT VERY FRUITFUL SEARCH"

All else aside, it must be said that history here belongs to those who *do* choose (a word Casanova consistently sets in quotation marks) to be translated, to self-translate, or to switch to English; not to those who remain, in Casanova's economic lexicon, "deprived," "destitute," "impoverished," and in her ontological lexicon, "nonexistent," "invisible." Casanova's is a history of the known, the visible, of those who chose English, sooner or later (and in one form or another), in a world in which it is natural to regard language as capital. It would be merely quixotic, perhaps, to want to write of those who, from the point of view of publication, have never existed—whose works, the possibility of whose works, remain beyond critical retrieval, in English or in any other language. Yet we might say that to construct an inclusive literary system, from the remnants that published literature preserves of literary activity, is to repeat the gesture of those who saw a North American continent lacking ancient or modern cities, and thus, in a way, lacking a history: essentially empty, despite the human lives that *had* recorded themselves there. To naturalize, by appeal to market forces, the death of languages, and thus the death of actual or potential literatures, is globalism of the very worst kind, that which helps to destroy its own object of study.

There are gradients here, which we can use to *imagine* the invisible. Consider the respective fortunes and the archival posterity, for example, of William Melvin Kelley's *Dunfords Travels Everywheres* (1970)—first published by a trade house (Doubleday), long out of print, bearing epigraphs from Melvin Tolson, from *Portrait of the Artist as a Young Man,* and from Amos Tutuola, and including chapters composed in a "Joycean" creole[73]— with Russell Hoban's *Riddley Walker,* a "cult favorite" preserved in a 1998 Indiana University Press expanded edition with afterword, notes, and a glossary keyed to the novel's "Riddleyspeak"—a mildly Saxonized dialect spoken in Inland, the England of the novel's postapocalypse.[74] At the time of this writing, the MLA Bibliography database of scholarship in literary studies yields two records for "Dunfords Travels Everywheres," twenty-five for "Riddley Walker."[75] Given that such aggregation of documented critical attention is dependent, at a base level, on the circuit of translation, broadly considered—and that it reflects that dependence in its choice of objects—we might suggest that what Venuti calls "the translator's invisibility" is not merely, as Venuti himself sometimes implies, a soluble problem: of equal rights for translators, either in terms of academic convention (translations counting as original, not "derivative" works for tenure consideration), or legally (in terms of intellectual property) and commercially (in terms of benefits to be obtained from holding or transferring intellectual property). Most authors, despite their ostensible primacy in literary production, *do no better.*

Let me close, then, by breaking the frame within which my own research objects, in this chapter, have unavoidably been situated. On his research into the career of Sir James W. Redhouse, the author of Turkish–English dictionaries published during the second half of the nineteenth century and still in widespread use today, the Ottomanist Carter Findley has written the following poignant reflection:

> One senses, first, that the mystery about Redhouse's personality and about many of the biographical facts has at times a significance of its own. True, it is due in part to fortuitous circumstances, such as the fact that he left no known surviving descendants or relatives, other than his second wife, to tell of him as a person, or that so little of his correspondence can now be recovered. But the circumstances that obscure Redhouse's traces at so many points were not solely fortuitous. There were occasions when anonymity was desirable or even became a necessity for him. . . . [B]y spending so much of his life either at the fringes or quite outside of English society, by making his way for so long in an Islamic society to which he could never be more than marginal, by serving as a "confidential medium," and by dividing his literary output, parts of it anonymous or unpublished, between two different cultures, Redhouse literally did become invisible to some degree, even to those of his contemporaries most interested in the fields of his endeavors. . . . The same factors that made Redhouse eccentric also affected his intellectual development, enabling him to achieve an extraordinary mastery

in Ottoman Turkish but denying him the more balanced perspective that a systematic education might have given him. As much as his early mentors in Istanbul and more than many of his academic contemporaries in Europe, Redhouse could only have become what he did by being largely self-taught and by branching out, or being pushed out, into untrodden pathways. The intellectual costs of such a formation are no doubt largely to blame for the debatable quality and miscellaneous character of Redhouse's occasional publications. . . . Redhouse's life thus hardly provides an ideal model for the modern-day student, and his intellectual formation cannot be said to provide any model at all, except as concerns the obvious benefits to be derived in the study of a language from prolonged residence in a country where that language is spoken. Yet, Redhouse did gain certain benefits from the peculiar path he followed, and they were benefits which an ideal academic formation could not have assured. The most fundamental point in this regard is that Redhouse really was, in other and broader senses than the one used thus far, a "medium of communication" between cultures. Indeed, his "invisibility" is a product to a degree not just of the confidentiality of so many of the messages he bore or of the anonymity of parts of his work, but rather of the very efficiency with which he and his works served this end of intercultural exchange.[76]

Redhouse's radical Turkocentrism (a kind of helpless partisanship grown—in Findley's account, at least—from a love for the Turkish language), the fragmentary and often impractical nature of his major projects, nearly all of which were left incomplete, and this "inhuman" role as efficient *medium* combined to obscure part of his life and work forever—withstanding even the formidable Findley, whose fifteen-page article contains 155 footnotes and cites twelve separate archival collections in Turkey, the United Kingdom, Germany, and the United States, in what Findley admits was a "not very fruitful search" for "widely scattered materials" and items that "did not exist." This "medium" who served the Ottoman Empire, whose linguistic proficiencies were cultivated in nineteenth-century polyglot Istanbul and propelled by Ottoman educational reforms, and who "proved himself able to write effectively in even the highest Ottoman style and to translate texts of repellingly technical nature into Ottoman,"[77] chose to give himself to Ottoman culture, literature, and language, rather than *taking* it, and, when he did address his fellow Europeans, to polemicize on its behalf rather than to explain and domesticate it.

Contrast this, now, with the book-world of Joycean modernist literary English invoked by both Burgess and Rushdie, as a commonly traded figure for intercultural exchange (and for that matter, for marginal academic formations) in the high modernity of Anglo-American literature. A world of encoded reference, guaranteeing translation in perpetuity by a scholarly industry created for the purpose that Joyce's actual works (like Eliot's and Pound's) certainly explicitly parody. Or, not a *world* of interminable discourse (which Redhouse's world also certainly was), but its perpetual-motion machine, the engine of an endlessly unraveled and reraveled "fascicular" modernity. Even reading in it all the enlightened and enlighteningly liberating subversions of parody, the immense literary-historical presence of the legacy of James Joyce, which Joyce achieved precisely by "devolving" *and still writing in* English, is nothing if not the literary testament of hypermnesic interiority or *Erinnerung* in Anglo-American and Euro-Atlantic capitalist modernity more generally.[78] If the answer to the Joycean question "Are we speachin d'anglas landadge or are you sprakin sea Djoytsch?"[79] must in some sense certainly always be generously both "yes" and "no," it remains an open question whether this sentence speaks even what Casanova calls a genuinely neutral "synthèse de toutes les langues européennes"[80]—or a piece of "broken English" that in its very *untranslatability* breaks for the Anglophone ear.

2

Translation Being Between

Nullum est hic Dictum, quod non dictum sit prius. Terentius.

Apes, ut ajunt, imitari debemus, quae vagantur, & Flores ad Mel faciendum idoneos.

Deinde, quicquid attulere disponunt, ac per Favos digerunt. Seneca Epist. 84.

Floriferis ut Apes in Saltibus omnia libant,

Omnia nos itidem Depascimur aurea dicta,

Aurea, Perpetua Semper dignissima Vita. Lucretius,

Legere et non Seligere est Negligere.

Lire, et ne point Noter, c'est Radoter.

Vergeefs is dan uw Werck gedaen,

Wanneer ghy Leest, en merckt niets aen.

Reading is null & quite of none effect

Unless we cull & for ourselves select.

The Chief & Choicest which we see,

Ev'n in Superlative Degree.

—FRANCIS DANIEL PASTORIUS, "Francis Daniel Pastorius,
His Hive, Melliotrophium Alvear or, Rusca Apium: Begun Anno
Domini or, in the Year of Christian Account 1696"

Translation is newly urgent and newly controversial today, in an era reviving narratives of incommensurability on a global scale. This book suggests that in order to read those narratives productively, we need to distinguish the study of plurilingualism, as a state or condition, from the study of translation as a procedure or operation.

From a Euro-Atlantic foundationalist and exceptionalist point of departure, one might do no better, of course, than to turn to literary history by examining the plurilingual literary traditions of medieval and Renaissance Europe, when Latin served as a transregional language across wide areas today sectioned by national borders and defined by national language cultures. In such writing, after all, what contemporary linguists would call "code-switching"—alternating between Latin and a vernacular—may well have been as common among the educated elite of the early modern Euro-Atlantic as it is today among those using English as a common second or foreign language. (Medieval macaronic verse, for example, commonly mixed vernacular with Latin words, or gave Latin markings to vernacular words, as in the eponymous example, the 1517 *Maccaronea* of Teofilo Folengo.)

Latin was not, of course, what we would today call a "native" language; it could only be acquired through education, and composing a work in Latin plus one or more Romance vernaculars (the individual differences between which were, of course, then far less developed) may have enabled a writer to reach a broader readership than could be reached in a vernacular alone, or possibly even in Latin alone. As Leonard Forster noted, in one of the earliest Anglo-American studies of plurilingual literature written from a postmodernist historical point of departure, the strong textual plurilingualism that today decisively *contracts* the scale of a published text's potential distribution to economically imagined mass reader–consumers might have worked, in the less literate era of Latin–vernacular amalgamation, to *expand* an imagined or actually existing reading public.[1] As the vernaculars developed through the Renaissance, on the other hand, plurilingualism in the form of self-translation from Latin may have served a similar purpose—broadening the range of "readership" for a text—but the most common tactic was to write in multiple languages in series, rather than in "switches" (Milton is an example of the Renaissance poet who writes in Italian as well as Latin and Greek and a Latinate English, but seldom uses anything like the burlesque "samplings" of macaronic style).[2] And as Latin yielded to French as the lingua franca of Europe during the seventeenth and eighteenth centuries, and Romantic devotion to national language emerged in the nineteenth, the disappearance of a locally "neutral" imperial language took with it the notion of such ostensibly "neutral" plurilingualism.

Rooted as they are in the earliest phases of the consolidation of what Benedict Anderson called "mechanically reproduced print-languages,"[3] early modern Euro-Atlantic plurilingual literary traditions can tell us little of direct consequence, for my arguments in this book, about the fully developed national-language constraints on plurilingual literary composition and publication in our own time—except, perhaps, in their negotiated afterlives in the mass-distributed vehicular print media of our own scholarship. The lines quoted at the beginning of this essay appear in the "Bee-hive" manuscript commonplace book composed by Francis Daniel Pastorius between 1696 and 1719, containing proverbs and quotations in Latin, German, Dutch, French, Italian, and Greek and intended for the private use of Pastorius's sons.[4] These lines also form the introductory selection appearing in Marc Shell and Werner Sollors's ground-breaking compendium *The Multilingual Anthology of American Literature,* a collection of North American documents from the turn of the seventeenth century to the 1970s that counts among its many mother tongues Massachusett, Lenape, Navajo, Arabic, and Chinese, in addition to European languages. It was through *The Multilingual Anthology of American Literature*—crossing my desk in the day-to-day textual traffic of a critical work flow tuned to the contemporary moment, and not by searching, for example, for the microfilm reproduction (with which I subsequently spent some time) in the collections of Penn State's Paterno Library—that I first stumbled, as it were, over Pastorius's hive.[5]

And so it is not, then, the textual condition of the "Beehive" in the originary archival format of the artifact held in Penn State's Rare Books and Manuscripts collection on which I want to reflect, here, but the contemporary editorial format by which *The Multilingual Anthology of American Literature*'s editors are constrained, in their project for the dissemination of evidence for an originary U.S. plurilingualism *through* it. For as it turns out, the "Beehive" is not only the first, but is also the *only* text, in this remarkable collection of primary sources, that is explicitly identified by the editors as a multilingual text, within a published book whose title (a key editorial and marketing "peritext") rings on the word's potent novelty in and for a structurally monolingual U.S. national culture. The other twenty-eight primary sources in *The Multilingual Anthology of American Literature,* by contrast, are identified not as *multilingual,* in the dedicated column in the volume's table of contents marking each text's categorial origin—but rather as composed in an original, non-English language from which each, in the collection's bilingual–multilingual format, is translated.

In no other case, in other words, is a primary source contained in *The Multilingual Anthology of American Literature* identified by the volume's editors as having been *composed by its author* in more than one language contiguously—by which I mean in or within, as it were, one compositional iteration.[6] And the collection is, then—as its subtitle, *A Reader of Original Texts with English Translations,* fully acknowledges—more a *multilingual anthology of texts* than an *anthology of multilingual texts.* The difference, declared here in the anthological composition and juxtaposition of materials but largely left to critical implication (*The Multilingual Anthology of American Literature* is intended, after all, to serve as a source of sources), is a small difference with significant power, I will suggest, to check the grandiosity of literary-critical claims made elsewhere for the decisive registration of new hybrid linguistic cultures in printed books of contemporary literature, the domain of literary scholars lacking the sociolinguistic and ethnological training (or motivation) to report on such cultures in real time.[7]

Taking this difference as its point of departure, the essay composing this chapter will explore the distinction between monolingual literary artifacts that become plurilingual *in* translation, and those that, in and by the light of a national literary standard, are plurilingual prior to translation—and which therefore are difficult or even "impossible" to translate, in the operational or procedural sense marking the reproduction and recirculation of a text, in book form, in the world-system of national-market "translation rights." I will suggest that this is a distinction worth making more carefully than is usual, and that the conflation of two different forms of linguistic difference—that embodied in the plurilingualism of plurilingual literary manuscript composition, and that generated in the translative circulation of a structurally monolingual print-distributed literary book-product or "work"—serves to obscure the material disciplinary-editorial practices that regulate the publication, and thus the dissemination, of contemporary readers' and critics' possible objects: in other words, the production of the contemporary literary archive.

THE HIVE AND THE MIRROR

The *texts* collected in the *book* entitled *The Multilingual Anthology of American Literature* may all be said to be meaningfully plurilingual in at least three fairly intuitive senses. They are plurilingual once in their juxtaposition with and to each other, in the internal linguistic diversity of the literary-critical and scholarly artifact published and archived under the title *The Multilingual Anthology of American Literature*. They are plurilingual again in their collective difference and individual differences from English, the federal language of the present United States (and thus, ex officio, of United States literature). Finally, they are plurilingual once more in the contingency of each individual text in the history of its own standardized national language—the French of Luigi Donato Ventura's 1885 *Peppino*, for example, which, if indeed composed by Ventura himself, is a French acquired as a third language by an Italian immigrant writing in the United States.[8]

Such forms of plurilingualism are artifactually comparative in nature, marking the difference of languages between and among individual texts in the synchronic space of the editorial collection entitled *The Multilingual Anthology of American Literature,* or else in the diachronic historiographic field of the development and standardization of a national literary standard for book publication, against and in which *The Multilingual Anthology of American Literature* as an editorial project takes its own (intervening) stand. As such, such forms of plurilingualism certainly constitute suppressed elements of variation in the history of a now structurally monolingual national U.S. culture, and Shell and Sollors are both sagacious and bold to point to the difference that recovering and rememorating the difference of European, African, Asian, and indigenous North American languages *as* United States languages might make. Arguably, however, the limit of any such project, in its presentability to even such a curious reader as that of *The Multilingual Anthology of American Literature,* is marked by the paradox that the texts the *Anthology* contains must be (and are) translated, so as to "return" to that originally plural culture of which they comprise suppressed elements (a paradox of which, as I pointed out in the essay composing this book's introduction, the editors are appropriately painfully aware). Of the work collected here, only the "Beehive" is a plurilingual text as it were in itself, sustaining alternation between what to a contemporary reader are unmistakably distinct national languages, in such proportion and density as appears to imply or demand a *plurilingual reader*. And with the exception of this inaugural exception as such, then, *The Multilingual Anthology of American Literature* is more properly to be understood, in terms of the archival terrain it surveys, as an anthology of *bilingual editions of originally* (entirely, or nearly entirely) *monolingual* texts.

Within the remarkably linguistically diverse format of the *Anthology* (a format whose presentation value is unavoidably reliant on novelty), the "Beehive" itself is even more remarkable then, in that, read as the presentation format of the anthology suggests it be read, as a text alternating sequences of English, German, Dutch, French, Italian, Greek, and Latin, it appears, at least in certain portions, to settle onto or in no single "base" or source language, to which other languages might be either quantitatively or qualitatively subordinated.[9] This, presumably, is why the "Beehive" alone merits the label *multilingual*, in *The Multilingual Anthology of American Literature*'s table of contents, which labels every *other* text in the volume with an original base or source language. This makes for the necessity of special accommodations at the level of the document, as well as in nomenclature. In presenting the "Beehive," Shell and Sollors's editorial strategy is, as with all the other content of the *Anthology*, to provide English translation of all material not in English in the original composition or publication. But rather than offering a facing-page translation, as they do with the *Anthology*'s other selections, Shell and Sollors resort here to endnotes translating the lines in Latin, French, and Dutch. The use of endnotes permits the excerpts from the "Beehive" to appear in the equilibrium of their original, interlinguistic difference, without the brute domestication of a facing-page English translation: one may consult the notes as one needs them, entirely, selectively, or not at all.

This strategy is entirely commendable, and indeed the only workable solution, given the actually existing and realistically imaginable editorial calculus of means and ends, here. My aim is not at all to quibble with this valuable product of the editorial–archival project that produced the *Anthology*, so much as to supplement the evidence it provides with reflection on some of the questions its framing (necessarily, and unavoidably) raises.

One such question, of course, is that of *reception* for a text that is originally plurilingual—in the sense that makes the "Beehive" unique among its companion texts—as distinguished from the reception of texts that are comparatively plurilingual (either synchronically, within the managed space of a particular archive, or diachronically, in the historiography of a standardized national language). One might suggest that between the translative rendering of the various languages of Pastorius's "Beehive," which homogenizes passages in languages other than English with those in English, and the more conventional operational or procedural translation of, say, Johan Person's "A Misunderstood People" ("Ett missförstådt folk," another selection in the *Anthology*) from its relatively homogeneous original Swedish, there is an indisputably meaningful difference. The tension between the very titles of these two works might, in fact, be understood to replicate the tension between *The Multilingual Anthology of American Literature*'s own title, promising *multilingualism,* and its subtitle, yielding *originals with translations.* Pastorius's text offers multiplicity, aggregation, repetition, and iteration, its language-surfaces like the clustered cells of a hive, without any obvious front, back, top, or bottom. "A Misunderstood People," by contrast, promises explanation, correction, facilitation: a framed window or mirror on each side of which immigrant and host languages have for the most part strongly fixed places.

For what in the course of this essay I will call *hermeneutical* (contemporary) translation theory, which offers "foreignizing" translation as a counterweight to translation as computational optimization, texts such as the "Beehive" present the beguiling appearance, I will suggest, of a nonoptimizable object—one whose "foreignness" is, in an interesting way, artifactually immanent rather than categorially comparative. I am going to ask why such texts, and the refinements and threats they offer to theories of foreignizing or "differential" translation, have received so little analysis in such translation theory (and by implication, in the transnationalist literary criticism that appropriates its core argument). My purpose here, again— this does bear repeating—is to supplement the valuable work of *The Multilingual Anthology of American Literature,* in two specific ways. First, I will suggest that one way to read the artifactual status of Pastorius's "Beehive," as what I am calling a *strong plurilingual text,* in a printed book regulated by a nationally monolingual editorial contract, is to see that, to speak partly figuratively, it *takes the position of the translator,* in a manner and to an extent that sets it apart from the *Anthology*'s other content. In doing so (and secondly), I want to draw attention to a consequent layering of meaning under the term "multilingual"—which has understandably, and entirely appropriately, become something of a squeaky wheel on the latest U.S.-based transnationalist critical bandwagon (and, as I indicate in this book's preface, a new marker of self-consciousness about the internal dynamics of the constitution of a U.S. imperial cultural homeland). In the disciplinary, archival, and material printed space of the *Anthology* itself, as a book product, the "Beehive" *itself* takes the position of Shell's third and liminal (or satanic) "hypothetical reader," here: "This anthology has three kinds of readers. One kind of reader knows the language in which the particular original work is written. That reader pays no attention to the English translation, or else reads it as a biased interpretation or as a work of art in its own right. The second reader does not know the language of the particular original work, and thus pays attention mainly to the facing-page English translation. . . . The third hypothetical reader knows all languages."[10]

"Proceed to Decode"

The cross-section of the contemporary moment within which I offer my analysis exposes several layers of sedimented postwar United States cultural history. I take it for granted here that the period after 1945—a common delimiter for scholars of United States and hemispheric Euro-Atlantic literature and culture—marks the convergence of a number of developmental factors: advanced or postindustrial "postmodern" finance capitalism; the vastly expanded scale of U.S. imperial military, economic, and cultural projects (and their ranks of influence); the dwindling of the British empire and the full course of the cold war, from the atomic age to what we call "globalization"; and the advent of computerization and computer science, in information theory and cold war–driven research in machine translation (the computerized transposition of human-authored documents from one rival hegemonic national language into another). I also take it for granted that in the same period, driven by new imperial technocratic imperatives, the culture of knowledge in the United States university changed significantly, largely to the benefit of applied science and to the detriment of the inapplicable humanities. The question of whether these structural changes are merely *reflected* in the cultural production of literature and the arts, or also partly produced by it is, along with the entire question of political and aesthetic vanguardism as reflective or productive of social change, an important one, to which anyone can only ever give a tentative answer. But in our culture of computerization, it seems to me that when we in literary studies make poetry—our commonsense exemplar of literary language—a figure for the untranslatable, we mean not only that poetry is the most sophisticated use of a *particular* human language, as our abiding historical Romanticism understands it (largely in national terms), but that it is the most human use of *any* language, in a world teeming with machine—that is, nondivine, yet non-human—languages. The untranslatable, as a figure for the Heideggerian "shadow" of Babel on our linguistic labor, is the *uncomputable,* that which cannot be binarized, that which best reminds us, so to speak, of human language's difference from code.[11]

In a recent rereading of the personae of Jean-François Lyotard as central players in our so-called postmodernism debates, Christopher Newfield has made the following points, which I will paraphrase in a necessarily somewhat reductive form.[12] Both humanistic and scientific knowledge alike, Newfield suggests, are today enclosed in what we might call a "grand narrative of optimization."[13] In this grand narrative of optimization, enlightened emancipation—ostensibly, the university's first reason for being—is supplanted by technical efficiency. Newfield argues that the real stakes of the postmodernism debates lay not in a struggle for prestige between the natural sciences and the humanities, or between the social sciences and the natural sciences. Nor, on the other hand, did the postmodernism debates produce real philosophical controversy concerning the status of knowledge or truth. Culture-war polemics in the academic and journalistic spheres, leading up to and through the so-called Sokal hoax of 1996, rather concealed a struggle for what Newfield calls "the protection of cultural knowledge from market optimization."[14] Lyotard, in Newfield's reading, argued relatively uncontroversially that the postwar elevation of applied science simply brings other modes of the production of knowledge into line with itself. "[Lyotard's] most basic point," Newfield concludes, "was not that knowledge lacks context-free foundations but that its defining context was now the drive to optimize."[15]

For a literary critic, I will suggest, nothing illuminates what Newfield calls the "drive to optimize" like the drive of early research in machine translation, in the social history of which techno-modernity and traditional culture might be said to bear down on each other, as it were, through language itself. In the exchange that developed between technical and literary figurations in which code and poetry, the translatable and the untranslatable, became two irreconcilable and interdependent cultures, we can find one origin, I would like to suggest, of the conflict of the postmodern literary humanities with the prestige of the sciences—if not always in fact with "science" itself. It is a conflict, I will suggest here and in the essays composing subsequent chapters of this book, that from the perspective of literary studies, as much as from that of "science," is absolutely and hopelessly romantic—a phrase I am going to use, here, in a complexly affirmative sense. In this phrase "hopelessly romantic," expressing bureaucratic contempt for those who refuse a disenchanted world, there is a temporality as necessarily mixed, we might say, in the vision of universally computed content as it is in the Romantic novelization of life in form. For "machine translation," a term used by engineers and humanists alike, is an anachronism—perhaps strategically, or perhaps unconsciously so—in which digital computation is symbolically married to time-bound and mortal heavy industry. I will return to this anachronism later in my discussion in this essay. For now, and as an anchor point of that discussion here, I want to suggest that regardless of the "side" from which it is viewed, what we have allegorized as the conflict between literature and science is neither hopeless nor "romantic," except to the extent that it is a proxy conflict for a conflict of modernities or modern temporalities that was never more alive than it is today, in the U.S. imperial critical attempt to appropriate and integrate transnational critical emergents posing symbolic threats to the management culture of the intellectual division of labor—and for which plurilingual literature, as a problem for print-capitalist criticism, serves as both a symbolic and a material spur.

One might, of course, locate any number of precedents for Newfield's gloss on Lyotard's concept of systemic optimization, in the traditions of early modern European continental rationalism. Universal language theories dating back to Athanasius Kircher's *Polygraphia nova et universalis ex combinatoria arte detecta* (1663), for example, can certainly be read as

projects to "optimize" the communicative function of languages by eliminating inefficiency through reduction.[16] But its most vivid illustrations are,
unsurprisingly, to be found in the postwar U.S. imperial field of Lyotard's
and Newfield's own primary concerns. It is the early history of research in
machine translation, I want to suggest, that offers some of the most compelling evidence of the postwar shift in the prestige of different forms of
knowledge in the university.[17] In the United States, the first application of
an electronic computer to translating natural languages was imagined in
1947 by Warren Weaver, who with Claude Shannon would shortly publish
a paper on the fundamentals of information theory, *The Mathematical
Theory of Communication.* In a letter to the cybernetics researcher Norbert
Wiener that year, Weaver imagined translation as a straightforwardly cryptographic problem, a problem providing its own readily technical solution,
on the one hand, *and* containing a grand political project, on the other:

A most serious problem, for UNESCO and for the constructive and peaceful future of the planet, is the problem of *translation,* as it unavoidably affects
the communication between peoples. Huxley [Julian Huxley, the first direc-
tor of UNESCO] has recently told me that they are appalled by the magni-
tude and the importance of the translation job.

Recognizing fully, even though necessarily vaguely, the semantic difficulties because of multiple meanings, etc., I have wondered if it were unthink-
able to design a computer which would translate. Even if it would translate
only scientific material (where the semantic difficulties are very notably less),
and even if it did produce an inelegant (but intelligible) result, it would
seem to me worth while. . . .

[O]ne naturally wonders if the problem of translation could conceiv-
ably be treated as a problem in cryptography. When I look at an article in
Russian, I say "This is really written in English, but it has been coded in
some strange symbols. I will now proceed to decode."[18]

Rebuffed by Wiener (and subsequently by the British literary critic and
proponent of Basic English, I. A. Richards), Weaver next approached a
Professor W. Prager in the mathematics department at Brown University,
seeking Prager's confirmation of an anecdote from cryptographic research.
That confirmation was incorporated into the July 15, 1949, memorandum

on machine translation Weaver sent to a large group of professional acquaintances, which retailed the anecdote without disclosing Prager's identity:

> During the war a distinguished mathematician whom we will call *P,* an ex-German who had spent some time at the University of Istanbul and had learned Turkish there, told W. W.[19] the following story.
>
>   A mathematical colleague, knowing that *P* had an amateur interest in cryptography, came to *P* one morning, stated that he had worked out a deciphering technique, and asked *P* to cook up some coded message on which he might try his scheme. *P* wrote out in Turkish a message containing about 100 words; simplified it by replacing the Turkish letters ç, ğ, ı, ö, ş, and ü by c, g, i, o, s, and u respectively; and then, using something more complicated than a simple substitution cipher, reduced the message to a column of five-digit numbers. The next day (and the time required is significant) the colleague brought his result back, and remarked that they had apparently not met with success. But the sequence of letters he reported, when properly broken up into words, and when mildly corrected (not enough correction being required really to bother anyone who knew the language well), turned out to be the original message in Turkish.[20]

Weaver's interest lay in the possibility that languages possessed properties—alphabetic letter frequencies, intervals, combinations, and other patterns—*"which are to some significant degree independent of the language used."*[21] Equally important for Weaver was the understanding that "the decoding was done by someone who did not know Turkish, and did not know that the message was in Turkish."[22] Computation's independence of culture here is understood to free the human operator of the computer from culture as well—a freedom re-expressed in the accurate manipulation of "foreign" languages without knowing them, on the one hand, and in finding one's own native language encoded, as it were, in such foreign languages, on the other. Such freedom is imagined throughout Weaver's correspondence and other writings of the period, many of which have been widely recirculated. In the July 15, 1949, memorandum, which refers to and reproduces his 1947 letter to Wiener, Weaver writes, "[I]t is very tempting to say that a book written in Chinese is simply a book written in English which was coded into the 'Chinese code.'"[23]

We might say that Weaver is an interesting, and even a sympathetic figure, in precisely the exuberance with which he thus proposed technical
solutions to extratechnical nonproblems (problems precisely not soluble
in the technical sense), which he *did* recognize in all their moral gravity.
Weaver readily granted literary language the organic cognitive prestige of
the uncomputable ("Pushkin need not shudder," he wrote, "[a]nd the
kinds of questions that enter in connection with the translation of the
Bible will continue to require at least fifty learned men"[24]), even if this
streak of epistemic prudence failed to prevent him from proposing perpetual peace through the automated translation of everyday public language,
which he understandably (if mistakenly) construed exclusively as a medium
of "communication." In Weaver's public and private writings, his initial and
quite reasonable reduction of the problem of automated translation to
scientific material—he was at times happy to admit the hopelessness of
machine translation for literary language—shades consistently into the
unique fitness of this *reduced* field of inquiry for the expansive project of
world peace, with rhetorical emphasis placed on the primacy of English
and the translating computer as a substitute for knowledge of languages
other than English.

Such a technocratic Pax Americana was of course the most tantalizing
fruit of the undisguised opportunism through which the United States was
able to displace a Europe in ruins from the world stage, and its shift of the
grounds of conflict at the core of the world system ran, as it often does,
through the circuit of the semiperiphery and at its expense. If William
Prager, the Brown University mathematician of Weaver's Turkish-language
anecdote, was able to write out a message in Turkish for the experiment,
that was because he was one of a generation of German émigrés, including
Erich Auerbach and Leo Spitzer, who taught at universities in Istanbul
during the 1930s and '40s, as the programmatically modernizing Turkish
state purged the universities of Turkish-born faculty.[25] Exotic competence
in the linguistic culture of what would subsequently become NATO's Eur-
asian flank served not only in such casual research roles as that described
in the encoding experiment, but in a more substantive capacity in early
computational linguistics, as well. In his 1949 memorandum, Weaver also
retails the story of the mathematician and logician Hans Reichenbach,
who, in Weaver's words, "also spent some time in Istanbul, and, like many

of the German scholars who went there . . . was perplexed and irritated by the Turkish language. The grammar of that language seemed to him so grotesque that eventually he was stimulated to study its logical structure."[26] On commencing such study, Weaver tells us (attributing the exclamation to Reichenbach himself), Reichenbach was "amazed to discover that, for (apparently) widely varying languages, the basic logical structures have important common features."[27]

Certainly, it is tempting (to inflect one of Weaver's own rhetorical tropes) to suggest that postwar Euro-Atlantic comparative literature shares with machine translation, as a culturalization of computational optimization, a common pretext in this irritating incommensurability of the Turkish language as emblem and memento of the struggle to define where Europe ends. For Auerbach (who, as Emily Apter's work on wartime intellectual emigration to Istanbul notes, seems to have avoided learning any Turkish) and for commentators on the Turkish exile of Spitzer (who did learn and use the language), that incommensurability appears to have been obscurely enabling, in terms that Edward W. Said has memorably re-rendered as "non-Occidental exile and homelessness."[28] No less so, we might note, in Weaver's appropriative portrait of Reichenbach here, where the incommensurability of Turkish provokes what Marshall McLuhan called "self-amputation," in the *creative discovery* of universal logical structures supposedly common to all languages, which might then, entirely conveniently, be manipulated by a computer.[29] In "The New Tower," a brief essay introducing a 1955 volume entitled *Machine Translation of Languages: Fourteen Essays,* Weaver glossed this effort with what one might call his characteristic false modesty:

> Students of languages and of the structures of languages, the logicians who design computers, the electronic engineers who build and run them—and specially the rare individuals who share all of these talents and insights—are now engaged in erecting a new Tower of Anti-Babel. This new tower is not intended to reach Heaven. But it is hoped that it will build part of the way back to that mythical situation of simplicity and power when men could communicate freely together, and when this contributed so notably to their effectiveness.[30]

The Language of Language

Weaver's contribution to *The Mathematical Theory of Communication,* a long general introduction to the technical paper authored by Shannon, is a study in technicist reduction yielding to something like romantic generalization. Weaver writes of a "fifty per cent redundancy" in the statistical structure of English, of "the most efficient kind of coding" as that which subtracts a "spurious" portion of information from the received signal, leaving what is useful. He admits that in one view, this reduction provides only "engineering details," and has little purchase on the "philosophical content of the general problem of communication."[31] But he nevertheless goes on to assert, in his own view, the reduction's universality: "[T]he mathematical theory [of communication] is exceedingly general in its scope, fundamental in the problems it treats, and of classic simplicity and power in the results it reaches. This is a theory so general that one does not need to say what kinds of symbols are being considered—whether written letters or words, or musical notes, or spoken words, or symphonic music, or pictures. The theory is deep enough so that the relationships it reveals indiscriminately apply to all these and to other forms of communication."[32]

The subtleties in Weaver's essay, which can be overlooked amid such mania, lie in his interpretation of Shannon's research, which redefined a technical concept of "information" in terms of *un*certainty—as a description of possible, rather than actual outcomes of communication. Information, in Shannon's counterintuitive definition, is not the actual content of an existing message, but rather a logarithmic measure of freedom of choice in the selection of a message to send. Any 2-choice situation between equal probabilities (a coin toss, for example) constitutes one bit or "binary digit" of information, that is, a unity expressed by the choice between zero and one, the outcome of which is encodable by zero or one. The outcome of a 16-choice situation is encodable in a binary number, four binary digits (bits) of information as a sequence of four zero/one choices (0000, 0001, 0010, etc.); a five-bit system encodes 32 choices, seven bits encodes 128 choices, and so on.[33] Each bit set thus affects the probability of a sequence producing a particular outcome. It is the unset states and the "free choice" they represent, diminishing as the sequence is generated, that for Shannon constitute information. Information is maximal at the point when data begins to be written to or retrieved from storage, or exchanged between other nodes of a communications system—that is, when the *least* amount has been transmitted—and vanishes entirely, as a quantity, when transmission is complete.

This, however, assumes a noiseless communications channel. Shannon chose to assume a *noisy* channel, which means that his emphasis was never on error-free transmission, but merely on, as he put it, "combating" noise: "If the channel is noisy it is not in general possible to reconstruct the original message or the transmitted signal with *certainty* by any operation on the received signal."[34] Repetition of the signal once (100 percent redundancy) provides a second iteration of the message, for checking against the first; if the two iterations differ, one needs a third (200 percent redundancy) in order to determine which of the first two iterations of the message contained an error. All this—Weaver calls it "ideal coding"—reduces transmission rates considerably, since identical data must be transmitted multiple times.

The introduction of controlled or partial redundancy, on the other hand, can add error detection and correction to the transmission process without reducing transmission speeds so considerably (this is the function of the eighth "parity bit" used in ASCII transmission). Controlled redundancy can also take advantage of statistical probabilities to achieve data compression. An alphabet, for example, might be encoded according to a statistical table of letter frequencies in U.S. English orthography. As in the transmission of a binary number representing a character in a code table, each letter selected when composing a word relates probabilistically to the previously selected letter in a set of relationships forming a Markov chain. In standard written U.S. English, the probability that the letter j will be followed by b, c, d, f, g, j, k, l, q, r, t, v, w, x, or z is zero, whereas the probability that a, e, h, i, m, n, o, p, s, u, or y will be chosen will be between zero and one. Presumably, by encoding a message using a code keyed to letter frequencies in English, the transmitter could "save bits" (and thus transmit faster) by not signaling any letter whose probability of sequential occurrence is one, since the receiver could fill in that choice with the same calculation.[35]

It is these advantages to be taken from the statistical properties of the *message* that seems to have suggested to Weaver the idea of an "interlingua" that could be used in automated translation. To Shannon's assertion that "the semantic aspects of communication are irrelevant to the engineering aspects," Weaver adds, "But this does not mean that the engineering aspects are irrelevant to the semantic aspects."[36] Meaning and information are to be considered separately—a bracketing that Shannon introduced to delimit his theory as a strictly technical problem—but now meaning is to be *accountable* to information, without the reverse obtaining. For Weaver, the engineer's communications channel, which deals solely with information defined, in technical terms, as statistical probability, is generalized to deal with the extratechnical, semantic problem of optimizing a message's meaning: "One can imagine . . . another box labeled 'Semantic Receiver' interposed between the engineering receiver (which changes signals to messages) and the destination. This semantic receiver subjects the message to a second decoding, the demand on this one being that it must match the statistical *semantic* characteristics of the message to the statistical semantic capacities of the totality of receivers, or of that subset of receivers which constitute the audience one wishes to affect."[37]

Shannon's concept of information provides a way, for Weaver, of theorizing the influence of context, or the entropy of unchosen messages, on meaning, or the message finally chosen—and thus of jumping from the technical problem of correct transmission to the "general problem of communication," and a distinction between communication and interpretation, which he forces from it.[38] The meaning of a message follows the transmission of a signal and its decoding by the engineering receiver; it is generated in interpretation by another agent, the semantic receiver, for an audience whose "statistical semantic capacities" are, presumably, known to that agent.

Weaver's confidence in the probabilities inhering in a "totality of receivers," no less than in English letter or word frequencies, is achieved by means of appeal to entropy as a concept linking the quantitative modes of mathematics and science to the qualitative modes of what he presumably regards as the aesthetic. This is for Weaver the grand implication of Shannon's association of information with uncertainty:

> One has the vague feeling that information and meaning may prove to be
> something like a pair of canonically conjugate variables in quantum theory,

they being subject to some joint restriction that condemns a person to the sacrifice of the one as he insists on having much of the other.

Or perhaps meaning may be shown to be analogous to one of the quantities on which the entropy of a thermodynamic ensemble depends. . . . [E]ntropy not only speaks the language of arithmetic; it also speaks the language of language.[39]

That in this generalizing of an engineering problem into an indiscriminate theory of all forms of communication, natural languages are regarded as static systems, and that we have no theory of how interpretation might affect patterns of usage, rather than merely conforming to them, are questions to be taken up by what I am calling hermeneutical translation theory. One can clearly distinguish here the interlinked, yet nonidentical strains of a science "placing entropy alongside beauty and melody" as a systemic quality *not* conventionally associated with positive knowledge, and of Newfield's "grand narrative of optimization," which reincorporates entropy into a design for efficiency, first in data transmission, then in Weaver's expansion of that design, in a mathematical theory of communication encompassing natural language as well.

TRANSLATION AS HERMENEUTIC

By "hermeneutical translation theory" I mean a body of work electively affiliated with poststructuralism, which produced a pointed revision of the "coding" model of translation and a renewed focus on interpretation as the transformation of knowledge. Such work takes its point of departure, in the words of Lawrence Venuti, from Roman Jakobson's underestimation of "the interpretive nature of translation, the fact that recoding [Jakobson's key term for translation] is an active rewording that doesn't simply transmit the foreign message, but transforms it."[40] Hermeneutical translation theory has supplanted Jakobson's work with innovative rereadings of essays by Schleiermacher, Benjamin, and Heidegger, which retain an understanding of language as essentially nonhuman (a legacy of structuralism) while refusing reductive analogies to code and coding processes.[41]

Although perhaps the most difficult to assimilate to this grouping, Steiner's *After Babel* is perhaps its strongest example of the rhetoric of the hermeneutical "turn" in and to translation. For Steiner, *all* acts of discourse are translations, and interpretation is an "original repetition," which no act of discourse precedes. We use language not only for schematic, informational "communication," but also—and in a sense that for Steiner is clearly primary—for privacy, fiction, counterfact, "alternity of being." "The French sense of *interprète*" commonly used to mean "translator," he writes, "is the vital starting point."[42] For Steiner, no linguistic universalism (that of Chomsky's transformational generative grammar, for example, just as much as that of the formalist linguistics preceding it) can account for actually existing languages, since it abstracts them into synchronic, mathematical, timeless form. If these universals in fact exist, it is more likely that human language diversity *resists* such biological universality, Steiner says, and the "organic subjection to death" that it entails, than that such structures express it.

Translation, accordingly, aims to produce not transparency but "translucency," an ambiguous and unresolved surface of simultaneous proximity and distance, affinity and difference with the source or original. Steiner's favorite examples are from the poems and translations of Hölderlin, "the most violent, deliberately extreme act of hermeneutic penetration and appropriation of which we have knowledge."[43] We might say that Weaver's technical limitation progressing to "literary" generalization meets its counterpart here, in Steiner's understanding of *all* discourse as translation, which nevertheless admits the interest and "potential utility of machine literalism." In routine understanding, Steiner allows, the "statistical bracketing" and pattern recognition of a code probably play some part, and "much scientific, technical, and, perhaps, even commercial documentation" "is susceptible to more or less automatic lexical transfer."[44] Yet finally, "the meta-mathematical view of language . . . will fail to account for the nature and possibility of relations between languages as they actually exist and differ. . . . No true understanding can arise from synchronic abstraction."[45]

Venuti, meanwhile, suggests that some of what might be taken for mere chauvinism, in the reductions of which thinkers like Weaver were so fond, conceals a systemic function. For Venuti, the expansion of scientific research and of commodity production and exchange during the twentieth century produce a culture "valorizing a purely instrumental use of language and other means of representation and thus emphasizing immediate intelligibility and the appearance of factuality."[46] "Foreignizing translation," the concept derived from Schleiermacher that Venuti sees revived in French poststructuralism, "seeks to restrain the ethnocentric violence of translation. . . . Foreignizing translation in English can be a form of resistance against ethnocentrism and racism, cultural narcissism and imperialism, in the interests of democratic geopolitical relations."[47]

Yet, despite its insistence on the special production of translucency and privacy, by translation taken *as* hermeneutic, hermeneutical translation theory has for the most part avoided that object of analysis seemingly *least* vulnerable to the computational optimization it so strenuously resists: what I am calling the strong plurilingual text. I will suggest that this apparent (but perhaps only apparent) blind spot, in a theory of translation that does its best to advance itself through the difficulty of translation, to but not beyond the verge of translation's impossibility, is a virtual analogue for the ethnological mode of a contemporary literary studies devoted, as Franco Moretti has put it, to "listening" to what the literary object is, so to speak, designed to say—and less agile when it comes to posing a question to that object's silent archives, about how they have come to be.[48] Interposing as much ethical difficulty as possible into translation, without denying its objects their constant circulation—and therefore avoiding those objects that resist it most—hermeneutical translation theory, in its integration of the public and private modes of address of an imagined world, perhaps paradoxically shares more with the literary object it so conspicuously *avoids* than with that which, adequately "contained" in a national standard, is in many ways more literally pliant to it.

THE STRONG BILINGUAL OR PLURILINGUAL TEXT

In the strong bilingual or plurilingual text, I will suggest, translation is already, and in advance, denied—but also, in a way, already performed. Denied, because the text includes in its "native" state, the state in which it comes to the reader, the schism that is the task of translation, which requests a translating agent. And *performed* to the extent that reading a text written in more than one language is, itself, already an act of something like translation, in the cognitive comparative "processing" of different languages. The strong bilingual or plurilingual text thus invites two seemingly incompatible structures of reading: one that reads such a text's movement centrifugally, as a movement of dissemination, in the refusal, as it were, to "say what it means" in one language; another, that reads it centripetally, in the recuperative construction of a synthesized, hybrid, or negative identity "expressing" that schism. The simultaneity of these effects, sometimes generalized at a level conflating national language politics with epistemological assertions about the nature of knowledge, describes what, in hermeneutical translation theory's signature turns of phrase, has variously been termed the "scandal," or the "misery and splendor," or the "impossibility and necessity" of translation.[49]

Translation implies both a translator, the agent who mediates the difference of specific languages, and a reader who is *translated for,* who demands that mediation. The translator is, of necessity, bi- or plurilingual; the reader *translated for* is of necessity monolingual, as regards the difference of *those specific* languages. Translation puts the difference of languages into question, by bridging them; yet it maintains and resolves that difference by completing the translation, which transforms one language into another, permitting the reader translated for to *remain* monolingual—to read the text only in her own language.

In the strong bilingual or plurilingual text, then, we might say we find not a relationship between a bi- or plurilingual translator and (with respect to *specific* languages) a monolingual reader, but something, instead, like the "reader as translator":[50] the reader already bi- or plurilingual with respect to specific languages. This is at the same time, we might say, an enabling and a divisive position. In the afterword appended to *The Multilingual Anthology of American Literature,* in a section entitled "Multilingual Translation," Shell compares *The Multilingual Anthology of American Literature* itself to an "international conference room," the site of "opportunity for diplomacy, trade, and intellectual exchange, but . . . also a site renowned for sparking wars."[51] The international conference room, Shell continues, "with its facilities for translation," permits social intercourse between parties that might otherwise be impossible. As peaceable as it may be, however, Shell points out, such intercourse can also take the form of conflict enabled or provoked by translation's dynamics of power, in the potentially coercive relation between who translates and who is translated.

If the "scandal" of translation is, then, its double function of extending communication (by making possible intercourse between persons differently monolingual) *and* of restricting it (in its function as intermediary, by permitting those persons to *remain* monolingual), then the strong bilingual or plurilingual text might be described as in one sense untranslatable (since to read it, one must already have been a "translator") and in another sense already translated (because in its "untranslated" state, the text already contains two or more distinct languages).[52] It implies not a nonreader, but a reader who is also, or already a translator: not a completely disseminated or "dead" reader, but a reader of complex coherence, who can move between and among different languages.[53]

Such translation already involves more than two languages: the two or more languages of the source, plus that (one, presumably) of the target. Even translation of the base or source language, in a "weakly" bilingual or plurilingual text, must move to a target language different from any of those languages in the source, otherwise one of the source languages "vanishes," as it were. Translation of *all* the source languages into one (different) target language, meanwhile, would simply eliminate those source languages, erasing their difference *as* different languages.[54] A strong bilingual or plurilingual text, therefore, within which one *cannot determine* a base or source language, presents one with something of a nonchoice regarding *which* language one might choose to translate. Since a strong bilingual or plurilingual text, as such, appears to demand reading facility in all its languages, resolution here would require one to choose one of three options: (1) rendering one language into the other, for a monolingual reader in *one* of those languages; (2) translating only one language, leaving the other untranslated, for a bilingual or plurilingual reader who knows one of the base or source languages, but not the other; (3) translating both languages into other languages, for a bilingual or plurilingual reader who happens to know *neither* of the base or source languages.

The first option, we might say, resolves the multiplicity of languages by doing away with it—while the second and third simply beg the question of translation. Would any publisher "in his right mind," one might ask, undertake a translation in order to reach a reader *also* bilingual or plurilingual, but in languages entirely different from the languages of the original?

THE IMPOSSIBILITY AND NECESSITY OF TRANSLATION

In its artifactual published form, we might say, the strong bilingual or plurilingual text renders that working paradox, or antinomy, beloved of hermeneutical translation theory: that translation is both *necessary* and *impossible*. Translation is *necessary* to the extent that there will never emerge one single and universal Language subsuming all other languages—insofar, that is to say, as we will always live in Babel's shadow, in the shadow of both the monumental desire for such a Language and the mediation in difference that fails to fulfill it. Translation is "impossible," on the other hand, insofar as such mediation in difference cannot *itself* be universalized, or positivized as a transhistorical operation or procedure across time and space. An extreme relativist position, holding that the difference of languages is complete incommensurability, would have to deny that mediation in which difference itself, in Derrida's phrasing, *is not*:[55] if a native English speaker believed that the referents of *Brot* and *pain* were substantively nonidentical to what she "knows" as *bread,* it is unlikely that she could learn to communicate in German or French. An extreme universalist position, meanwhile, that holds that the difference of languages is always reconcilable, conceives mediation as that which *overcomes* and resolves that difference: thus the proposition, on the basis that *Brot* and *pain do* have the same referent as *bread,* that the duplicate terms—in effect, the duplicate *languages*—be eliminated by reduction. As Weaver put it, in a subtly Eurocentrist conceit echoing Ferdinand de Saussure's own referents of choice, "A South American has, in general, no difficulty in recognizing that a Norwegian tree *is* a tree."[56] Hermeneutical translation theory, we might say, insists on the generalized difference of languages, on their original differentiation from (and thus repudiation of) any organic, original Language of the past, without admitting their resolution in a schematic-technical Language of the future. Interpretation, and translation conceived *as* interpretation—in its own self-understanding, at least—is that mediation of difference that does not resolve difference, but keeps it in play.

Translation, that is to say, functions within Newfield's Lyotardian "narrative of optimization" to the extent that it is conceived, schematically, as reduction of a base or source language to content passed as a message to a target language—or reduction of the base or source language *directly* to the target language, as in Weaver's notions of Russian or Chinese as "English coded with strange symbols." It is in this optimized computational functionalism that Venuti sees translation as a key enabler of Anglo-American cultural globalization, including both the dissemination of books translated from English and the projective integration of media control in developing countries by transnational media conglomerates.[57] For Venuti, insofar as income from foreign rights in translation sales is not reinvested, the transnational publishing industry merely performs in the mode of resource extraction. The democratic goal of a cultural materialist translation practice, he argues in terms derived from the work of Deleuze and Guattari, is to "minoritize" or "shake" the global linguistic hegemony of U.S. English.[58] This means *not*, Venuti is careful to emphasize, acquiring a countermajority over global English—overturning or counterturning it by opposing to it a "minor" vernacular—but rather "proliferat[ing] the variables within" global English, exploiting its "multiplicity and polychrony." Ethical or "scandalous" translation, Venuti suggests, submits English "to a local differentiation, as assimilation to the heterogeneity of a minor position."[59] Translation, for Venuti, is thus "uniquely effective in exacerbating the tensions of colonial discourse," because to move between colonial and indigenous languages is potentially to undermine the hierarchy in which colonized identity as "mimicry" is formed.[60]

One might say that in its artifactual published (book) form, the strong bilingual or plurilingual text seems to *enact*, rather than *argue* such "minoritizing" translation—inserting other languages in visibly internal parallel opposition, rather than urging them to proliferate serially from within. The very concept of a readership defined broadly by legibility within a national linguistic standard—regardless of whether it be understood as complacently hegemonic or successfully minoritized—is to some extent placed under erasure here. The strong bilingual or plurilingual text, that is to say, destroys the weaker plurilingual text's given basis for differentiation between a language of content, which controls *what* is said and remains translatable, and untranslated "foreign" languages of form, incident, or mere ornament. One might say that the strong plurilingual text is untranslatable in the strict sense, or translation-resistant to the extent that, as with idiom and nonsense, *the effort expended in dealing with problems of the transfer of content might be better spent learning the language(s) of the source.* The strong bilingual or plurilingual text, that is to say, is structured by that imperative, to know or to learn the languages of the source, in place of or prior to translation. It is, in Venuti's terms, *already* "foreignized." As such, one might say, it points in two directions, legitimating both the fantasy of original or universal language—of the subsumption of all languages under a metalanguage (organic or technical)—*and* the fantasy of escape from language into absolute difference or privacy.

Such texts are uncommon today, for reasons that might be assumed to be plain. One might say that the problem of *translation* for such texts forms a semiabsurd corollary to the problem of their publication (and potential readership) in the first place. Yet even one of the most obvious literary modernist precedents, Pound's *Cantos,* is for the most part passed over by both Steiner and Venuti, for analysis of the more substantively monolingual translation dynamics at work in Pound's *Cathay* or the Cavalcanti poems[61]—an odd refraction, perhaps, if, as in the work of both critics, it is the unacknowledged complexities of nationally monolingual translation, obscured by mathematical models of communication (be they structuralist–semiotic or capitalist), that are mobilized to undermine just such models. The strong bilingual or plurilingual text, which "embodies" the scandals of translation, would at the very least seem to present itself as an auspicious research object here.

WORLDS OF LANGUAGES

What I am calling the strong bilingual or plurilingual text requests a notion of translation, and of reading *as* translation, that accounts for its proportional equality of languages and deals responsibly with the cosmopolitan fantasies, as well as the fantasies of local resistance, that it enables. If monolingual translation can be thought as a bilingual encounter between two nations or national cultures, then literary plurilingualism, which might involve alternation between, or cycling among, more than two languages, can be thought as the encounter between several symbolically constituted linguistic "nations," or national linguistic cultures, simultaneously.

It is at this point entirely trivial, perhaps, to observe that projects for a universal language will always be haunted and upset by what Benedict Anderson termed "the fatality of human linguistic diversity."[62] What I want to emphasize, nevertheless—and to associate with the artifactual published form of the strong bilingual or plurilingual text—is the vital sense, in Anderson's schema, of *expansion toward a limit.* Anderson argued that in its fictive juxtaposition of disconnected events in the "homogeneous empty time" of Euro-Atlantic modernity, the "print-capitalist" production of the newspaper and novel enabled imaginations of the nation as a social group whose members might never meet each other, but who were linked by a common language. In Europe, this national language was consolidated "from above," out of the spoken vernaculars, for "dissemination through the market," "below" the Latin of elite bilinguals.[63] The new "mechanically reproduced print-languages," for Anderson, provided a sense of social belonging larger than the region, yet smaller than the world: "The potential stretch of these communities was inherently limited, and, at the same time, bore none but the most fortuitous relationship to existing political boundaries."[64]

In the Euro-Atlantic context in which Anderson formulated his schema—and that provides the irreducible intellectual and methodological inheritance of literary studies in the United States—we might think of the strong bilingual or plurilingual text as "frozen" at this moment, between expansion past the field of the local and reconsolidation as an expanded field of locality. We might say, in other words, that it reflects both the expansion of a field of literary exchange, in material book publication and distribution, and that which frustrates exchange, placing a limit on it. The incommensurability of national languages provides a global market for translation, which seems at the same time to serve the limit of a given national language (in mandating monolingual translation) and to supersede it (in demanding bilingual or plurilingual agents, as the performers *of* that monolingual translation). It follows from Anderson's schema that the nation requires not merely a subnational, but also a supranational frame of reference, just as the monolingual translation, circulating in a market for monolingual translations, is produced by a bilingual or plurilingual translator, and thus refers additionally and nonincidentally to the plurilingual. The "stronger" a bilingual or plurilingual text, one might say, the more explicitly rendered this paradox of *expansion toward a limit*. This, perhaps, is how, in Venuti's own account, Friedrich Schleiermacher's theory of "foreignizing" translation can serve a Prussian nationalist and imperialist project on the one hand, and evolve an anti-imperialist, "ethnodeviant" translation ethic at the very same time.[65]

"Was muß man machen, Tiefe zu erzählen?"

I have argued that in the book production of contemporary literature, the strength or weakness of the plurilingualism of a published literary text is largely a measure of its conformation to editorial standards of publishability determined by measures of marketability (including marketability in and for translation rights), themselves determined by benchmarks for growth and profitability within necessarily segregated national-language markets linked by (and in) translation. One might, then, speak of scales and degrees of such conformation, in the authorial and editorial negotiation of the right to "visible" archival existence that is publication, in such a system—and of the editorial custody that mimics and generalizes the conventions of culturally literate discourse in U.S. print media.

The weakest bilingual or plurilingual text, by such conventions, might be one merely seasoned, so to speak, with foreign words or idioms, in the everyday citational literacy that makes use of such elements as markers of education or objects of aspiration to the prestige or cultural capital of specific foreign languages, or of plurilingual competence itself. Here we might distinguish in both the common usage built on elite or educated public media discourse, and in specialized academic or other technical discourse, between two groups of borrowings. The first group might be thought as *assimilated* borrowings, which are no longer commonly emphasized or translated in printed text (in U.S. English common usage, "zeitgeist," for example, and in specialized discourse "mise-en-abyme"). The second group might be thought as partly or incompletely assimilated borrowings, which still tend to be marked with typographical emphasis, and attached to explanatory translations or attributions (*la dolce vita,* for example, or *bon vivant*). Reproduced in common usage, the borrowings of specialized discourse tend to appear in familiarized forms, followed by a translation and perhaps an attribution, such as "a French expression meaning 'focal reduplication,'" just as new borrowings into specialized discourse are "domesticated" in the same way ("Shklovsky's notion of *ostranenie* or defamiliarization"). Access to foreign languages, and comfort or authority in their use, accounts for borrowing the word in the first place; implicit here, perhaps, is not merely the knowledge of another language, but additionally a sense that the word in the foreign language is somehow more "just" than its native equivalent.[66]

One might begin, then, by asking how, where, when, and why foreign words are or are not naturalized in various specialized discourses, as well as in the often ephemeral realm of common usage. Why do we instinctively distinguish assimilated from unassimilated borrowings, using typographical conventions to mark a word's or a phrase's immigration status? In U.S. English, "zeitgeist" is today typeset with a lowercase "Z," bears an anglicized pronunciation, and is seldom marked explicitly any more as a foreign word. On the other hand, there is *la dolce vita,* which despite its rough equality of cultural currency is more commonly suspended between quotation marks or set in italic type, receives explanatory translations or attributions, and compels us to mimic Italian pronunciation. *Zeitgeist* is a translatable concept, of course, in the sense that it can be applied anywhere, whereas *la dolce vita,* with its companion idiom, *il dolce far niente,* stands for a global southern, a continental Mediterranean, a national Italian, or a regional Roman attitude: any and all of which are understood, in a United States context, as culturally Other. U.S. Americans, to their pride and despair, do not live *la dolce vita,* and italic type signifies a desire for the words along with their inadmissibility.

Many weaker bilingual or even plurilingual literary texts are resolutely idiolectic in this very sense. That is to say, they tend to translate and gloss words and phrases in a "foreign" language, in subordinating apposition to its native counterpart. As I have already noted, such domestication is hardly peculiar to U.S. English or Anglophone editorship in and of itself, but is in fact a structuring convention of the nationalized languages of book publishing generally (within a global publishing market that is certainly dominated by Anglo-American conglomerates[67]). Thus reports the narrator of Emine Sevgi Özdamar's "Mutterzunge," the bilingual opening text of her celebrated plurilingual German–Turkish collection of the same name:

Ich sagte: "Was muß man machen, Tiefe zu erzählen?" Er sagte: "*Kaza geçirmek,* Lebensunfälle erleben."[68]

I said: "What must one do, to recount deep things?" He said: "*Kaza geçirmek,* experience accidents of life."[69]

The Turkish idiom *kaza geçirmek* (to have an accident), the focus of this anecdote, is paraphrased in German here for a German-speaking, and by explicit indication *not* Turkish-speaking, reader. This appeal to monolingual German readers, within a German–Turkish literary-productive context, is made from the position of a minority language, on behalf of a minority culture, in the direct sense in which the onus is on Turkish emi-grants living and working in Germany to learn the German language. Yet to the extent that the bilingual narrator (here, under duress) engages in *both* foreignizing and domesticating behavior with respect to her "Mut-terzunge," she provides both the titillation of the foreign and its instant domestication: the double move of the discourse of exoticism. The fact is that no one thus served is moved to learn a new language:[70] the sanc-tioned reasons to learn such a "minority" language (law enforcement, espi-onage, ethnography) require little in the way of such help from the native informant.

Gloria Anzaldúa, to take a counterexample, makes fewer such gestures of overt accommodation. Her *Borderlands/La Frontera: The New Mestiza* switches "from English to Castilian Spanish to the North Mexican dialect to Tex-Mex to a sprinkling of Nahuatl to a mixture of all these," for entire prose paragraphs and passages of poetry, while also employing untrans-lated mixed phrasing on the sentence level: "Through our mothers, the culture gave us mixed messages: *No voy a dejar que ningún pelado desgraci-ado maltrate a mis hijos.* And in the next breath it would say, *La mujer tiene que hacer lo que le diga el hombre.* Which was it to be—strong, or submis-sive, rebellious or conforming?"[71] While it is possible for an Anglophone reader with no knowledge of U.S. Spanish to infer the topic here—the contradictions of a culture of male control over women's bodies—these "messages" themselves, in their idiomatic vocalization of (disputed) cul-tural mores, remain purposefully concealed from that reader—with a sim-ilar situation prevailing, of course, for the Hispanophone reader with no knowledge of English.[72]

We might return here to the radical language distribution of Pastorius's "Beehive," noting the most important difference between the forms of "sur-vival" of these texts: that both *Mutterzunge* and *Borderlands/La Frontera* belong to the late twentieth century, that they were written for publi-cation, and that they remap the artifactual relationship, in book publica-tion, between a legally and culturally dominant national language and a designated minority language (Spanish in the United States; Turkish in Germany). We might note also that the "Beehive" and *Borderlands/La Frontera* nevertheless resemble each other more closely, in their respective embodiments of the translation problems of hermeneutical translation theory, than either resembles the *Cantos,* for example, or Özdamar's "Mut-terzunge"—each of which, we might say, for specifically different reasons, in different contexts, and from different directions, moves to exoticize, via a double movement of foreignizing and domestication, the "foreign" languages it incorporates.

TRANSLATION BEING BETWEEN

Despite the challenges they pose to their own archival posterity, in contravening the monolingual editorial conventions of the global literary system—a lesser challenge, arguably, in the case of *Mutterzunge,* and a greater one in the case of *Borderlands/La Frontera*—both works can be said to be fairly securely emplaced in contemporary literary history and historiography, to the extent that each has attracted a great deal of attention and commentary in both the literary public and the university-based scholarly spheres. The same cannot be said of the next work I will discuss, the Swiss British writer–scholar Christine Brooke-Rose's novel *Between,* originally published in 1968—which is a liminal text, we might say, both in the plurilingual strategies it deploys on the page and in its entirely tenuous life in both print and critical commentary.

Narrated by an interpreter working in various capacities for postwar international governmental and academic organizations, *Between* is organized by images of international and interlinguistic circulation and patterns of association formed in the violent disjunctions of travel. The text mixes German and French into its "base" or source English, with short passages in Italian and bits of dialogue and phrasing in Danish, Dutch, Spanish, Polish, Portuguese, Romanian, Provençal, Czech, Slovene, Serbo-Croatian, Bulgarian, Greek, and Turkish—all without (in any of these languages) using forms of the verb *to be.*

Between's performative plurilingual virtuosity is balanced by this grammatical elision and liquidation, on which Brooke-Rose commented in an archly avowed autocritical swan song entitled *Invisible Author: Last Essays.*[73] Assessing her own body of work as a kind of extended lipogram, Brooke-Rose reflected at length in *Invisible Author* on the long and productive career that had left her work largely unread by and unknown to both the common reading and the literary-critical public. Describing the consequences of her failure to draw attention to the experimental constraining structures by means of which she composed many of her later novels, Brooke-Rose distinguished between masculinist and feminist approaches to the negativist form of literary performativity embodied in the lipogrammatic procedures of her Francophone contemporaries in the Oulipo group—whose mechanization of literary composition, Brooke-Rose argued, replicated the duplicitously demonstrative productivism of the Joycean high-modernist modes it claimed to displace. Discussing Georges Perec's composition of *La disparition* without making use of the French letter *e,* Brooke-Rose remarks that "Perec told of his lipogram and got lots of attention, then and ever since, just as Eliot printed footnotes to *The Waste Land* and Joyce was careful to leave keys that soon overcame . . . the mystification about meaning, keys that initiated and continue to feed the immense Joyce industry." Of the grammatical lipogram structuring *Between* (published a year earlier), by contrast, Brooke-Rose says, "I said nothing, and was more than spared the industry: no one noticed."[74]

To disclose the lipogram, to render it visible, is, Brooke-Rose argues, to return it to the territories of the organic humanist discourse of masculinized creative originality, leaving a "key to the industry" guaranteeing archival posterity in and through a similarly masculinized scholarship. She reminds her reader that the antinomian consciousness that narrates *Between,* in contradistinction, dissolves itself in the colliding plurality of national languages that constitutes her in her work as a verbal intermediary, caught in the flow of time in language—though as a public consciousness and the fictive narrator of a book that did succeed, however weakly, in being published, she also necessarily manipulates that plurality, reconsolidating it in the cosmopolitanism of a polyglot agent. We might say that the dual registers of *Between,* which quite cannily and accurately reflects on its own future as a published artifact, turn on and around this limit.

The narrator, a simultaneous interpreter, works in her native languages, French and German. "She lives," as Brooke-Rose writes in her commentary on the novel in *Invisible Author,* "between languages, between conferences, between places, in airplanes and hotel rooms, which look more and more alike."[75] Her acquired English, the language of her British companion and lover, Siegfried, joins her native languages in an exuberant Europhone idiom of interlinguistic riddle and innuendo:

Zut alors says Siegfried grown slightly bald somewhere between New York and a paunch pahr dessue le marshy. Pupate? Pupate? Que cherchez-vous madame, ah, l'ascenseur. Oh mademoiselle, they have not blossomed yet, the season has not yet come. Achten Sie auf den Original-verschluss. Heil-und-Tafelwasser. Das österreichische PRE-BLAUER. Sauerbrunn. . . .
—Man denkt in Deutsch wann mann in Deutschland lebt.
—Auf Deutsch darling.
—Und since man spricht sehr little Deutsch unlike my clever sweet half born and bred on Pumpernickel, man denkt in eine kind of erronish Deutsch das springt zu life feel besser than echt Deutsch. Und even wenn mann thinks AUF Deutsch wann man in Deutschland lives, then acquires it a broken up quality, die hat der charm of my clever sweet, meine deutsche mädchen-goddess, the gestures and the actions all postponed while first die Dinge und die Personen kommen. As if languages loved each other behind their own façades, despite alles was man denkt darüber davon dazu. As if words fraternised silently beneath the syntax, finding each other funny and delicious in a Misch-Masch of tender fornication, inside the bombed out hallowed structures and the rigid steel glass modern edifices of the brain.[76]

Other Germanic or Romance languages pepper this narrative too, in what the interpreter terms "smatterings," seasoning the texture of thought itself, as well as of her erotic banter with Siegfried. Along with the English–German–French–Italian core, these "smattering" or seasoning languages form a cluster of complex nativity, we might say, within the larger languagescape of *Between*—less a center than a network of the familiar that draws from ceaseless movement and circulation a form of stasis and a "base."

This expansion toward a limit—what I earlier called the "frozen" moment of the strong bilingual or plurilingual text—is partnered with a visual idiom of stillness in movement, of peaks of circulation at which circulation appears to cease. A jetliner is a "great pressured solitude" floating "motionless" and "immobile" over the "halo" of propellers, blades blurred; air-conditioned or centrally heated hotel rooms are filled with "insulated silence"; traveling west over the Atlantic Ocean is an "endless day." Images of what the narrator experiences as a kind of timeless or time-stopping sunlight are abundant, glinting on the metal wing of the plane, striping the airport hallways, pouring through curtains into a hotel room. Her

horoscope reads *Sie haben Appetit auf Neues:* for frontierlessness, for the
"freedom of the air," for "frequent changes of partners loyalties convic-
tion,"[77] for "the flickering local variation on the presentation of opposite
viewpoints on every aspect of an instant world."[78] Looking at a billboard
advertising laundry soap, she thinks to herself, charmingly: "Più bianco
than what? We live in an age of transition, perpetually between white and
whiter than white. Very tiring. Zoom."[79]

"Between" is, in fact, the first word of the first and last sentences of this
novel, its first sentence being a mock-Joycean extension and variation on
the last. Each sentence presents the jetliner, its body (with, inside it, the
passenger's body) "floating" in flight, "between doing and not doing." "In
some countries" at the borders of this circulation, the narrative consciousness observes, "the women would segregate still to the left of the aisle, the
men less numerous to the right. But all in all and civilisation considered
the chromosomes sit quietly mixed among the hundred and twenty seats
or so that stretch like ribs as if inside a giant centipede. Or else inside the
whale, who knows . . ."[80] The exhausts of the jet engines are "invisible in
their power save for a tremor against the blue," the propellers "invisible in
their speed save for a tinted halo," in the sky "no cloud and from this seat
no reef of nature no manmade object passing to show that the plane flies
immobile at eight hundred and thirty kilometres an hour." The plane's
position is purely mathematical; in "the deep blue of high sky," motion
cannot be seen.

Polish, Czech, Slovene, Serbo-Croatian, Bulgarian, Greek, and Turkish
compose another category of "smattering"—language picked up in travel
or from a phrase book, deployed alternately as gestures of primitive fluency and (more often) comic obstacles. Encounters with these languages
arise from the narrator's searches for entrances and exits to and from hotel
rooms, elevators, and women's restrooms. Here, the blocking effect of
foreign orthographies is linked to the body, to movement on the ground,
to the counterpoint of physiology and its regular functions with the
placeless environments of global circulation. As the interpreter struggles
with inscriptions in (faithfully typeset) Greek and Cyrillic, other motifs
of organic or physiological interruption surface. Her hotel room number
assignments, in different cities, countries, and continents, seem to reveal
a pattern. The reader's attention is directed to her body, to the medal of

Saint Christopher, patron of travelers, nestled between her breasts; to the in-flight meal tray "full of half-eaten trifle and the crumbs of roll"; to the fat hands and bald or fluffy "head-tops" of passengers; to the narrator's physical sensations when the plane hits the runway or when she wakes in a hotel room at dawn. There is a series of behavioristic gags (a dog barking in Dutch, a cock crowing in Portuguese, a car revving in Danish) and a photograph snapped on the plane, "with a tip of nose in the foreground and maybe a dark green shoulder or curve of bosom even and the enormous wing spreading back moving at high speed over the Danube quite blue from der Luft and gone."[81] Such images recur cyclically, sometimes suggesting organic rhythm, at other times mechanized iteration. And at times, the narrator's physiological and technical idioms merge, the jetliner figured as a whale or a helix, the interpreter "all channels alert eyes ears mouthpiece and fingers through her long auburn hair."[82] Neither the physiological nor the technological idiom is universalized here; the narrator finds refuge neither in pure being, in the regional stasis of her thinking and speaking body, nor in ceaseless becoming, her globalized flow in and through placeless place. One is left with a "globo-local" world of partial or concrete universals, from which particulars precipitate as national character traits.

This systemic and dialectical image of the modernity that is the narrator's actual field of labor does, however, find its limit in *Between*. In fact, one might say that in many ways, the true concern of Brooke-Rose's novel is more the border or seam of that modernity with its continental outside—the "betweenness," one might say, of the Bosphorus Strait—than its play within "Europe" *as* just such a closed political, cultural, linguistic, and religious system: and that this is the substance of its symbolic conflict with the closed order of a technocratic Euro-Atlantic high modernist and postmodernist literary tradition, with the care it took to leave "keys" to the critical and scholarly industry of its own perpetuation. In *Between*'s sequence set in Turkey, the foreign words and phrases (as well as the place-names that are both words and things) of the narrator's "smatterings" are less virtuosically assimilable as unfamiliar elements, advancing instead toward a kind of productive incommensurability.

To be sure, this is an incommensurability experienced by *Between*'s European protagonists, masculine (or masculinist) and feminine (or feminist) alike, with high anxiety. The otherness of Turkey and of Turkish people, their ways of life, and their language, provokes in Siegfried a noticeable intensification of the spectacular encyclopedist mode through which he negotiates and performs his own postwar European cosmopolitanism. Siegfried's improvisations here make crudely explicit use of caricature, in the assertion of cultural difference—a tendency in which the narrator is silently complicit: "Unless he says but now we have moved out of the hard bed area into the softness of the east come live with me and join my harem here in Istanbul in heavy heat dein Brust like a mosque domed on the night sky my hallowed structure like a minaret piercing the Milky Way and hats geschmeckt?"[83] Siegfried takes up position as his lover's guide, declaring his preference for the Süleymaniye mosque in Istanbul and an admiration for Arabic calligraphy ("so much easier to contemplate than images because devoid of sense, to us at least"), as well as enjoying gossipy asides on the scandal of the Turks (they are impious Muslims who can't read Arabic and enjoy drinking). In a scene that may be a dream sequence, the European delegation is entertained with a performance by a group of male dancers while a separate group of female dancers, waiting their turn, waits visibly in the wings. Addressed in French by one of the delegates, the women answer haltingly, "les hommes pas permission kadın, kadın, er, femmes danser en public." A crowd of delegates, led by Siegfried, then chants in primitive Turkish, "Kadın! Kadın! Kadın!" ("Woman! Woman! Woman!") until the women, interpellated and emboldened by this demand for modern equality, step eagerly out onto the stage.

It is by recalling this "chant" that the interpreter, searching in a subsequent sequence for the "Turkish ladies,'" will eventually—but not without assistance—find her way to the building's restrooms. Along the way, the narrator recalls a billboard advertisement in Turkish containing the phrase "Lux sabonu hayranım" (mildly ungrammatically, "I'm a fan of Lux soap"[84]). Misappropriating the word *hayran* (possibly having misheard *hanım*, "lady"), she asks an unidentified interlocutor for directions to the women's toilet, using the phrase "*Hayranım lutfen*" (a more or less nonsensical utterance that would be difficult either to translate or transpose). Clearly, the "joke" here, if there is one, is on the narrator—and it is, straightforwardly, a humorous mistake, the humor of which operates in the displacement of the alien traveler by the essentially opaque foreign word. In a deliberately introjected counterprojection to the confidently masculine crowd chanting the transparent name of Woman, Turkish here serves to constrain the narrator's spatial and social mobility, in the Lacanian limit-drama of doors marked for "gentlemen" and "ladies."

Compare this with a parallel narrative in which the interpreter (now in Rome) must submit to an interview with a Vatican functionary in order to begin the process of having her marriage annulled. As the narrator restages it, this endeavor involves actual or imagined interviews, in several Western European languages, concerning birth control methods and their frustration of the natural purpose of marriage. Here, the narrator's jokes are unquestionably "in" jokes, turning on a series of idiomatic culturalist euphemisms for contraceptive devices, whose humor is tied to a narrower and more specifically circumscribed context of reference (Germanic–Latinate, European, and Catholic). The centrifugal linguistic slapstick of mangled Turkish in the nonsense phrase "Hayranım lutfen" yields here to a kind of Euro-Atlantic centripetal cosmopolitan wit:

E allora, what methods did you use?

—Comment? Ah. Hé bien mon père, d'abord une—je ne sais pas comment ça s'appelle en français.

—Dites en allemand mon enfant, ou en anglais.

—A sheath, at first, then a Dutch hat, er, cap.

—Non capisco.

—Vous voulez dire, madame, une capote anglaise?

—Non mon père. Je crois que capote anglaise veut dire ce que les anglais appellent French letter.

—Una cosa di gomma?

—Si.

—E l'altra cosa, più tardi?

—Je ne sais pas monsignor.

—Dessinez, s'il vous plait. Ah si, si, la conosco. Va bene. Scusi, grazie tanto.[85]

One might imagine these scenes of language on a vector of internationalization linking the core of an expanding European community to the foreign entity at its continental border. In the opaque word KADIN, the narrator, fluent in multiple European languages, makes a fresh confrontation with the unknown: a confrontation managed at once with humor (and humility), and at the same time through complicity in a comically typical, touristic act of self-distancing. It is the exhilarating and traumatic moment when, on first learning a foreign word, one is thrust into involuntary solidarity with those for whom that word is *not* foreign, at all—and before (in the condensation of that expanding field of experience) the word becomes part of an idiom one's own.

Between is a work cosmopolitan in its internal figurations and provincial in its possibilities for circulation as a material artifact. Its implied reader, one as idiosyncratically plurilingual in a particular spectrum of European national languages as itself, would be likewise formed by the condensation of an expanding language field, in a second-order localization or reterritorialization. *Between* must "lose" in translation, not because it has purified a national language so as to help it resist translation into any other, but because it has *exceeded* translation conceived as the mediation of any two national languages.[86] Translation being between *two* languages, it follows that a work such as *Between* moves toward untranslatability in the latter, metastatic and liminal sense (despite the fact that it never quite relinquishes English as a base language), which goes a long way to explain why theorists of translation, even when they insist on translation as deeply and ethically difficult, seem to avoid taking such texts as their research objects. The invisibility of the "invisible author" of *Between* would necessarily extend to any *agent* of translation, as well.

I want to close with an anecdote from machine translation research that marks this dynamic, as it were, in reverse. Victor Yngve, who directed a machine translation project funded by the National Science Foundation in 1953, included in the text of his progress report for that year the following product of an experimental automated translation from German into English, which purposefully left articles and other function words untranslated in a test of the system's optimization for efficiency:

Die CONVINCINGe CRITIQUE des CLASSICALen IDEA OF PROBABILITY IS eine der REMARKABLEen WORKS des AUTHORs. Er HAS BOTHen LAWe der GREATen NUMBERen ein DOUBLEes TO

SHOWen: (1) wie sie IN seinem SYSTEM TO INTERPRETen ARE, (2) THAT sie THROUGH THISe INTERPRETATION NOT den CHARACTER von NOT-TRIVIALen DEMONSTRABLE PROPOSITIONen LOSEen. CORRESPON DS der EMPLOYEDen TROUBLE? I AM NOT SAFE, THAT es dem AUTHOR SUCCEEDED IS, den FIRSTen POINT so IN CLEARNESS TO SETen, THAT ALSO der UNEDUCATED READER WITH dem DESIRABLEen DEGREE-OF-EXACTNE SS INFORMS wird.

Regarding the "success" of the experiment, Yngve's conclusion, as reported by John Hutchins, was as follows: "Those who knew no German at all were able to grasp only the subject matter from the translated stems. They were generally unable to get much idea of just what was being said about the subject matter. On the other hand, people who knew a little German grammar, after they had recovered from their mirth, demonstrated that they were able to understand quite well and fairly rapidly what was being said."[87]

Machine translation, in other words, worked quite well, provided that those translated for *already knew the source language.* The same could be said of the social operations producing the strong bilingual or plurilingual text, which arrives from the literary humanist end of the spectrum of value, here. The uncanny convergence of such "machine language" with the textuality of *Between*'s narrator's love scenes with Siegfried suggests, perhaps, that the drama we find here is not—or not only—a struggle for primacy between exponents of humanity and efficiency, but also over how (definitively) to confirm machine failure, in a kind of declining Turing test: can we distinguish the artifice of machine translation from the breakdown of that social institution, a national language?

3

Containment

In August 1959 the magazine *Atlantic Monthly* described a technical, military, and cultural intelligence blunder that had sparked panic in the United States two years earlier, and which must sound down the echo chamber of history now, toward years' worth of untranslated Arabic-language interceptions languishing in a National Security Agency vault somewhere. Technical details relating to Sputnik I's radio system, the article claimed, had been published by the Soviet Academy of Sciences in a Russian-language amateur radio magazine to which many U.S. libraries subscribed, but of which only the U.S. Air Force had made a (classified) translation. In a demonstrative instance of what we might call information pathology, or the excess of recognizable or usable knowledge by compiled data, the U.S. Navy's satellite tracking system—constructed, as part of the Naval Research Laboratory's faltering "Project Vanguard," without that readily available (if "encoded") knowledge—had proved unable to eavesdrop on Sputnik I.

I begin with this anecdote—which turns on the hiding in plain sight, as it were, of language understood as culture—in order to open the question of language as a container, in the seemingly incompatible vehicular and constraining senses of that term, of translatable or untranslatable knowledge, the object and stock-in-trade of professional research. In the postwar cold war culture of the United States, I have already suggested, that question was structured by aggressively competing visions of the relationship between sociolectic and technocratic forms of technicity, which crossed (or collided) in such spectacular failures of "human" or cultural intelligence as are invoked by the figure of Sputnik I overlaid with "9/11," and which then (as now) served as incitement to doubling down by both the theoretical partisans and the practical monomaniacs of both cultures. In the short term, then as now, such problems of cultural difference as are presented by the *open secret* of Sputnik I are approached, we might say, by means of what software programmers call a "patch," which changes the behavior of a specific component while purposefully leaving unrevised the larger system in which it is embedded.

The *Atlantic* article's author, David O. Woodbury, retailed two motifs of postwar public policy discourse on machine translation that reflected the early drive, in that research, toward the goal of completely automatic computer translation of natural or human languages. The first of these sounds that familiar refrain of global capitalist modernity confronted with the inscrutable productivity of its socialist other: the need to match and exceed the pace of both known and imagined Soviet scientific innovation, with which U.S. research was imagined to advance only in step. The second stressed the inadequacy of human staffing to the scale of intercepted enemy knowledge production:

> Since Sputnik I, a crash program by the National Science Foundation has been turning out an estimated 100 million words per year of technical Russian translation alone, but this is less than half of the text we should be handling. Little has been done with other important tongues. It is impossible to obtain enough translators, especially the trained people required for work in technical fields. Such people as there are cannot be spared from their chosen professions. About ten years ago Dr. Warren Weaver of the Rockefeller Foundation, foreseeing the situation, suggested that the enormous routine job of translation might be done by machines. The idea was quickly taken up by linguists and electronics specialists in America and England. Today, the computer, or electronic brain, is well along toward picking up the burden of machine translation, known as "MT."[1]

What is most interesting in this construction of crisis is certainly not the comically time-bound optimism regarding "electronic brains" (which we, who live with personal computers that are as much bloated and sluggish *bodies* as they are anything else, can openly laugh at today). What is interesting, rather, is the barely detectable tension here between a hemispheric figure defined by the Russian language of the Soviet enemy, on the one hand, and the invocation of "other important tongues," on the other. In the previous chapter, I described how Weaver, the prime mover of postwar United States "MT" research and a tireless advocate of its enabling violations, wanted to make MT crucial to the peace-keeping operations of new postwar world governmental organizations, enhancing international and intercultural communication, as he put it, "for the constructive and peaceful future of the planet."[2] It would be tempting to read the dashing of Weaver's hopes directly from the postwar hubris with which he framed them, blending triumphalist U.S. liberal idealism with the equally triumphalist scientific reductionism ready to hand (even when apparently hesitant) in the shaming victory of U.S. atomic weapons research. The more proximate cause for the militarist diversion of MT, of course, was the arms race of the deterrent world-system, figured in document-processing terms by the author of the *Atlantic* article, for whom the crisis condition was the outpacing of U.S. reading capacity by Soviet writing. If funding for MT research gradually became easier to secure through the early 1950s, as this imagination of unprocessable input–output asymmetries gained traction, it was the 1957 Sputnik I launch that galvanized U.S. effort all at once to what we might call the *monolingual* military application of MT to Russian technical literature.

Ironically, perhaps (if one is seduced by simple cause and effect), it was the Russian-to-English MT demonstration at IBM's New York headquarters in 1954, covered prominently in U.S. newspapers, that focused attention on MT in the Soviet Union itself, prompting the revival of Petr Petrovich Troyanskii's neglected proposals for mechanized translation dating back to the 1930s.[3] Three major and numerous minor Soviet research groups were created immediately following the IBM demonstration, and work on an English-to-Russian system began promptly in January 1955 at the Institute for Precision Mechanics and Computer Technology in Moscow.[4] Although the internal linguistic diversity of the USSR and its sphere of influence meant that Soviet MT research was from the start more categorically diversified than its U.S. counterpart, English-to-Russian carried the primary emphasis of Soviet work of the 1950s and '60s, and as in the United States, Soviet first attempts were "brute force" methods, bringing maximum hardware and software computing power to bear on the noncomputational complexity of the translation problem.[5]

The meticulous archival work of John Hutchins on the origins of MT research makes clear that what we call the cold war included war in, of, and for (human) language as a "code" to rival repositories of defense-industrial knowledge, and that computers, in addition to directing extrahuman-scaled, wholly automated offensive and defensive systems of weaponry, were put to the task of processing ever-increasing volumes of documentation produced by human researchers in excess of their own capacities for reception. Insofar as the weaponized materiality of the arms race was dependent, on this sense, on surveillance of enemy research, and insofar as the transmission and preservation of research took place in documents composed in human languages, it is not at all far-fetched to speak of a confrontation between the English and Russian languages, in what Paul N. Edwards, borrowing from the literary criticism of Sherman Hawkins, termed a geoinformatic "closed world" structured by technical and geo-strategic metaphors of containment and automation.[6]

Let me suggest now that the natively located humanistic study of U.S., British, and Euro-Atlantic Anglophone literature, as an effort of human or humanist intelligence, has been and is every bit as bound, in this sense, by its linguistic closure as its counterparts in the world of military technocratic espionage. We might say that in that sense, the rise and fall of what McLuhan jokingly called a "Pentecostal condition of universal understanding and unity," in fully computerized "instant translation,"[7] is something of an allegory for the rise and fall of the postwar strain of United States exceptionalism whose professional cultural expression in the social-, literary-, and mass-culture historiographic formations of U.S. American Studies is, even today, a site of struggle over the definition of U.S. national culture *in* both historically North American and diasporic U.S. languages— to say nothing of the languages of genuine rivals to U.S. imperial power. (Indeed, we might ask how it is that that legacy of a natively located U.S. literary studies most directly interrogative of U.S. cold war culture seems to have established and reproduced itself, with great success, in the absence—or perhaps the denial—of any imperative to literary or literarist training in the language of the great enemy.)

Edwards suggests that the material–ideological apparatus of the confrontation we call the "cold war" was a structure of closed informatic systems for military strategic early warning and automated response, entwined with emblematic and iconic contrasts at the material/immaterial horizon of the concept of "information" itself. Constructed with necessarily predetermined and prelimited data structures, which "collected" information from and on the enemy's spatial field of material operation on the one hand, and rhetorically *produced* it on the other, cold war systems both fabricated and deferred the reality of global armed confrontation in "gaming" simulation[8]—a dynamic we might think as translative in its both necessary and impossible modes of equivalence. Within such an understanding of the translative production of information, one might see machine translation as both a technical project and an imaginary, closing on itself as a massive infusion of defense funding turned it definitively toward a single language pair (English and Russian), assigning one language the fixed position of input or source, and the other that of output or target. The technical problem of automating translation itself enters the system of contained confrontation at that point where captured enemy documentation, amassed in material form, needs to be *read* in a manner that most efficiently extracts its embodied content—and purposefully blocks the reflexive effects of such "reading" (for example, incitement to language acquisition).[9]

Edwards adapts Martin Van Creveld's concept of "information pathology" to name the (bathetic) failure of high-tech input–output systems to accommodate quotidian unprogrammed inputs: that which, in the comedy of human–machine errors, "does not compute," not because the conditions of a problem are too complex, but rather because they are too simple. Edwards's favorite example is Operation Igloo White, run in Vietnam by the U.S. Air Force from 1967 to 1972 at an annual cost of $1 billion. From the Infiltration Surveillance Center in Thailand, U.S. operators monitored the sounds of vehicles, the body heat given off by living creatures, and even the odor of urine through a network of computerized sensors installed along the Ho Chi Minh Trail. Computers relayed the geographic coordinates of such signals to U.S. planes flying over the jungle, controlling the release of munitions over targets invisible to the pilot and his own instruments. Yet many of the "kills" counted by the air force, which a 1971 Senate subcommittee report concluded far exceeded the number of available targets, were apparently executed on tape recorders playing recorded truck rumblings, or bags of urine planted or emptied near the system's sensors by the Vietcong.[10] In Igloo White's closed system, as Edwards interprets it, "kills" were completed attacks as produced, preprogrammed outputs—as victims of which an *actual* truck, and the tape recording of a truck engine, were informationally equivalent.

It is in just this way, we could say, that as machine translation is substituted for human fluency, it maintains the source language in precisely its incommensurability or inaccessibility *as* source. Not because machine translation "doesn't work," but because the cultural knowledge thus relocated to the machine will, in the best of all technical implementations, remain there, as inaccessible to its users as it was before. (In delegating language acquisition to a computer that you operate, you get translations whose accuracy you can't yourself verify.) While early researchers complained that "lay" expectations for MT discounted the controlled or closed environment in which they measured success, much early popular writing on machine translation in the United States was in fact surprisingly culturalist in this deeper sense, which suggests that computation's foundering on culture is not in fact a soluble problem, but a culture itself. In the glee with which newspaper and magazine journalists imagined the translating machine foundering on human idiom, there is not an argument, strictly speaking, but a kind of enjoyment of the unexpected or the unknown.

Here is Hutchins, editorializing on this point:

Critics and sceptics have been fond of repeating alleged mistranslations, howlers which no human translator would perpetrate, in order to ridicule the whole enterprise. The most popular example has been a story involving the translation of two idioms from English into Russian and then back again from Russian into English: *Out of sight, out of mind,* and *The spirit is willing but the flesh is weak.* According to some accounts the first came back as "invisible insanity" and the second was "The whiskey is all right but the meat has gone bad"; according to others, however, the versions were "Invisible and insane" and "The vodka is good but the meat is rotten"; and yet others have given "invisible lunatics" and "the ghost is willing but the meat is feeble." There have been various other permutations and variants; such variety is typical of hearsay, and indeed, some accounts give the languages as German and English, and others assert they were Chinese and English. Nevertheless, the supposed translations are repeated to the present day as genuine examples of the "literal-mindedness" of machine translation.[11]

One might say, with justice, that Hutchins enjoys these anecdotes as much as anyone else. But also that he implies that such stubbornness, whether in everyday humans or professional humanists, reflects a fundamental misunderstanding of the technical enterprise, a misunderstanding that is simply out of joint, unsynchronized with technocratic modernity as a historical fait accompli. We might suggest, in contrast, that this culture of apparent "antimodernity" is in fact a competing modernity, neither part of a singular modern nor its real "primitive" other. In the linguistic imaginary of the early cold war "system," dominated by faith (however brief and tenuous) in brute-force technical solutions to linguistic difference, we might think of literature as a form of information pathology, superfluous from the standpoint of efficient communication or document processing and representing an exception (perhaps permanent) to preprogrammed outputs. The author of the *Atlantic Monthly* article is perhaps typical of journalists (and not only journalists) covering machine translation, then as now, in closing his article with a figure of literary language as the final (unattainable) cultural object of computational desire:

> The ultimate in translation machines is thus not too hard to imagine. The final word—and no informed engineer would be surprised—will be the machine to which one can talk in one language while it simultaneously intones the translation in another, perhaps several others at once, depending upon what buttons are pushed. And if someday this ultimate robot, made a little tipsy by its own cleverness, should hear the lines
>
> > 'Twas brillig, and the slithy toves
> > Did gyre and gimble in the wabe,
>
> we might find out what Lewis Carroll really meant.[12]

In what follows, I examine literary devices for the "automatic translation," predominantly of a language represented as Russian, in several literary works of the period. My readings will suggest that Anglo-American cold war literary plurilingualism allegorizes in language the technical and geostrategic confrontation between the United States and the Soviet Union, mediated by the category of national language as repository of encoded knowledge and determined by the sociality (or asociality) of computerized translation. Though none of these works necessarily takes machine translation as a specific theme, or other aspect of their reproducible content *as* works, the authorial–editorial formal strategies through which each one, from within English, manipulates representations of the Russian language, in particular, can be said to illuminate that sociality as Weaver and others expressed it early on, in the project for fully automated and human-independent MT.[13] In its literary aspects, I will suggest, the particularly linguistic confrontation staged here between English and Russian recalls the dynamics of both the initially euphoric phase, and later, the deflationary phases of arms-race machine translation research, in its attempt to "recode" Russian (and other languages) *as* English. Thus, while none of these works ought to be read, either thematically or formally, as a monodimensional historical allegory, I will suggest that the unambiguously fixed position of Russian as an "input" language here cannot be discounted, either, in its literary coproduction of cold war hegemonic language politics.

Naïve or sophisticated understandings of authorial or editorial "intention" are less useful, for my purposes here, than attention to the material constraints of literary book publication and circulation (by which, as we will see, even a *personally* "strong" plurilingual author is as tightly bound as anyone else). In my examples here—literary works chosen as exemplarily suggestive, rather than synoptically definitive—Russian is translatively "contained" within a rival language, for a monolingual or Euro-Atlantic plurilingual reader constructed by the editorial–artifactual form of the published book, in what we might call a literary-humanist *enactment* on the material printed page, rather than reflection in narrative symbol, of the technocratic dream of fully automated MT. One the one hand, we might say, such literary or literarist enactments as are found in these three works *resist* the coding model of fully automated MT, by staging precisely the failure, or the "impossibility," of translation as "universal understanding and unity." At the same time, on the other hand, they support and reproduce or coproduce that coding model, in their own very aggressively monolingual preprocessing of foreign input as domestic output.

Containing *A Clockwork Orange*

"Nadsat," the speech personality Anthony Burgess invented for his 1963 novel *A Clockwork Orange,* is probably best described as a literary standard English into which are mixed many words transliterated from Russian as well as a few from German, some English slang, and some outright neologisms. In a way, the proliferation of pseudo-scholarly supplements to the novel, beginning with the Nadsat glossary appended to the first U.S. edition, is itself an element of *Clockwork's* logic of restricted excess, the closure that ensures Nadsat will be perfectly comprehensible to any Anglophone reader willing to postpone the gratification of full comprehension for a few pages.[14] *Clockwork's* narrating agent, Alex, whom we might read as a complex of fictive narrator (in the sense traditional to formalistic narratological approaches) and print book *editor,* takes plainly visible care to present each Russian-language borrowing in varying contexts and grammatical positions, so that with repetition its foreign sense may be clarified and its glossarial mapping to an English equivalent encouraged. The plurilingualism of *A Clockwork Orange* might be said to be "weak" to the extent that Alex strives so visibly to absorb foreign words into his expanded *literary* English, subtended as it is by the intensely monolingual play of pun, infantilism, and slang, the anticipated recognition of which is configured to imply and construct a reader-as-native-speaker.

Nadsat's borrowings can be divided into several categories. The weapons carried and used by Alex and his "droogs" are designated with Russian words: britva (razor), nozh (knife), oozy (chain, from *uzh,* snake). So are violent actions: crasting (stealing, from *krast*), dratsing (fighting, from *drat,* to kill), oobivatting (*ubivat,* to kill), tolchocking (*tolchok,* a blow), razrezzing (*razrvat,* to rip). Nadsat also contains an abundance of Russian words for body parts: glazz (*glaz,* eye), goober (*guba,* lip), groody (*grud,* breast), litso (face), gulliver (*golova,* head), rooker (*ruka,* hand), rot (mouth), yahzick (*yazyk,* tongue), zoobies (*zuby,* teeth). Many of these words are either chosen or transformed to repellent effect: "goober" suggesting phlegm or chewed food, "groody" dirtiness, "rot" rot, and so on. And finally, there are the social categories: baboochka *(babushka),* banda (gang), brattie (*brat,* brother), cheena (*zhenshchina,* woman), veck or chelloveck (*chelovyek,* man), devotchka (girl), malchick (*malchik,* boy), millicent (*militsiya,* policeman), plenny (*plenniyi,* prisoner), ptitsa ("chick," from *ptitsa,* bird). On the one hand, the interpolation of Russian words in itself constitutes a kind of linguistic violence done to the novel's own native English: particularly for the reader with no knowledge of Russian, this violent interpolation of a foreign language interrupts reading by leaving referential holes in the story's linguistic surface. Where weapons and acts of violence are concerned, the borrowings serve to mystify violence, constructing it as opaque to representation. In precisely this form of mate-riality—in their way of "standing off" the surface of both the text of *Clock-work,* and the *book*—Russian words also serve to soften or deflect attention from violence, on something of the principle of the military euphemism, which conceals extrajuridical killing behind such emotionally opaque technical jargon as "antipersonnel" and "collateral damage." (This is the function performed in reverse by *Clockwork*'s own English euphemisms, most notoriously "the old in-out-in-out," which evades the legal definition of rape by corporealizing it.) Words for parts of the body, meanwhile, seem chosen to evoke both the monstrous and the mechanistic: "rooker" sug-gesting a black bird or perhaps a claw, "glazzies" artificial eyes, "rot" and "zoobies" something organic but misshapen or decaying. The ambiguity of reference built into *Clockwork*'s transformations at once sharpens and blunts the grossness of these foreign parts and appendages.[15] Nadsat thus functions generally both to perform and to obscure violence, to realize it translatively *in* language (and in language's lapsarian representation of things), and to reconstruct it as unrepresentably foreign: conducted with foreign implements, upon foreign parts of bodies belonging to foreign people whose social positions are located in a foreign habitus.

At the same time, however, the native speaker of English is invited to take euphonious pleasure in the monolingual polyphony of puns ("sinny" for "cinema" and "charlie" for chaplain, as in Charlie Chaplin) and port-manteau words ("skrike," scratch and strike, "chumble," chatter and mum-ble), as well as the schoolboy infantilism of "eggyweg" (egg), "skollywoll" (school) and "appy polly loggies" (apologies).[16] There are modulations from contemporary into mock-biblical and Elizabethan English: "O my father. . . . Fear not. He canst taketh care of himself, verily."[17] And the novel is full of disguised and undisguised British cultural allusions: the masks the gang members wear include faces of Disraeli, "Peebee" Shelley, and Henry VIII; there is a Marghanita Boulevard (Marghanita Laski) and a Boothby Avenue (Bob Boothby).[18] While some transformations from Russian, such as "slooshy" and "devotchka," are left relatively intact as interpolated foreign words, others are anglicized to the point of seeming—or becoming—native English neologisms: "horrorshow," for example, the inverted affect of which conceals its derivation from the Russian *kharashó* ("good"), or "yarbles," in fact a truncation of "yarblocko," Burgess's transformation of *yabloko*, apple.[19] There is also the evocation of Swift in "gulliver" (from *golova*), the culturally specific diminution (and transgendering) in the transformation of *militsiya* to "millicent," and the slang scatological ring in English of "Bog" (*Bog*, God). Such extreme domestications merge tracelessly into the novel's English for all but the most committed lay enthusiasts and scholar–detectives. (One might also reflect here on *Clockwork*'s narrator's name, Alex, and the names of his "droogs," Dim, Pete, and Georgie, which suggest both Russian and English names.[20] "Alex" also suggests a Latinate pun: *a/lex*, outside the law, outside the word.)

To be sure, Nadsat "disturbs" English—but not without also (and constantly) reassuring it. Geoffrey Aggeler cites one such iconically "disturbed" passage, noting that as intensely literary English, it "would lose everything in translation":[21]

> As I slooshied, my glazzies tight shut to shut in the bliss that was better than any synthemesc Bog or God, I knew such lovely pictures. There were vecks and ptitsas, both young and starry, lying on the ground screaming for mercy, and I was smecking all over my rot and grinding my boot in their litsos. And there were devotchkas ripped and creeching against walls and I plunging like a shlaga into them, and indeed when the music, which was one movement only, rose to the top of its big highest tower, then, lying there on my bed with glazzies tight shut and rookers behind my gulliver, I broke and spattered and cried aaaaaaah with the bliss of it. And so the lovely music glided to its glowing close.[22]

Burgess himself, in his role as autocritic and self-explicator, suggested that this refamiliarization of Russian borrowings was a construction for "brainwashing" the reader, providing her a lesson or "primer" in brain-washing: "You read the book or see the film, and at the end you should find yourself in possession of a minimal Russian vocabulary—without effort, without surprise. This is the way brainwashing works."[23] This, we might say, is a paranoid inversion of Adorno's notion of the essayist reading "without a dictionary," like "someone in a foreign country forced to speak its language,"[24] and it is somewhat disingenuous (though to be sure, what author's view of his or her own work is not?) on at least two counts. First, because the *deep* subrogation or reprogramming implied by the weight Burgess gives here to "brainwashing" is hardly to be imagined in *Clockwork* as a published literary artifact: given the editorial repositioning, punning and slanging play, and outright translation that the work's Russian bor-rowings undergo, within a containing referential context keyed to British culture, one might say with justice that there is never any real danger of Russian, the parasite language, really "taking over" its host.[25] Second, be-cause this (exaggerated) power of the foreign word is in fact one compo-nent of a strategic appeal, very much in the "Joycean" high modernist mode, to the flexibility and incorporative power of a native language, and is thus, in a quite substantive way, a celebration of that language (English). It was foreordained, in a sense, that the dust jacket of the 1962 Heinemann edition would proclaim that "it will take the reader no more than fifteen pages to master and revel in the expressive language of Nadsat."[26]

A close look at *A Clockwork Orange*'s opening pages reveals just how compulsorily autotranslative Nadsat must be as a literary idiom, and how comically desirous assertions of its resistance to reading must finally be. Each of the novel's three divisions opens with an idiomatic and strongly *voiced* line of English dialogue: "What's it going to be then, eh?" As an equiv-alent, in its narrative context, for "What shall we do tonight?" the utter-ance "What's it going to be then," along with the interrogative interjection "eh," establish the narrating agent's English as regionally specific: British, then English; possibly Canadian (then Ontarian); certainly not U.S. Amer-ican. The monologue that follows, and which is sustained throughout *Clockwork*, is quite intensely idiomatic in this sense: "There was me, that is Alex, and my three droogs, that is Pete, Georgie, and Dim, Dim being really dim, and we sat in the Korova Milkbar making up our rassoodocks what to do with the evening, a flip dark chill winter bastard though dry."[27]

We might take note of how "droogs," here, is immediately clarified, by "that is Pete, Georgie, and Dim." The referent of "rassoodocks" (from *rassudok*, mind), by contrast, isn't glossed—but it's far from difficult to infer from context. Reading *Clockwork* with an attentive eye (and, perhaps more to the point, *ear*) for such things, one might divide the novel's Russian borrowings and neologisms into three classes: those glossed or even directly translated by Alex, the narrator; those whose meaning can be inferred from context, as here, with little damaging ambiguity (even, as here, on their first appearance); and those whose meanings can be guessed precisely only after multiple iterations in multiple contexts.

The first class is surprisingly common, and lends a subtle metafictional life to the novel at the editorial level itself, with Alex seeming to monitor his exuberant idiom for comprehensibility, as though anticipating a literary audience for whom Nadsat as an invented language is already an issue. No further than the third paragraph of *Clockwork*'s first chapter, we encounter the first of many semipedantic glosses of "Nadsat" words. Describing the codpieces each member of the gang wears, Alex explains:

> I had one in the shape of a spider, Pete had a rooker (a hand, that is), Georgie had a very fancy one of a flower, and poor old Dim had a very hound-and-horny one of a clown's litso (face, that is). . . . Then we wore waisty jackets without lapels but with these very big builtup shoulders ("pletchoes" we called them) which were a kind of mockery of having real shoulders like that. Then, my brothers, we had these off-white cravats which looked like whipped-up kartoffel or spud with a sort of a design made on it with a fork.[28]

"Rooker" and "litso" are parenthetically translated from Nadsat–Russian into English, while "shoulders" is translated *into* Nadsat–Russian (*plecho*, shoulder) and the German "kartoffel" is provided with a slang English equivalent, "spud." A bit later, while the gang is assaulting the "doddery starry schoolmaster type veck," we encounter another definition: "In the trousers of this starry veck there was only a malenky bit of cutter (money, that is)."[29] (Context provides an inferable referent for "malenky"—*malyenkiy*, small—as well.) Other examples include the following: "It was nadsats mostly milking and coking and fillying around (nadsats were what we used to call the teens)";[30] "these nagoy (bare, that is) cheenas and vecks";[31] "Then I tooth-cleaned and clicked, cleaning out the old rot with my yazhick or tongue";[32] "better than any synthemesc Bog or God";[33] "a creech of nadsat (teenage, that is) malchicks and ptitsas."[34]

Nadsat words are also translated in staged parallel shifts between its youth argot and "adult" English, such as when Alex speaks with his "Post-Corrective Adviser," P. R. Deltoid: "'The millicents have nothing on me, brother, sir I mean.' 'Cut out this clever talk about millicents,' said P. R. Deltoid."[35] Alex himself shifts registers at a time of confrontation, when he breaks ranks with his own droogies: "'And what will you do,' I said, 'with the big big big deng or money as you so highfaluting call it?'"[36] Such self-translation drops off in the novel's second section, at a point when Alex might assume his reader has begun to acquire a sense of his idiom.

It would seem important to note, in this connection, that Alex has all along asserted the *fluency* of Nadsat by contrasting it with the babble produced by others "deeper" within the youth subculture than he. Even when grownups find the argot incomprehensible—or, like Drs. Brodsky and Branom at the Staja (prison), regard it with tolerant scientific curiosity as a quaint class-tribal dialect, Alex goes out of his way to mark (and dismiss) as "nonsense" the ravings of a synthemesc doper in the Korova Milkbar, who utters such strings of language as "Aristotle wishy washy works outing cyclamen get forficulate smartish" and "Urchins of deadcast in the way-ho-hay glill platonic time weatherborn."[37] In so doing, Alex insists by contrast on the manifest comprehensibility of his own idiom. Quite unlike Nadsat, this drugged nonsense-talk mixes slangy wordplay with terms drawn from the specialized lexicons of technical knowledge production, and is pitched so as to form another, far more resistant opacity, in contradistinction with Nadsat borrowings. Such strings of "nonsense," along with the interpolation of Alex's and others' prisoner ID numbers into strings of dialogue, in scenes at Staja ("Just you wait, 7749222"; "Ah, little 6655321"), in fact constitute one of the few material disturbances of *Clockwork*'s otherwise insistently fluently *vocalized* language.[38]

Nadsat is thus best understood as an incorporative vocalized idiom, in which one can certainly (by Alex's standards, at least) become "fluent," and which absorbs the substitution of semantically congruent words from a foreign language, Russian—yet rejects as *nonsense* strings of grammatically incongruent words in its native base (English). This, we might say, is a distinction that emplaces the novel inextricably within the structural history of cold war hemispheric language politics, in their deeply, even fatally translative and *machine*-translative aspect. If Burgess once claimed that he chose Russian "merely," as he put it, because Russian words blended more harmoniously into English than French or German, elsewhere he also stated that he chose Russian as the principal or only "other language" of power in the cold war.[39] Read through the force field of this pair of contradicting statements of (casual or strategic) constructive intention, *Clockwork*'s literary texture might be read as an enactment of the military-cultural deficiency that lent the first wave of machine translation research such gravity: an insufficient literacy in the Russian language among native speakers of English relative to the volume of scientific technical literature then being produced in Russian. That is to say that if Nadsat embodies a paranoid vision of English contaminated by Russian through the ostensibly spontaneous confluence of criminal youth subcultures, it *also* stands for the specific sociality of machine translation understood, in its earliest stages, as an autonomous technical problem of cultural knowledge, soluble by computational brute force. As a translative negotiation of two historically national-imperial languages, Nadsat embodies medially the division of the world into U.S. and Soviet spheres of influence, configured to mirror that historical balance of power that we called "deterrence."[40]

As such, *Clockwork* necessarily constructs a confrontation between English and Russian, acquiring what we might call reversible specificity with respect to those two particular languages. This affects what one might call *Clockwork*'s "translation situation." That is to say that while one might certainly translate *Clockwork*, and even translate it well, into other languages—and that one might even, in so doing, preserve the cultural context of political confrontation between hemispherically hegemonic languages—*Clockwork*'s own medially linguistic historical specificity, in the cultural conflict of English and Russian, remains irreproducible in any language(s) *but* English and Russian. A Russian translation of the novel, reversing *Clockwork*'s native configuration of administrative and administered languages (and substituting English loan words for the Russian loan words in the original), thus preserves that medially linguistic historical specificity as declared by the very "name," Nadsat, of the work's idiom—

though the only way to completely "reverse" the novel would perhaps be to change British cultural, geographical, and historical references to Russian ones.[41]

Clockwork's double movement, then, as a plurilingual literary artifact, is this. We can hardly avoid reading the novel's broadly "Joycean" idiom, in the intensely masterly incorporative and improvisational manipulation of English as a *container* of other languages, as irreducibly but "reversibly" specific in its index of the historical confrontation of U.S. English with Soviet Russian—and as such, as *blocking* complete or "free" translation, as content, into forms unable to index that specificity. At the same time, we cannot ignore the myriad ways in which, disavowing opaque *nonsense,* Alex, the novel's custodian of the Nadsat idiom or speech personality, works to *enable* or *unblock* complete or free translation. This, we hardly need to point out, is only one strategy or form of enactment of cold war language politics, and while its essential conservatism need not necessarily be understood to limit the value of *Clockwork* for literary history, it need not be defended as an inevitable posture, either. It would have been possible—indeed, in the cultural context of the cold war, as it is bound to early research in machine translation, it might have represented another linguistic-political choice altogether—for Burgess to have composed his novel in a less overtly Joycean, "idiom neutral" English, or to flatten the national-cultural specificity of the mother tongue by other means.

Oh, Merde

Published in 1966, a few years after *Clockwork* first appeared, Robert A. Heinlein's *The Moon Is a Harsh Mistress* tells the story of a libertarian revolution in a former penal colony on the moon in the year 2075. It is narrated by Comrade Manuel (Mannie) Garcia O'Kelly, a computer engineer who speaks an English from which both definite and indefinite articles, as well as the occasional grammatical subject or impersonal verb, are frequently dropped, as if to suggest either English learned as a foreign language by a native speaker of Russian, or the imitation of Russian grammar in English: "My old man taught me two things: 'Mind own business' and 'Always cut cards.' Politics never tempted me. But on Monday 13 May 2075 I was in computer room of Lunar Authority Complex, visiting with computer boss Mike while other machines whispered among themselves."[42]

Mannie's ethnic background and Earthside national affiliations are mixed—U.S. (itself an Irish/Latino mix), Australian, and Tatar or Uzbek—but in Luna society's culture of polyandrous marriage, pointedly divided between English-speaking and Russian-speaking cultures, one grandmother from each. Like Nadsat, Mannie's "Luna English" is a defamiliarized English, estranged from itself through lexical and grammatical contact with Russian. But where in the Joycean idiom of Nadsat this contact may be described as primarily additive or supplemental, Luna English is largely subtractive, deleting grammatical functions that serve to mark English fluency and euphony. Rather than anglicizing a large number of Russian borrowings, Luna English borrows a small set of token words wholesale, posing questions of speech verisimilitude, and of ambition thereto, impossible to answer in the linguistic frame-within-frame of the novel's idiom. One might ask oneself, for example, if those Russian interjections common to Luna English mark the Russian fluency (over the language horizon, as it were, of both text and book of *The Moon Is a Harsh Mistress*) of the character who interjects them—or if they are to be taken as tokens common to the linguistic-narratorial agent of third-person omniscience, which recasts national-language categories in national-language allegories: "Am not going to argue whether a machine can 'really' be alive, 'really' be self-aware. Is a virus self-aware? Nyet. How about oyster? I doubt it. A cat? Almost certainly. A human? Don't know about you, tovarishch, but *I* am."[43]

"Nyet" and "tovarishch," here, suggest mixed language and cultural fluency, we might say, without doing much to release Russian from constraint to allegorical type. Luna English includes similarly transparent portmanteau words and neologisms in the common idiom of mass-market science fiction, often translated internally by Mannie (much as Alex, when he worries his auditor won't understand, obligingly translates certain Nadsat terms): "So-called computermen—programmers, really—of Authority's civil service stood watches in outer read-out room and never went in machines room unless tell-tales showed misfunction."[44] Neologisms for technical equipment or information processes ("talk-talk," "read-out," "tell-tales") are anachronized or primitivized for maximum semantic transparency, while the subtractive subcompetence of small distortions—"went in" in place of "went into," "misfunction" instead of "malfunction"—invite editorial monitoring from *Moon*'s constructedly fluent Anglophone reader.

If Luna English speakers' outright solecisms are both rarer and more interesting, they serve this end no less well:

> "Not funny?" "What? Oh, every funny!"[45]
>
> "Not?" "Very not."[46]
>
> Before I was done, two little boys flanked me and added shrill endorsements,
> along with clog steps. So I tipped them and told them to be missing.[47]

It is Mike the computer, meanwhile, who speaks perfect idiomatic
English, without any Russian grammatical distortion or solecisms (though
he does say things like "Bolshoyeh thanks!"). But this is perhaps less
potentially distinctive than it may seem, given the quite fluent saturation
of Mannie's Luna English with Commonwealth Anglophone nativism, in
the form of punning slang ("dinkum thinkum," Mannie's word for computer), categorical usage ("bloke," "maths," "pig-headed"), British cultural
references (to the *Encylopædia Britannica,* for example, and quite possibly to *A Clockwork Orange* itself), Anglophone puns ("Use it once, you're
a wit. Use twice, you're a halfwit"), and U.S. dialect (as when an African
American type yells in italics, "Git!"). Such Anglophone fluency is a trait of
the novel's most emblematically cosmopolitan character, Wyoming Knott,
who "looked Svenska and had British last name with North American
first name but could have been Russki"[48] and sprinkles her conversation
with phatic tokens of Russian, German, French, and Cantonese. Tellingly,
perhaps, her introduction to Mannie—and to the reader—comes through
a complicated (if banal) Anglophone pun-against-pun: "Call me Wye,
Mannie—but don't say 'Why not.'" This linguistically enclosed homophonic humor forms the substrate in *Moon* within which distinctly "foreign" words, interpolated into Wyoming's Luna English, function to type
her at once as linguistic secret agent (obscuring her social specificity with
the mystique of espionage) *and* as a paragon of *Moon*'s (and Luna English's)
linguistic Anglocentrism—which is clearly and uncomplicatedly reserved
as a dominant mode. Nowhere in *Moon,* after all, does *any* character speak
more than a few words at a time in a language other than English, and even
then, such language, as deployed on the page, is nearly invariably tokenis-
tic and phatic: greetings, expressions of thanks or dismay ("Oh, merde"),
or toasts when raising a drink.

Luna English, then, even (or especially) with the "cosmopolitan" variations added by Wye, functions, like Nadsat, to offer the Anglophone reader a nativized experience of a "foreign" language and of the *difference* it stands for, without demanding or requiring any effort to contact that difference. To be sure, where Nadsat is a kind of super-English, gathering and integrating loan words as supplements to an already highly idiomatic native polyphony of youth slang, formal address and archaic and modern, as well as futuristic vocabulary and phrasing, Luna English is a sub-English, tending toward idiom-neutrality in its solecisms. But *both* super-English and sub-English here tend to serve as English primordialities: Luna English is *contrivedly* awkward, "spoken" on the pages of *Moon* as a second language, the solecisms of which are certainly best noted by (and most diverting to) a native Anglophone ear. Both solecisms and foreign words here might be thought as the objects of a linguistic commodity fetish, concealing language's differential sociality behind the magical autonomy of the defamiliarization effect, akin to having actors playing Germans in a U.S. film speak English with a German accent for the sake of typological realism.

Taken together, these two works demonstrate, we might say, something of the cost of posterity in a closed system of "deterrent" dynamics. As Weaver's political cosmopolitanism coexisted with an intellectually provincial technical solution, and as the plurilingual potential of early machine translation was overtaken by the monolingual imperatives of cold war defense funding, each of these novels exposes Anglophone readers to Russian, homeopathically contaminating English with, and thus *containing,* English's rival as a language of hemispheric power. One might say that the textual gesture of opening, of mixing one's own language with the Other, is a linguistically "cosmopolitan" or potentially extranational gesture, while the containment effect of literary idiom, which operates in the linguistically nationalized realm of the publishable book, is (necessarily) xenophobically nationalistic. In homeopathically contaminating English with Russian, then, *Clockwork* and *Moon* perform two mutually contradictory operations at once, one centripetal and one centrifugal with respect to the difference of the different languages they combine and juxtapose. Each of these plurilingual novels figures an untranslatable historical specificity in and *as* language, in generating a complex of linguistic effects that together index an irreducibly historically specific *medial* confrontation between the linguistic categories of two political systems of belief at war with each other—and in envisioning their "impossible" mixture, in the interdependent stasis we once called deterrence. Each work embraces translatability (and translation), in turn, in imagining that combination as a victorious transformation of one of those systems into the other—that it imagines itself, as it were, winning the war.

The stylized literary language produced by this double movement, in each case, more than resembles the automatic machine output of early experiments in computerized translation from Russian to English, which produced target language (Russian) shadowed or colored, boldly or slightly, by the source. If U.S. machine translation research (even in its later dystopian, human-assisted forms) thus served as a functional substitute (and funding diversion) for a program of more widespread and laboriously acquired human social fluency in the Russian language—thus serving paradoxically to *maintain* Russian as an "unknown" language, transferring fluency to the machine agent—each novel in its own way simultaneously undermines "brute force" technicity, and the linguistic power struggle that funded it, *and* reinforces it. In this movement, the literary construction of russicized English, as a programmatic social gesture confronting Anglophone readers of a novel with homeopathic Russian contamination, converges with the machine production of russicized English, in the *failure* of an optimally autonomous technical task. To the extent that each novel, as a consumable literary commodity, relieves its gratified reader of the demand for any social knowledge of the Russian language, it is perhaps unexpectedly closer to the founding ideological precept of MT as expressed in Weaver's observation to Norbert Wiener: "When I look at an article in Russian, I say 'This is really written in English, but it has been coded in some strange symbols. I will now proceed to decode.'"[49]

One might read Weaver's political cosmopolitanism as a fair analogue for the Anglophone literary exuberance of both novels—which, with Weaver, imagine the world's hegemonic and subaltern languages in something more than readily instrumentized translative relations. One might with equal justice point to the technical imperative overtaking (or perhaps cofounding) that imagination, deleting the sociality of linguistic difference and the exogamous elective affinity that, as Adorno put it, *drives* us to foreign words.[50]

A Law Is a Law

Given each writer's subfluent working knowledge of Russian, such movement can be said to have been elective in Burgess's and Heinlein's cases, though unquestionably buttressed by the imperatives of the publishing industry against which Burgess noted he (vainly) strove; in the case of Nabokov, a native speaker of Russian who composed most of his major late work in English, one might speak more decisively of such movement in terms of structural coercion. As the second novel Nabokov wrote and published in English and the first composed while residing in the United States, *Bend Sinister* is, we might say, perhaps the most conflictedly Joycean of Nabokov's works in style in its forms of reflection on plurilingualism as active conflict both among languages themselves and with the monolingual imperatives of book publication.[51]

Bend Sinister is set in an invented "Padukgrad," where a fictional Slavic Germanic macaronic and neologistic language called simply "the vernacular" is spoken. This "vernacular" is not an element of the novel's own literary texture but is rather indexed or represented within that texture, which consists of standard literary English broken by words and phrasing in German, French, Russian, and Latin, with longer sentences, exchanges of dialogue, and verse fragments in French and Russian. Of the patterns with which these other languages appear, one may observe that French is clearly contradistinguished from both English and Russian, marking the speech of ostensibly Francophone characters, or the social class and level of education (or aspiration thereto) of ostensibly non-Francophone characters. When ostensibly employed by this latter group, French words and phrasing tend to serve either as metonymic cultural markers or as literary *mots juste*, the carriers of a cultural-linguistic specificity unavailable in the novel's textual English. Instances of this particularity range from the quotidian ("the very small and not overabundant sandwiches and some triangled *bouchées*"), to more deeply encoded levels of reference ("those mirrors of infinite space *qui m'effrayent, Blaise*"; "Flaubertian *farceurs*"). Still other deployments of French, such as "the *enfant terrible* of the sixties," are used parodically, as plurilingual clichés emptied of meaning.[52]

Though French words and phrases are invariably italicized in editions of *Bend Sinister*, entire sentences and exchanges of French dialogue, equally invariably, go untranslated. French thus at once takes the mutually exclusive roles of secret language, inaccessible to the monolingual Anglophone reader presumed in various strategic ways by the novel's hyperconsciousness of itself as a book published in the United States in U.S. English, *and* of a language presumed *for* that reader—in conspicuous contrast with Russian, words and phrasing in which are consistently translated, paraphrased, and pedantically (and of course parodically) glossed. Compare these two passages (from the novel's midsection and closing section, respectively):[53]

> *"Et voilà ... et me voici ..."* he said with an infantile little whine in his voice. *"Un pauvre bonhomme qu'on traine en prison."* Oh, I don't want to go *at all!* Adam, isn't there anything that can be done? Think up something, please! *Je suis souffrant, je suis en détresse.* I shall confess I had been preparing a *coup d'état* if they start torturing me.[54]

> *"Yablochko, kuda-zh ty tak kotishsa* [little apple, whither are you rolling]?" asked the soldier and added:
> *"A po zhabram, milaĭ, khochesh* [want me to hit you, friend]?"
> *Tut pocherk zhizni stanovitsa kraĭne nerazborchivym* [here the long hand of life becomes extremely illegible]. *Ochevidtzy, sredi kotorykh byl i evo vnutrenniĭ sogliadataĭ* [witnesses among whom was his own something or other ("inner spy?" "private detective?" The sense is not at all clear)] *potom govorili* [afterwards said] *shto evo prishlos' sviazat'* [that he had to be tied]. *Mezhdu tem* [among the themes? (Perhaps: among the subjects of his dreamlike state)] *Kristalsen, nevozmutimo dymia sigaroĭ* [Crystalsen calmly smoking his cigar], *sobral ves' shtat v aktovom zale* [called a meeting of the whole staff in the assembly hall] and informed them *[i soobshchil im]* that he had just received a telephone message according to which they would all be court-martialled.[55]

Playfully transcoding the scholar's philological dedication to rooted linguistic priority and verisimilitude, Nabokov's narrator frequently lards his glosses with interpretive hesitations such as "The sense is not at all clear." Of course, he also "misleads" the credulous reader of *Bend Sinister* with both neologistic and false glosses: "Krug played football [vooter], Paduk did not [nekht]"; "The style, the begonia [brilliancy], will be yours, of course."[56] The narrator's play with such faux amis, of course, is encoded both orthographically and phonetically so as to camouflage itself from the constructed reader of *Bend Sinister,* the Anglophone–Francophone Euro-Atlantic reader ignorant of Slavic languages to whom such glosses are (disingenuously) offered. Strictly speaking, this reader is neither the subject nor the object of the narrator's pseudo-scholarly tricksterism, which, as with Alex's disavowals of "nonsense" in *A Clockwork Orange,* turns on the subordination of echolalia to the virtuosic play of truth with lie in hypersense: an intricate display of literary and literary-critical "capital" undermined, but never fully disavowed, by parodies of its conspicuous consumption or waste. Even the untranslated French in *Bend Sinister* includes plainly calculated clichés, bald cognates ("Je regrette but a law is a law"), ornamental citations, and phatic exclamations, seldom concealing *information* crucial to the novel's plot line (such as it is).[57] One might observe, without impugning the novel's art, that its literary parodies of plurilingual superfluency as class privilege function precisely to contain the abyss of verisimilitude posed by Nabokov's ambitions, and that this makes it the very type of modernist literary self-reflection on what Pascale Casanova, ventriloquizing Kafka (and Deleuze and Guattari), calls "the impossibility of not writing"[58]—and by which is really meant the impossibility, in the scene constituted by the literary-historiographic gaze, of *not writing for publication.*

Bend Sinister's internal representations of translation themselves converge centripetally on the book's foreign words and phrases, invoking translation as a conversion fated by the format of the published book itself. When Professor Krug shouts, "Stoy, chort [stop, curse you] . . . for the first time that night using his real voice,"[59] we realize that Krug's "real" voice is discontinuous with the Francophone voice in which he occasionally appears to think—and with the English, as well, into which that French is transposed and transformed. Krug's "real" voice, here, is Russian, or else the simulacral russianized "vernacular" of Padukgrad, a national-yet-not-national state *and* state culture; and it is that "real" voice that is the prime object of a utopian-realist parody that re-represents and diminishes it. Sometime later, when Hustav, the armed representative from "headquarters," arrives to arrest Ember, Krug's rival translator of *Hamlet,* Krug speaks to him in periphrastic English, thus marking off their exchange up to that point *as* a translation. Hustav is recast, in this encounter, as a monolingual barbarian who cannot properly identify the foreign language Krug speaks:

> "This idiot here has come to arrest you," said Krug in English.
>
> Hustav, who had been quietly beaming at Ember from the threshold, suddenly frowned and glanced at Krug suspiciously.
>
> "But surely this is a mistake," said Ember. "Why should anyone want to arrest me?"
>
> "*Heraus, Mensch, marsch,*" said Hustav to the valet and, when the latter had left the room:
>
> "We are not in a classroom, Professor," he said, turning to Krug, "so please use language that everybody can understand. Some other time I may ask you to teach me Danish or Dutch. . . ."[60]

In a way, this passage stages the final consequence of the novel's plurilingual strategem (and predicament): a kind of capitulation, achieved through parodic protest, to the impossibility of publishing a strongly plurilingual work of literature. On the ambivalent use of "affective" Russian in Nabokov's body of work as a whole, Antonina Filonov Gove has observed: "One can suppose that code-switching would tend to have the effect of disrupting textual continuity, and that for monolingual readers this would serve to lower the level of emotional response to the passages in question. It is further likely that the full pathos of several key passages in *Bend Sinister* will be missed even by readers who know a substantial amount of classroom Russian."[61] Gove discounts, perhaps, the extent to which *Bend Sinister*'s interpolated Russian is familiarized by Nabokov's narrator's editorial and parodic translation, as well as the possibility that *other* kinds of affective response, such as that excited by a carefully circumscribed exotic unknown, may combine with the suspicious resistance projected onto Hustav, for example, in his metafictional figuration as (nonideal) reader. But for that, the conclusions Gove draws from this observation are no less salient:

> The lack of access to a normal range of readers can be an acute personal and artistic problem for an émigré writer. A tragic case in point among Russian émigrés was Marina Tsvetaeva. Nabokov's change to English as his literary

medium, presumably motivated in part by a desire for a less limited readership, eventuated in a new, probably unforeseen, reader problem. In the process of developing as a writer in English, Nabokov has evolved a style that incorporates the cognitive and expressive riches and delights of a versatile monolingual. Among other things, the author finds himself with the capability of varying the expressive nuances of his text by his choice of linguistic vehicle. . . . [O]ne may ask whether the cost of using this superb expressive resource is not disproportionately high. It may be that an awareness of the costs in readership led Nabokov to moderate the affective use of Russian in his later novels.[62]

Nabokov, containing his Russian for publication in English, points through archival memory to Tsvetaeva, the untranslatable poet of "vivre dans le feu," the suicide whose burial place is unknown, whose writings were banned, lost, whose correspondence was sealed until the year 2000.[63] And if *Bend Sinister*'s conflicted resignation *to* publication and its posterity points us in this way to Tsvetaeva, whose fragile legacy scholarship is only now beginning to retrieve, one can only wonder, perhaps, to whom or what to point from there.

THE CASE OF ARNO SCHMIDT

One of the most systematically extreme and conflicted forms of Joycean cold war plurilingualism in Euro-Atlantic postwar literature may be that characterizing the work of Arno Schmidt, who bent the essential conservatism of Joycean "fascicular" plurilingualism to its nadir in the antimodernist refusal of publication. Schmidt's literary fictions are set in the present or future of a culturally, ideologically, and linguistically partitioned Germany, and traversed by a deeply divided plurilingual impulse. On the one hand, they are intensely, categorically, and nationally monolingual, bound to the untranslatable intricacies of idiomatic and colloquial German, the mimicry of regional German dialects, and intensive phonetic and syntactic play, in a hypervirtuosity orchestrated by an unapologetically centralized first-person narrative-authorial fictional subject who is happily and substantively identical from one of Schmidt's works to the next. On the other hand, Schmidt's fictions, which often imagined the problem of Europe (if seldom the problem of the extra-European) as a problem of incommensurable national publics, led him, through the structural logic of their own literary production, to diminishing visibility as a publishing author, in reflection on the unsuitability, and indeed, the impediments of book publication to his work.[64] Schmidt's oft-remarked "untranslatability" from German (which in no way blocked his own prodigious achievements as a translator), in the autonomous plurilingual erudition through which he cultivated secession from imagined literary publics, made him at once a typical and an unusual expression of the double bind of the avant-garde, with the deliberate publication of his late work in typescript facsimile standing as a radical, if incomplete gesture of withdrawal from book publication itself.[65]

As manifest in Schmidt's management of languages on the page, the structural anticipation of this late secessionist gesture might best be observed in a group of publisher-typeset novels spanning the middle period of Schmidt's body of work. Published in 1960, KAFF *auch* MARE CRISIUM is one of four novels set partly or entirely in an apocalyptic cold war future, where even nuclear warfare has not resolved the conflict between the United States and the USSR, but rather extended and deepened it (for example, by relocating it to other planets similarly divided).[66] The "Kaff" of the novel's title stands for Giffendorf, the rural northern German town where the narrator, Karl Richter, and his companion, Hertha Theunert, visit Karl's aunt, and where Karl improvises for Hertha's amusement the story of Mare Crisium, site of a U.S. moon colony in the year 1980.[67] While this narrative displays a kind of Germanophone Euro-Atlantic linguistic ecumenism, as Karl weaves words and phrasing in English, French, Italian, Spanish, and Latin into his German while mimicking his aunt's and companion's Platt and Silesian dialects, a second narrative, interwoven into the first, takes place at Mare Crisium and turns on comic figurations of the untranslatable incommensurability of U.S. English and Soviet Russian.

Schmidt breaks many words down into individual morphemes, glossing them inventively and reassembling them into words using the mathematical equals sign as a connective declaring a seriality Schmidt found missing in subordinating "Websterian" compounds.[68] Reading Joyce's style through Freud, Schmidt developed a study of "etyms," quasi-primordial linguistic elements of the subconscious that, like slips or puns, speak of, for, and in the drives. In the etym theory as embodied in Schmidt's practice of literary composition, we might say we find something of the double movement at work in Alex's insistence, in *A Clockwork Orange,* on Nadsat as separate but equally, idiosyncratically fluent idiom. Resisting, in its etymic disassembly of language, the figurative unity of its intention, Schmidt's practice moves on the one hand toward the radically non- or aliterary autonomy of language speaking by, and from, and out of, itself, rather than from or of a human subject. Restoring that unity, after the fact, in the idiomatic fascicular bundling of reassembled words, his practice restores to incipiently autonomous language its idiomatic literarity.

Schmidt criticism, as devoted to the Joycean mode as was Schmidt himself, often places the greatest weight on this dynamic *in* Schmidt's exuberant German—but it might as profitably be noticed at work at the epistemic *limit* of Schmidt's foreign-language borrowings and interpolations.[69] With the exception of Russian, languages other than German that appear in KAFF *auch* MARE CRISIUM tend to *serve* Karl in his hyperfluent intellecto-verbal virtuosity and the encyclopedic powers of literary- and intellectual-historical improvisation that go with it: a quality marked in this text, as in many of Schmidt's others, as both masculine in and of itself, and as a point of conflict between Karl and both Hertha and Karl's aunt, Tante Heete. French, for example, serves as a carrier of literarity, with titles and emblematic place-names from the novels of Jules Verne, for example, citationally interpolated into Karl's dialogue with Hertha.[70] French words—and, occasionally, Greek—also serve as metonymies for both French national culture and for Southern continental clichés of sexual profligacy.[71] Literary Latin, meanwhile, appears (perhaps symptomatically) at those moments when U.S. Anglo racism, projected onto the Missouri "moonie" George Harris (who, finally separated from any contact with African Americans, has forgotten the English word "black"), is both caricatured and appropriated.[72] Karl's most conspicuous and metonymically energetic display of plurilingual erudition comes after just such a little burst of Latin, as Hertha, shocked by the managed racial purity of the U.S. moon colony, prompts the following "edjumucative" exchange:

> *"Und bloß Yankees* ?—*Weder Creolen,* noch Mulattn ; noch=ä—sag Du ammall noch Sortn." / : Mestizen ; Metifen ; Calpan Mulatos ; Zambos ;

Cascos ; Cabern ; Tresalven ; Zambaigen ; Cholen ; Saltartras ; Postizen ; Coyoten ; Giveren ; Cambujos ; Harnizen ; Barziden ; Albarassaden ; Castizen : Terzeronen Quarteronen Quinteronen Octavonen. . . . . / "Hör auf." sagte sie schlicht. / Dann siegte aber doch die weibliche Neugier wieder : "Albarassaden ?—Das'ss'a hübscher Name : Wie sind'nn da de Elternteile ?" : "Mulatten & Cambujos." : "Mulattn iss klar : Neger & Europäer. Aber 'Cambujos'?" : "Mulattinnen & Zambaigen." : "Und Zambaigen ?" : "Amerikaner & Zambos." : "Und Zambos?—Du: kommt nich beim Keller anne 'Zambo=Maria' vor ?" : "Entschtehen, wenn 1 Neger 1 Amerikanerin bürschtet."[73]

"And nothin' but Yankees ?—No creoles, nor mulattos; nor=uh—okay, you tell me thother variashuns." / : mestizos ; métis ; calpan mulattos ; zambos ; cascos ; caberos ; tresalvos ; zambaigos ; cholos ; saltartras ; postizos ; coyotos ; givers ; cambujos ; harnizos ; barzidos ; albarassados ; castizos : terzeroons quadroons quintroons octoroons. . . . . / "Stop." She said flatout. / But then female curiosity won out again : "Albarassados ?—What a pertty name : what's the pairntage there ?" : "Mulattos & cambujos." : "Mulattos is clear : negro & european. But <cambujos> ?" : "Female mulattos & zambaigos." : "And zambaigos ?" : "'mericans & zambos." : "And zambos ?—Say : isn't there a <Zambo=Maria> somewhere in Keller?" : "Are the product of 1 negro balling 1 'merican=girl."[74]

One might celebrate all this, on the one hand, as a liberating chain of signifiers for miscegenation—its drift a vivid declaration of the taxonomic instability of racial type—and impugn it, on the other hand, for what it certainly *also* is: a masculinist display of encyclopedist virtuosity that rigidifies the gendered relation of Karl with Hertha even as it pits earthly North American human racial diversity against that of a lunar U.S. monoculture. This, however, is only an exceptionally exuberant example of the insistently Joycean treatment that foreign words receive in Karl's self-consciously pedantic monologues, which surround them with explanatory translations, nativizing puns, interlinguistic homophonic jokes, and neologistic play—one language excepted.

Russian, by notable contrast, is something of a blank other in KAFF: a signifier of the blundering ignorance and incomprehension dividing U.S.

and Soviet formations, rather than Western philosophical and literary erudition and its scenes of seduction. As he prepares to visit the Soviet colony,
Charlie, the U.S. librarian who is Karl Richter's lunar alter ego, refuses, in
high comic form, the very notion of learning any Russian:

> Ich wollte doch, vorsichtshalber, wissen, was "Bitte : Essen !," oder so was
> ähnliches, auf Russisch heißt. Und er (kalt ; gefühllos ; man merkte eben
> die Satem=Eltern) : Wenn ich den Wunsch nach einem Imbiß verschpüre,
> möchte ich nur sagn : "Wascha=wsoki=blagorodjai wiliki präwosch : kodi-
> etexwoj tackdalscha."—Ich bat ihn, er möge diesen fürchterlichen Satz auf 1
> Schtück Papier schreibm, das ich mir um den Hals hängen und vorzeigen
> könne : zu erlernen vermöchte ich ihn nicht ; wollte es auch nie versuchen.[75]

> I just wanted to know, by waya precawtion, what "Food : please !," or the like
> might be in Russian. And he (cold ; callous ; you could sents the Satem=
> parents) : If I should feel the urch for snax, all I needed to say was :
> "Vasha=visoka=blagorodjy vellicky prevosh : koditexvoy tackdalsha."—I
> asked him if he would write this dreadfull sentents on a piece of paper for
> me, so I could hang it around my neck and sho it : I was incapable of learning
> it; didn't even want to try.[76]

In the faux-honorific "Wascha=wsoki=blagorodjai wiliki präwosch :
kodietexwoj tackdalscha" ("Your high, noble, exalted excellence, and so
forth"), Russian shares a comic affiliation here with the nonsense that
stands at the other end of Joycean idiomatic plurilingual fluency. In fact,
Karl very explicitly pits Joyce as "gleichzeitich modern *und* verschtänd-
lich" ("at the same time modern and understandable")[77] against Gertrude
Stein, whose voice is parodied in utterances marked as echolalic foils to
Karl's hyperfluency:

> "PROSECUTORS *prosecute the prosecuted=ones : should the* prosecuted=ones
> prosecute their prosecutors-" (Und so ging es noch eine gute Weile fort, in
> Gertrude's schteinichster Weis' . . .).[78]

Karl's apparent sympathy for the USSR's Turcophone internal Others,
and his mockery of monolingual Americans (Charlie's visit to the Soviet

colony is in fact punishment for proposing the study of Russian in U.S. schools) are run through the circuit of his U.S. alter ego, for whom the Russian language is comically opaque, and Russian speakers' mangled English is comically transparent. When he can't understand the "Baddelabopp=a=bopp" of "Der=ihre Mäulchen," Charlie chastises himself insincerely, "Leiderleider : verfehlte Erziehunk" ("Shame=shame: flunkt education").[79] Even the comic thread through which Charlie is duped by Rashevsky (the Russian speaker who teaches him "Wascha=wsoki= blagorodjai wiliki präwosch : kodietexwoj tackdalscha") returns control to Karl's monologue of seduction, channeling identifications based on power differentials—English as triumphant, Russian as "loser" language—into the performance of fluency again. The carefully circumscribed exposure through which Karl stages Charlie's "surprise" at the fact that to ask for food in Russian does *not* in fact require an impossibly complicated honorific form of address, is as apt a figure as any here for the *containment* of the experience of the foreign.

4

Language Memoir and
Language Death

Perhaps it is no more than a critical commonplace now that in doing our "work," we scholars are pinned between the rock of literary privacy and the hard place of the public sphere—that we have to work, if work we are to have, *in* that in-between: writing itself (writing *about* something) being that being-caught, forced from the testimonial local into communication, released to the network (from that moment forward packet-switched, re-produced, open to recombination, the threat of the simulacrum, the possibility of not, after and at all, having testified anything). My proposition in this penultimate essay, which finds the effects of that commonplace somewhere between antidisciplinarian outrage and ho-hum academic realpolitik, is a simple one: language memoir *is* language death. That is, "language memoir"—a record of the experience of second- (or third-, or fourth-) language acquisition, performed for a home–abroad readership tacitly or expressly shaped as a market, in which we can recognize one of the new literary genres of globalization—is a kind of living *in* dying: what Derrida, in a commentary on Benjamin's now fatally overread "Die Aufgabe des Übersetzers," called "sur-vivre," in a bit of semitranslatable play translated as "living on."[1] Further: to pursue this antinomy to its useful depth is not, as one might suppose, to be restrained to hermeneutic (if certainly multiple) *meaning*. Quite to the contrary, I want to suggest, it is to ask concrete and practical questions about effect, or intensity, in the constitution and reconstitution of literary works as research objects. From here the way lies more open, I think, to permutational modes of questioning, which neither stand nor fall, as so many of us do these days, on either the autopoietic self-evidence of irreducible difference or the necessarily forced provenance of communicative reason.

What does it mean, for example—I will pose this, here, as a *disciplinary* question—to stake a claim for "language memoir" as a new genre, as we scholars have done only too recently? In attempting an answer, here, I want first to examine in turn each of two possible points of stress in this phrase, so as to mark the meaningful *and* effective tension between them, which forms, I will suggest, what Adorno would call a *Kraftfeld* in the disciplinary agora *and* the classroom of globalizing or comparative multi-ethnic and cross-cultural literary studies today. Subsequently, I will argue that this tension is not exclusively or necessarily even primarily textual, or endemic to all modern or postmodern uses of language as such, or some variation on a familiar variation thereof—but rather that it is a material tension, at once produced by and reflected in the structural constraints of U.S. book publishing today.

Language Memoir as Language

We might first choose to read the phrase "language memoir" as *language* memoir: as memoir, that is to say, whose generic frontier is marked, possibly expanded, or otherwise modified by an encounter with language as a limit: an encounter that can be positivized as an "experience," perhaps only as what the narrator of Emine Sevgi Özdamar's "Mutterzunge" calls *Lebensunfälle* or life-accidents. The story—the *disciplinary* story—of *language* memoir is this: searching in vain for truly personal accounts of language acquisition, the writer, critic, literature professor, and language instructor Alice Kaplan—or, somewhat more accurately, Kaplan's narrator[2]—locates in twentieth-century French and U.S. literature an entire existing genre of autobiography structured by narratives of language acquisition, for which she proposes the phrase "language memoir."[3] At once a *result* and a *creation* of research, language memoir as a new critical category of published, but substantively unrecognized texts enables us, Kaplan's narrator suggests, to see the special character of the social experience of language acquisition obscured by other, methodologically dominant interpretive practices. For all their obeisance (in certain modifications, at least) to the notion of the constitution of the subject in language, Kaplan's narrator implies, such interpretive practices, *as* scholarly practices, remain deeply, even fundamentally estranged from the perspectivist subjectivity of writing practice as such, and thus from the process producing their own objects of study.[4]

As a corrective intervention into the production regime of literary scholarship, this gesture establishes an analogy, we might say, between second-language acquisition and creative or original literary production, as explorative practices for which one refrains from defining optimal or optimized *applications* in advance. And as such, we might read it as attempting to clear space, in a way (or generate new territory), for such second-order practices, within a disciplinary structure both parasitic and violently disavowing. On the one hand, then, "language memoir" names an existing, thus far uncategorized literary tendency and/or an actualized body of works marked by that tendency: a division of knowledge hidden within another, more expansive division or classification, as yet insufficiently differentiated. Something "invisible," in other words, in the scholarly optics of autobiography and memoir as such. Kaplan's narrator relates how, seeking accounts of *experience* rather than *expertise* in language learning, she "read as many scholarly disquisitions as I could find on second language acquisition—linguistics, sociology, education—and I found methods and statistics and the occasional anecdote, but nothing, really, about what is going on inside the head of the person who suddenly finds herself passionately engaged in new sounds and a new voice, who discovers that *'chat'* is not a cat at all, but a new creature in new surroundings."[5] Framed quite self-consciously here is a paradox—or rather, what I have been framing in this book as an antinomy, to emphasize its nonsoluble character as a putative problem. For if the impatience here for recognition of "what is going on inside the head" of a person learning a new language—that is, for "real" experience, rather than experience as (disciplined) knowledge— is another way of marking that field as a remediable lapse in scholarly discipline, the narrative in which it is embedded, of the *birth* of experience from the lack of spirit (as it were) of scholarship, moves experience from its position as basis and background of knowledge to a position in the lead: the "new creature in new surroundings" of the language memoir itself. What is presented here as the *discovery* of language memoir is, in a not at all conspiratorial sense, in fact its *creation*: that *writing* of its own operations that scholarship cannot acknowledge, at the cost of no longer being scholarship—of being merely, so to speak, one of the most sophisticated literary forms of personal writing. This, we might say, is the premeditated substantive intervention of Kaplan's narrator into the critical dynamic she both embraces and rejects, and which I'll propose we use as a basis for reflection on the conflict, in critical desire, between language acquisition as (as Kaplan thinks it) a creative practice, and translation as a procedural means to a positively determined end. In this narrative of experience irrupting into knowledge, we might say, we see the co-constitutive possibility and impossibility of knowledge as discipline, dividing and subdividing a field of experience that can always be divided *again*.

On the other hand, then, "language memoir" names something new: an *emerging*, rather than a merely obscured or overlooked form. As such, it can, in the critical afterlife of Kaplan's essay, be incorporated into an existing transdisciplinary rubric (ever-"increasing" globalization) without losing its own intrinsic novelty, as archival discoveries in historical research fields inevitably do. This double gesture, unique to the study of *contemporary* literature and culture, is performed from the other side, as it were, by scholarly commentaries on the language memoir that followed Kaplan's (narrator's) first, insistently personal *essay.*[6] The generic division between the personal and the scholarly forms of the essay, I want to suggest, is crucial to reading this double inflection of "language memoir."

For this experience—"what is going on inside the head of the person"—is presented, by Kaplan's narrator speaking *as* (personal) *essayist,* as an experience of the division of identity, of language acquisition as "a leap into a new persona."[7] The Whorfism of the writer chasing "experience" here is a disseminating or centrifugal force splitting the disciplinary–generic premise for the *Bildungsroman*—for Kaplan's narrator speaking *as scholar* (she is both), language memoir's principal literary-historical and taxonomic antecedent. For Kaplan's narrator as personal essayist, *Bildung* is the entry into the social order of a second, or third (etc.) self—of multiple selves, into potentially multiple and coexistent social orders. Here, we can see, is escape from the low identarianism of sociologized reading, which historicizes the false universal subject of *Bildung* without seriously testing reflective structures of ethnic, national, or class identification. But for Kaplan's narrator as scholar—she who invokes the *Bildungsroman* in the first place, in a comparative-critical gesture—*Bildung* (the literary-historical and literary-critical concept, not the experience) is necessarily a habituation or reconciliation of multiple selves, with each other and with the unicity of "a" or "the" social (literary-historical, literary-critical) order. You cannot know that what you are living is *Bildung,* while you are living it; to be recognizable as such—that is, to be historical—*Bildung* must be embodied (arrested) in a *roman,* in the novelization of experience. This is why, I want to suggest, Kaplan's narrator, meditating on this antinomy, carefully presents us with language memoir as a genre of *published writing*—as a body of artifacts—rather than as a practice of "life writing."[8]

Kaplan's narrator-as-essayist strenuously resists the idea that either communication or "empathy" is the goal of language learning: as a record of that goal and its realization, what language memoir records, she says, is the very violence of the self splitting in real experience: "Students learn [languages] out of desire and fear and greed and a need to escape."[9] And yet it's difficult, as she seems to acknowledge, to ignore the systemic *monolingualism* of a new genre *recording for publication,* and thus unavoidably positivizing, its author's (experience of) plurilingualism. In so many of Kaplan's own examples, after all, the *language* memoirist (in the first emphasis) is really a language *memoirist* (in what is now a second)—the "last persona," so to speak, one who inherits previous languages, but no longer speaks them: who chooses *one* language to speak, a language that henceforth represents in itself or "contains" her previous languages. Much of what, in a critical idiom, we can sensibly term "language memoir" today is kept in print by the commercially powerful trade division of a tripartite U.S. publishing industry, whose imprimatur shapes the teaching of contemporary literature even as its editorial practices disqualify it (for good reason!) as an archive of scholarship on that literature. And as it happens, most of this body of published writing on the indisputably profound real experience of the plurilingual condition contains very little *artifactual* plurilingualism, of a categoriality reflective of everyday life in many parts of the globe today, including the cosmopolitan metropolitan and migrant labor zones of the United States itself.

This simultaneous discovery–creation and canonization of a new genre is a process that operates, then, in a field *constituting* its discovery, rather than *being constituted by* it: that is the key to its self-consciousness as "personal" criticism, unwilling to pretend otherwise. And what Kaplan's narrator as personal essayist knows quite well, then—and what she is telling us, indirectly—is that there has never been, nor could there ever really "be" such a genre as *language* memoir, in the more than honorably dis- and anti-identarian sense. This record of an experience splitting the *national*-language self—for all of Kaplan's narrator-as-scholar's examples were published in the official language of a nation-state, thus in a national book *market*—is itself a national language allegory, in which the plurilingual subject whose story it is, tells (can only tell) that story in (to) a national language market, which mandates that the story be told in *one* (national) language.[10]

LANGUAGE MEMOIR AS MEMOIR

It is this tension, perhaps, that marks Lea Ramsdell's and Margaret K. Willard-Traub's pointedly forensic, rather than generative uses of the terms "linguistic autobiography," "scholarly memoir," and "autobiographically inflected text," all of which resist the stronger taxonomic claims implicit in Kaplan's coinage. Which is not to say that scholars are necessarily or inherently more careful, on this account, than journalists or creative writers. On the contrary: most of the vocabulary of culture at large in the literary public sphere, we might say, has its origin in debate within the ivory tower, for which purposes new terms, genres, fields, periodizations, and entire disciplines are handily invented (indeed, we might say that the profession thrives *only* through such acts), in a determination that Kaplan's narrator notes herself:

> What I was looking for was not theory, but fiction. When I turned to fiction I found, to my delight, that there is an entire genre of twentieth-century autobiographical writing which is in essence about language learning. . . .
>
> As I keep writing I remember more and more of these language scenes from my favorite books, until all of literature starts to seem like a "language memoir."[11]

Here, the discovery of language memoir as genre is amplified into the simultaneous dissemination of that genre in Literature and its expansion *as* (or into) Literature itself, the very paradigm of literariness. It is perhaps in sensing this extent to which her own subject, "scholarly memoir," is something of a danger to itself that Willard-Traub, for example, goes out of her way to redefine genre as material, rather than formal: genre, that is to say, whose genericity consists precisely in its materialization, and thus dissolution, of the scholarly praxis of taxonomy: "In attending to . . . multiple aspects of identity . . . such reflective texts compose a *material genre* by stipulating a linguistic transaction . . . often absent from traditional academic discourses demonstrated by scholars and learned by students."[12] Indeed, the prime figuration of "scholarly memoir" as *material* genre, in Willard-Traub's essay, is anti- or countergeneric. Inasmuch as scholarly autobiography, Willard-Traub implies, is only fully autobiographical when it is anti-autobiographical—autobiography, in other words, that calls into question the re-presentability of the autobiographical self, itself—genre here can only be formulated as a negation of genre, as a negation of the scholarly practice of the taxonomic study of genre.

One way to exit this impasse, I'll suggest, is to consider one or more of the materialities of genre that Willard-Traub invokes, but (in my own reading, at least) doesn't pursue to any great length. Rather than asking whether the genre of autobiography, for example, is inherently stable or unstable, we might ask what conditions cause it to appear stable or unstable—to generate discourses around its authorization and verification. The intensified commoditization of the book under new structural market pressures, we could say, imposes certain such conditions on (*for*) publishable autobiographical writing (as a *condition* of publication), demanding implicit or explicit guarantees of reliability and candor from the text's narrator—and culminating, for the moment, with the noncelebrity memoir, which in the absence of any other given authority demands more and more intense (and impossible) identifications of a literary work's narrator with its author. In that identification itself, perhaps, we can then see a correct reading of the specific materiality of contemporary autobiography as mediated by the book publishing industry—and in Willard-Traub's resistance to such "common sense," the articulation of possibilities *relative to* that materiality.

In claims for the recovery or novelty of a new genre, meanwhile, there is surely some element of what Douglas Hesse, in an "assay" of the long-since resurgent personal essay, described as the "land rush" and even the "colonization" projects implicit in competition for professional status and prestige.[13] The *ideology* of literary nonfiction, as Hesse finds it in the "rise of the personal essay" during the 1990s, requires claims for the organic freedom of essay-writing from generic convention, on the one hand, and for its (new or recovered) place in the taxonomy of genres—that is to say, claims for it *as genre*—on the other. In like fashion, we could say, language memoir stakes a claim on the volatile bifurcation of the self in multiple language acquisition—that is its story—even as it stabilizes and eliminates that volatility by organizing its textual effects. To the extent that Kaplan's narrator's formulation pits psychic experience ("what is going on inside the head of the person") against research ("as many scholarly disquisitions as I could find"), it seems to reproduce familiar claims for the unmediated nature of the personal. To argue for the recognition of unrecognized, unmediated experience-against-theory-as-genre is, we could say, equally contrary to common sense: a genre is a rule, and a rule can never be free.

But if, as Paul De Man argued, autobiography *as* genre is not a genre at all, but "a figure of reading or of understanding that occurs, to some degree, in all texts,"[14] then it is this bivalence itself, we might say, that generates Kaplan's narrator's incommensurable formulae for "language memoir": once, as a blank space in the taxonomy of genres, an unrecognized or undiscovered element of a closed system; again, as that which proliferates within all elements of the system, exceeding and opening it again: "all of literature" becoming, or revealing itself as, language memoir.[15]

LANGUAGE DEATH

We might name this negative tendency—the death drive, as it were, of language memoir *as* genre—"language death." Like "language memoir," "language death"—the title of a short and urgent book by David Crystal, author of *English as a Global Language* and *Language and the Internet*, among other works—is a provocative *phrase,* at once announcing a new form or pattern, purportedly *in* the world, and a new mode or "meme" of discourse *on* that form or pattern. If, with Kaplan's narrator-as-(personal)-essayist, we suppose memoir a record of "real" experience—experience as lived, rather than as mediated by scholarship—then "language memoir" draws our attention to a specific dimension of that real experience: linguistic experience, the experience *of* language (language *memoir,* in its second, material sense). Alternately (more radically, and impossibly), as we have already indicated, the "language" in "language memoir" *is* the mediation of that lived experience, is language *as* the mediation of experience (*language memoir*, in its first and ideal sense). That, we might say, is the provocative ambiguity of the phrase "language memoir," what I earlier called its double inflection: in the redundancy of this idea of a linguistic turn in (of all things) writing, it begs the question of what (recorded) experience is *not* mediated by language.

What does the phrase "language death" do? To start, it grafts (biological) death into language, a form of sociality that we don't conventionally think as an organism—even if we don't go so far as (with De Man, for example) to counterdetermine it as inhuman. The semantic shock, as it were, of the phrase "language death" is thus constituted once by a turn in thought (can language die?) and again by a question about forms and fields of critical discourse: can we *speak* of language as though it can die? More to the point, perhaps, it asks us to ask ourselves what is at stake in speaking of language as dead (or living), and when (and why) we begin doing so.

For Crystal, language death is, and names, an unprecedented contemporary historical event. Citing documents drafted during the 1990s by the International Linguistics Congress (1992), UNESCO's Endangered Languages Project (1993), and the U.S.-based Endangered Language Fund (1995), among other new non- or quasi-governmental organizations, Crystal observes:

> The need for information about language loss is urgent. As the quotations from the various professional groups show, we are at a critical point in human linguistic history, and most people don't know.
>
> Language death is real. Does it matter? Should we care? This book argues that it does, and we should. It aims to establish the facts, insofar as they are known, and then to explain them: what is language death, exactly? Which languages are dying? Why do languages die?—and why apparently now, in particular?[16]

Here, Crystal echoes the double inflection of Kaplan's narrator's "language memoir." Both *Language Death*, the text, and "language death" can be read as diagnosis *and* prognosis, paradoxically invested in repetition *within* or *of* the rupture it claims and demonstrates. In fact, as with language memoir, we could say that the poetry of the phrase "language death" lies precisely in this doubling, in the economy of discourse that maintains a critical conversation ("the quotations from the various professional groups show . . .") against the agon of the avant-garde (". . . most people don't know").

The key point of assertion in Crystal's gambit is, in fact, the sentence beginning "As the quotations from the various professional groups show." For it might be more accurate to say that what the quotations from the mission statements of professional (in this case, quasi-governmental) organizations do here is *define* a crisis, rather than disclose one. To say this is to see that the gambit turns on a subtle, yet meaningful equivocation. I point this out not because I mean to cast doubt on Crystal's claims, which seem to me likely to be true, and necessary to take seriously. What I want to point to, rather, is the way that scholarly discourse, even (or perhaps especially) in the antischolastic or nonspecialized idiom Crystal adopts here, answers its own obligation to speak, for better or for worse, where there *may be* silence (is there any better definition of silence than "language death"?) and to design speech, after a fact, to obscure it. This systemic or self-regulating quality of scholarly discourse, its intolerance of silence, is of course one key to the practice of "worldly" criticism, in the progressive sense that includes speaking truth to power.[17] But it is also, we could say, an intensive mode of structuration of the past and, at times, the present and future as well, with results that are (intentionally or unintentionally) regressive.[18] It is this that allows us to see in these provocative, stylized critical objects, "language memoir" and "language death," the language *compulsions* of scholarship itself—and to argue, by way of inverting and joining them, that the one "is," in a sense, the other: that is to say, that language memoir *is* language death.

Archive Fever

In thus formulating a provocative thesis-phrase, I am after all only appropriating *explicitly* patterns of emphasis latent in contemporary scholarly culture, as well as their counteremphases in the so-called literary public sphere. For Crystal, writing in the mode of the public scholar (that is to say, for a wider or "general" audience), makes straightforward and self-conscious use of an analogy, now effortlessly discredited by the scholarship to which *this* (my own) essay addresses itself, between biological life and the active use of a language.[19] "To say that a language is dead," he writes, "is like saying that a person is dead. It could be no other way—for languages have no existence without people."[20]

To read this carefully is to see that the bogus biological analogy, in a double voicing bearing the stamp of (condescending) editorial "care" for what general readers can understand, is supported by a far more sensible (to us) claim: that language is social, and that patterns in language use, including the social termination of its use altogether, are forms of the social (and not, for example, effects of an autonomously operating system). To read for such double voicing—an end run, as it were, around the censors of market-optimized prose—is to mark ourselves with the sensitivity we scholars pride ourselves on, through which we can elicit unintentionally progressive effects and counterdesires from even (especially) classic literary monuments to class power. While as I have said (and will say again shortly), I cannot regard this habit as utterly collusive in the naturalization of that power—for that too is symptomal, of a nonsocial System—it is also true that in our attention to such satisfyingly unwelcome disturbances in a text, we sometimes fail to notice the materiality of gestures by which that disturbance is controlled: gestures, that is to say, that in the main intervene between writing a "text" and its publication. For the *Verfremdungseffekt* of the phrase "language death" clearly foregrounds the analogy (language is a person), rather than the supporting or qualifying claim (language is social)—and this, I think, is clearly intended. Crystal is more than glad to acknowledge his vanguardism here: "the phrase 'language death' sounds as stark and final as any other in which that word makes its unwelcome appearance."[21]

I'll have more to say on this in a moment. For now, I want to highlight two arguments that emerge from Crystal's discussion. The first, which extends the biological analogy of living language, is the notion of a "living archive." Speakers of a living language, Crystal reasons, "become" archives of the linguistic history of a community—mortal archives, that is to say, which cannot outlive their archivists. And since archive and archivist are identical, death here—the perishing of Crystal's hypothetical "last living speaker"—is obliteration, the erasure of an entire communal history.

"When a language dies that has never been recorded in some way, it is as if it has never been."[22]

Why, then, we might ask, resort to the figure of the archive—in other words, to analogy again—if it must be qualified, in Crystal's words, as "unlike the normal idea of an archive"?[23] Crystal points to two distinct forms of response to incipient language death, each of which operates within (or constructs) a different time scale. The first response is to convert the living or mortal archive into an archive proper—that is to say, a material ("dead") archive, equipped to survive—before it is too late. The second response—anticipating, as it were, a language death yet to come—is to work to *prevent* language death, by intervening in the economy (or the economics) driving it. If the first impulse here preserves what we call "history" in its ostensibly natural form, the past, the second, we could say, traps it in the amber of an eternal present. Insofar as it invites (indeed, invokes) stabilization, language maintenance inevitably mandates *standardization*.

Material archives, then, are in Derrida's terms "topo-nomological," marking the boundary or the transition between the private (a space where things are reserved and stored, out of view) and the public (a space where things are instituted, regulated, and authorized, in exposure). Among other things, this means that the transition from private to public "does not always mean from the secret to the nonsecret"[24]—that the constitution of a material archive is also always its destruction, erasure (that is its "fever"). Crystal's notion of *a* language as "living archive" encourages us, first, to see language itself as "living," and secondly, as including in its "life" the valuably inert sedimentation of culture we associate with institutions. Derrida's figure of *mal d'archive*, by contrast, asks us to consider that the archive itself is already "alive" in the specific sense in which the dynamics of institutional sedimentation invoke "drives" *against* life. (It also invokes a "human" pathology—the fever one might suffer *from* the archive, or the fever *to* archive.) Where for Crystal, language as "living archive" is threatened by not being recognized as such—with the protections accruing to cultural institutions—for Derrida, the archive is threatened precisely *in* its constitution and protection as such. As a technical structure, it perpetuates itself by determining in advance what can be archived (what can be recognized): it *produces* as much as it records.[25] That production is both "life"—autonomous self-creation in circumscription or "worlding"—and "death" as circumscription, as self-erasure; and the nonindependence of science or a philosophy from their material archives *in writing* is also, we might say, the nonindependence of literature from its mediation by *publication*. The "living on" (*sur-vivre*) with which Derrida translates Benjamin's *fortleben* describes the living death of writing (in the ordinary sense, as *preceding* publication) *in* publication, a living death at once an analogy and, in the case of plurilingual literature, a *problem* for translation.

The second argument that emerges from Crystal's analysis, meanwhile, is formulated in an attempt to answer the question, *Why* attempt to prevent language death? Why, indeed? As he pointed to two forms of response to language death in his first argument, here in his second he provides two different answers. The first answer is grounded in, or forms, an ecological or ecosophical analogy: what we need, Crystal argues, is a "green linguistics" and a global language policy informed by it—a diversity of languages in interrelationship being necessary for stability in the system of global culture *just as* the diversity of species is crucial to the stability of the global (biological) ecosystem. Here, Crystal pauses at a point more than germane to language memoir, in the Whorfian aspect Kaplan's narrator-as-essayist lends to it, as well as to a distinction one might profitably draw between "strong" and "weak" plurilingualism in published writing. Weighing linguist Geoff Pogson's genetic analogies for language diversity, Crystal observes: "A notion such as 'cross-fertilization of thought' sounds very simple; but it is far more than allowing oneself to be influenced by the occasional foreign turn of phrase—as when English speakers make use of such words as *élan* or *chic*. For bilingual (or multilingual) individuals, there is the permanent availability of two (or more) hugely different perspectives on large areas of life."[26] Interestingly, perhaps (if not necessarily symptomatically), Crystal immediately deradicalizes this thought, resorting to the double-voiced reading of what I have called the "proliferation thesis," in a fundamental conflation of local dialect variation with national ("official," publishing) standard: "And even monolingual people are historically multilingual, in the sense that their language will contain loan-words reflecting the history of its contact with other cultures. English, for example, has borrowed huge numbers of words from over several hundred languages, and hundreds of languages have in turn borrowed huge numbers of English words."[27] It is difficult, of course, to imagine that "Nuestro Himno," the Spanish-language

version of "The Star-Spangled Banner" sponsored by British impresario
Adam Kidron, would have provoked the reaction it did in April 2006 if it
had merely been transposed into a local or historical dialect variation of
U.S. English, or a register of English heavy with jargon or obvious loan
words. (It makes little difference to those who see the Spanish-language
version as "un-American" that, as Kidron put it in an AP wire story by
Laura Wides-Munoz, "American immigrants borrowed the melody of the
'Star-Spangled Banner' from an English drinking song."[28]) Still, in antinomian fashion, Crystal's second answer to the question, Why prevent language death? fairly neatly inverts the ecocritical emphasis on diversity.
Here, rather than stress the interdependent stability of the whole system,
Crystal appeals to the need for integrity in its individual parts. The other
reason to prevent language death, he suggests, is that language stabilizes
and "expresses" identity:

> If we turn the concept of diversity over, we find identity. And everyone cares
> about their identity. A Welsh proverb captures the essence of this section's
> answer to the question "Why should we care if languages die?":
>> Cenedl heb iaith, cenedl heb galon
>> "A nation without a language is a nation without a heart."[29]

It is only the plainest *and* grossest irony, perhaps, that a Welsh nationalist
proverb must be cited in translation for the Anglophone monolingual
audience presumed or produced by that translation, in support of the
claim that (national) language death *matters*. But Crystal's essay (for it *is*
an essay) is at its most interesting, I think, when he abandons the biological and ecological analogies for social-systemic order, and the national
and national–ethnic analogies for identity, for the simple claim that *languages are intrinsically interesting*: that we might as well grant, to the sociality of difference carried by language, a maieutic form of intrinsic value.
The notion that incommensurable difference is social is, I have been suggesting all along, what we might call an antinomy of literature—perhaps
especially, of globalizing or "world" literature and literary studies and its
putatively new genres. It is, perhaps, a claim standing too squarely within
the ideological antipodes that seem (still) to drive so much literary-critical
debate today, from an aggressively market-driven critical pragmatism quite

happy to see the uncertainty principle passed to the new anthropology, to an inverted absolutism of difference (though it is almost never really that) in post-poststructuralist "ethical" orientalism and back again.

Still, I am far from the only one making it. Timothy Brennan, for example, has recently argued for recognition of the incommensurability of political "cultures of belief"—chiefly, that of twentieth-century socialism—as a *value* of difference equal to that granted routinely, nowadays, to ethnic particularity. Brennan's notion of incommensurability here combines intensity of approach in the subject (one form of which is language acquisition) with intensity of structure (i.e., presumed complexity) in the object. What he resists, then, is a kind of facile affirmation of the "translatability" of difference, on the one hand, and an equally facile insistence on its untranslatability, on the other.[30]

To summarize briefly: Brennan argues that we can recognize the recognition of incommensurability in cultures of belief as progressive precisely to the extent that it *drives* translation, as the bringing of incommensurabilities into contact. Emphasis on the incommensurability of cultures of belief can also, of course, serve the imperial function of the "politico-exotic," which helps to prevent or to preempt contact—especially when, as in Heidegger's writings, that emphasis is coded in terms of a linguistic a priori. Though I'm not entirely willing to follow Brennan into the polemic that writes Heidegger up as a foreign influence to be excised, the argument driving it is more than compelling. That argument promotes *successful,* rather than failed translation, in the intensified form of "conversion," a term Brennan seems to select quite purposefully from among the varieties of religious experience. What we need, he suggests, is that "complete rethinking"—a transformation by, for, *in* difference—that makes for religious common sense, yet is presumed alien to comparison (comparability) in the liberal secular belief culture of literary and cultural studies. Conversion, in this sense, is a collision of incommensurabilities, precisely *not* their maintenance in separate life-worlds; the incommensurability of (ethnic, national, class . . .) difference is not *beyond* commensurability, but *resistant* to it: a gap bridgeable by rigorous, but not by casual contact. Conversion, in other words, not the impossibility of conversion. For Brennan, this is emphatically a material problem—a problem of book publication and book markets:

It is difficult to talk about the cultural closure or uniqueness of worldviews without appearing romantic. And yet it appears to many of us who study the Spanish-speaking Caribbean, for example (and to take only one case), that its culture possesses a social language that gives to its users a license to poetry, bluntness, or passion that audiences in North America cannot read without ironic distancing or embarrassment. Contrast this state of affairs with classic translation commentaries. George Steiner's *After Babel,* for example, confronts a host of translation difficulties from the vantage point of a withering cosmopolitan urbanity that seems relatively minor when measured against the task of rendering the simplest African or Arabic "proly" fiction into a cogent, marketable English-language text. Proly fiction is not necessarily the brute, unmetaphorical narrative of harsh experience or autobiographical confession that we know from so many dismissive or patronizing reviews in the West, but a fiction that often is immersed in an alternative value that constitutes an experimentalism.[31]

Crystal's final answer to the question "Why prevent language death?"— "because languages are interesting in themselves"—is re-expressed (or we can re-express it) here in terms of "alternative" value—the vanishing of which, we might add, the ecological analogy for language death ironically serves to naturalize, even while protesting it. In the end, Crystal's notion of language as a "living archive," elaborated in a "public" idiom, and Brennan's notion of secular conversion, *fully* legible only to veterans of academic theory wars, are complementary ideas—forming a zone of tension across personal and academic genres, like Kaplan's narrator speaking now as essayist, now as scholar.

If (for now) I end here, at what might seem a merely formal (or generic) point—essays versus articles—that is because these two cultures, of the public and the academic intellectual, themselves form a/disciplinary cultures of belief linked by zones of incommensurability-in-contact that neither facile market-rate interdisciplinarity nor deep territorial superspecialization can (or should be allowed to) conceal. In an often brutal performance of high critique popping with intricately referenced snap, Brennan's most persuasive moment, for me, comes in an elliptically related but plainly formative personal anecdote: one that turns on the *unpublishability* (by fiat of a journal editor) of an early critical-intellectual project of his own (an English version of an essay by Sandinista National Liberation Front interior minister Tomás Borge). If I may be taken, for the moment, as a fairly typical (if perhaps pointlessly self-conscious) professional reader, we might ask ourselves, as I have been asking myself here, if the most interesting question we can ask of "language memoir" is not what it *is*—and how we can get in on it—but what, in a somewhat less than obvious sense, it is *not:* what we lose, in other words, rather than gain in its constitution as such, and how that loss is imbricated in regimes of publication for which producers of intricately *writerly* scholarly prose, like Brennan, at once sign and countersign, in a practice of essayism at the top of an anti-essayistic profession. In the "translative" relation between plurilingual experience and monolingual publication, I am saying, we find something like the tension between "creative writing" and the discipline of contemporary literary studies, a tension that in some ways we can see approaching a head today. That (as Kaplan's own work shows) we cannot posit the "creative" process as the opposite of the scholarly enterprise, but must see in it its own deep investments in critical reification, is only one of the subsequent turns we might take.

5

The Other Other Literature

This book has "worked" at the intersection of an apparently formal problem with a material problem. In literary and cultural studies, any such intersection pits the fact against the process of production of our own research objects, in a conflict that, we might say, we have devised many ways to acknowledge without really analyzing—insofar as analysis brings us sooner or later, and uncomfortably, to the discipline we exercise on those objects, and on ourselves as their analysts, in our disciplinarity. The positivism latent even in our most pliant conceptions of scholarship is, we might say, both an acknowledged and an unacknowledged ground of conflict at the intersection of research methodology with the reproduction not of methods so much as institutional positions for researchers. The pathos of this mix of assent and denial, of what one might call blindness in insight, is nowhere more abjectly figured than in the dispersions of global critical consciousness made a local imperative, carefully shielded from the bite of the anticolonial critique of the academy itself. What Haun Saussy describes as comparative literature having "won its battles," in its dissemination to fields like United States studies,[1] is understandably felt as a loss by those who now hold the high ground. In U.S. literary studies, assent takes the form of a distinction between the U.S.A. as legal object, or entity, or actor, and "America" as a representation, or perhaps an imaginary, long since lost to the jurisdiction of U.S. citizens (and in fact never having belonged to them at all). Denial, meanwhile, ensures that making a career in what we call "American literature," either as its critic or as its primary producer (or as both), means asserting such jurisdiction, in any number of ways and at any of many available levels of intensity.

It is perhaps in an embrace, rather than in a discounting of this antinomy of critical practice that Gönül Pultar writes of the "ethnic fatigue" legible, for example, in the work of Turkish American poet Seyfettin Başçılar, who has resided in the United States since 1966, writing poetry in Turkish that is published in Turkey.[2] The very aesthetic or habitus, as much as the settings, images, and themes of Başçılar's poetry is arguably as U.S. "American" as it is Turkish, and Pultar asks us to ask ourselves if it is so certainly *not* American literature, even (or especially) if it is written in one of the languages that less than one-tenth of one percent of the U.S. population, at the time of the 2000 census, could read. In Pultar's outsider's reading of the contemporary U.S. literary and literary-critical scene, what she calls "ethnic fatigue" is a product of double consciousness as a *medium*, rather than as a given object of critical discourse. For Pultar, the non-Anglo whiteness of Caucasian Turkish–Americans, which makes them "too good" for affirmative action, combines with a both contingent and persistent incommensurability, in the mediation, more than the mere civil status, that is migrancy from the non-West. In Turkish American writing, as Pultar reads it, the repression of that incommensurability returns in the form of what she calls a "weariness" with writing in English. Pultar thus "translates"—perhaps one should say "untranslates"—for contemporary U.S. literary studies the Turkish poetic trope of *hüzün*, as she reads it revalued in Başçılar's poetry, as one figure for a non-Anglophone American literature.[3]

I think we have to think this *secession* from a critical scene as something more than confrontational self-immolation performed at the gates of the art institution. That is a modernist critical figuration of the avant-garde which, whether it ridicules the drive to invisibility or grants it real value, presumes that silently single regime we call our modernity as its arena of operation. Americanists, for example—even (or especially) comparative Americanists—must accept, indeed assume, that "our" writers may turn—may *have* turned—from the U.S.-based literary-critical scene toward those of competing modernities, without yet also renouncing the figure "America" and their claims on it. And that in the violently mixed and conflicting temporalities that *can* form a lived everyday (at least if one is persuaded by

the arguments of Harry Harootunian)[4] reside both criticism's best challenge, and its unpreventable failure, in a sense that is far more easily
acknowledged than it is lived. It is not a matter of saying that global literary
studies is the cultural policy of empire, but rather of recognizing the indis-
cipline in the expansion of any field, which both unsettles and resettles its
critical wilderness.[5] "There is a relation," Diana Taylor has argued, "between
how one lives America and the naming and conceptualization of a field of
study." Taylor asks us to ask ourselves how a repertoire of deeply and fatally
performative cultural and critical practices, as "live embodied behaviors,"
encounter the "scripted genres" of the archive in our work—an encounter,
Taylor implies, that must change that work in some substantive way.[6]

One might also listen to what writers turning *to* the American scene from
its remaining outsides have to say to it, even (or especially) in translation—and to the special form of alert silence that often receives them. If
Turkish *hüzün* can be "translated," as Pultar translates it, into a kind of
"American literature," then we might think that translation as also yielding
access to a gesture and mode of reading we might call "untranslating," and
whose object is neither the original nor the translation as given research
objects, but the movement between them, which can never itself properly
be an object, since it is also the limit of criticism caught in the act.

One might, for example, build on Pultar's brandishing of this Turkish
signifier against a U.S. literary-critical scene so inward looking that it over-
looks the other in its own midst, by looking at its inversion in the English
translation, produced by the United States publishing industry, of the
memoir that launched the Turkish Nobel laureate Orhan Pamuk onto a
world stage.[7] To the extent that the "untranslated" critical object *İstanbul:
Hatıralar ve Şehir/Istanbul: Memories and City,* here, is not, and perhaps
never could be, precisely the same artifact as the "original," we might speak
of an attenuation of the authority of guardians of national literary culture that replicates from the "other other" side, as it were, Pultar's "ethnic
fatigue." In its counterfactual untranslation, in the editorial English translation of Pamuk's memoir that circulates in the form of a material object,
the book, *hüzün,* as both a glyph and a sign, goes radically out of joint, losing its status as precisely that cultural property it is used, both sincerely
and ironically, to mark.

One might read Pamuk's memoir as, among other things, an essay on the affective dynamic of contemporary Euro-Atlantic, and especially U.S., professional ignorance of Turkey: a condition linked to the fundamental incommensurability, as Pamuk's narrative persona sees it, of imperial with postimperial perspectives. But that reading will carry with it consequences for reading itself, I will suggest, that cannot be effectively quarantined by scholarly expertise. Where Pultar's free conceptual translation of *hüzün* concentrates in the idea of the "American" a critical mass sufficient nearly to destroy that idea, Pamuk's insistence on the cultural untranslatability of *hüzün*, as marking an affect inaccessible from within the academic cultural legacies of Western European empires, similarly poses both a challenge and a question to those cultural legacies as embodied in the U.S. university today. Lost, because untranslatable for a reader implied by exclusion from the memoirist's native language, *hüzün* is found, in a way, in its suspension in the text's necessary translation and untranslation from that language. This dynamic we might call a "double writing," once for a bilingual capable of "receiving" the writer, without anywhere being implied as her reader, and again for the monolingual reader that the text *does* imply. As such, we might say, it is perhaps something of the dynamic of criticism itself, as commentary that hesitates between the performative or ludic mode of literature and the constative discipline of a literary education.

One might ground a reading of *İstanbul: Hatıralar ve Şehir/Istanbul: Memories and City* in the emphasis on figures of relation between core and peripheral areas of the global system in Pamuk's recent work, including the 2002 novel *Kar (Snow)*—and in its focus on the gaze of "Western eyes."[8] It is also bound to the amplified cultural field created by the award of the Nobel Prize for literature, at a time when Turkey found itself very much on the global stage for (among others) academic literary critics and other cultural brokers, who understood themselves as charged with saving Pamuk, the "good" Turk, from his bad countrymen. In the libidinal investment of all this consecration, Pamuk's works now arguably circulate well beyond the range within which fieldbound adjudications of how well or how badly his work has been translated, or constructions of *Bildungsromanen* linking these recent books to the early- and mid-career work, are the first and last matters at hand.[9] To mark this eclipse of acquisitive expertise, in the fundamentalist sense of that term, one might propose for analysis here an effect, called "untranslation," observable only in the work as it circulates in translation, dependent on that artifactual status, and constituting a form of immanent critique of that dependence, in the rigidity imposed on actually or potentially plurilingual writing *by* translation. "Untranslation," in this sense, might signify neither the translation accessible to "all of us" reading the target language, nor the source accessible only to native and trained informants, but rather the play-in-relation of the original and the translation, in the transnational and trans*actional* book market which alone allows either to circulate.[10]

İstanbul: Hatıralar ve Şehir/Istanbul: Memories and City is organized by a comparison of culturally marked and culturally incommensurable forms of affect. At times, *hüzün* is a modality of the narrative persona's individual psychic life, the Sunday sickness of the Westernized bourgeois interior of the nuclear home and the maternal embrace in which he tells us he passed his comfortable childhood. At other times, it is a mode of historical consciousness joining him with the city across class lines in a cultural collectivity at once hidden from, and very much exposed to, Western eyes. Presenting himself as a European-style public critic and intellectual, rather than as a scholar, the memoir's narrator stages a set of what we might call missed encounters between two groups of dead writers about the city—one group not Turkish so much as *İstanbullu*, the other not French so much as European. (In other words, he is a comparatist, taking the role of a mediator or, depending on how one thinks it, even a medium.) If, as Pamuk's narrator argues, writing from inside Istanbul and writing from outside it are in meaningful ways utterly incommensurable, such incommensurability is not an expression of quantitative or scalar difference in accumulable positive "knowledge" of Istanbul. For Pamuk's narrator it is a matter, rather, of the difference between Turkish and Western forms of what we call melancholy, as *mediator* of the production and transmission of knowledge about "Turkey" and about "the West" itself.[11] *Istanbul* confronts the modern imperial ethnographic European retrieval of a Constantinople lost to the Turkish horde with the modern postimperial autoethnography of republican Turkey, in the gulf separating the *hatıralar* of Turkish Istanbulite writers, including Pamuk himself, from the City-object of Western writings about the late Ottoman Empire.

These writings—the Turkish travel memoirs of Lamartine, Nerval, Gautier, Flaubert, and others—are juxtaposed and compared with the Istanbul essays and memoirs of Turkish modernist writers such as Yahya Kemal, Abdülhak Şinasi Hisar, Ahmet Rasim, and Ahmet Hamdi Tanpınar. Where Gautier's European experience of melancholy in Istanbul universalizes an individualized form of affect, it points, the narrator implies, to an incipiently "global" Europe of expanding imperial nation-states, within which the modernizing demolition of Paris is that of empire rising.[12] Tanpınar's Turkish experience of *hüzün*, by contrast, in the decline of empire, particularizes a communal affect as the experience of imperial collapse and shrinkage onto the nation-state—and national language. *Hüzün*, then—the untranslated, untranslatable modern Turkish word interpolated into the "English-destined" text of a Turkish world writer—stands for the loneliness of national language in an imperial world: a signifier of Ottoman Turkish contraction onto the "pure" Turkish republic.

Pamuk acknowledges that his use of *hüzün* draws on Tanpınar's own use of the term (as well as of a related term and concept, *hasret*) as an affect of imperial decline, but he takes it over for his own, strategically imprecise purposes here. These purposes themselves might be said to include a strategically imprecise form of appeal to the "world" in "world literature," for the Euro-Atlantic core constituency of whom, at least, the Turkish and Ottoman historical and literary-historical context of Pamuk's body of work is largely invisible—and for whom Istanbul's appeal is precisely that of a "world city" disembedded from five centuries of rule by Europe's enemy.[13] As what I am calling "untranslation," rather than self- or auto-translation, Pamuk's *hüzün* is insistently specular, in this sense, a production of the critical (and self-critical) gaze in its imbrication with "comparatized" modes of desire produced by a global culture industry and its universities. Where it is turned on demonstrative intensities of local color, in interpolated information genres such as a five-page concatenation of street tableaux and the entire chapter devoted to Reşat Ekrem Koçu's *Istanbul Encyclopedia*, the fluency thus invoked is pointedly contrasted with the futility of neoimperial English instruction, whose product is merely and literally digital. "I am speaking," the narrator insists, "of the third-class singers imitating Turkish pop stars and American singers in the pavilions, and of the first-class singers, of the bored students in never-ending English classes who in six years have been unable to learn to say anything other than yes and no."[14] Characterizing his U.S. expatriate teachers at Robert College in Istanbul as "leftists" who "had volunteered to come to Turkey to educate the ignorant third world children of faraway poor countries,"[15] he builds on the incommensurability of their political naïveté with an anecdote about the students' response, which turns on the opaque homonymy of an English word with a colloquial Turkish word: "To one teacher who often said 'You are pushed' to illustrate how society pushes out a good person who does not submit to it, some jokers in the class answered 'Yes sir you are pushed' at every opportunity, the American teacher not knowing that the last word was the same as a derogatory expression in Turkish."[16] In the juxtaposition of *hüzün* with the happiness of "the happy people of America or Europe,"[17] there is a complicated form of extranational desire and affiliation—of "comparatism," perhaps, in the less than professional, but also more than merely bureaucratic sense— which demands accounting. As a concept of an affect, *hüzün* itself is a placeholder—though a place in motion, to be sure—for the incommensurable, and as such, is there to do what the narrator wants the untranslatable Turkish word *hüzün,* in its "untranslation" in English translation, to do, which it cannot do: to be both merely and superlatively a glyph, an opaque object lesson in the incommensurability of the East, condensed in Istanbul, with the West.

But a pure incommensurability would be a blank in history, an impossible book, a waiting that prevents the writing of the book. And so *hüzün* is not, after all, the affect of a homogeneous metropolitan–national collective, as the memoir's narrator wants to construe it—and it cannot be translated completely within extranational metropolitan–hemispheric comparison. For the narrator in fact *does* translate *hüzün,* when he offers as an equivalent the *tristesse* of the independently enlightened or the properly instructed Western visitor to Istanbul. The French term, which the narrator knows quite well is as difficult to render in English as is *hüzün*—and which will therefore be left untranslated for U.S. readers, for example, as well—is a melancholy converted from individualized to collective pathos:

> Here *hüzün* is much less a feeling of melancholy [*melankoli*], meaning a
> single person's mental state, than something like what Claude Lévi-Strauss

described in *Tristes Tropiques.* If Istanbul, lying on the forty-first parallel, little resembles tropical cities in its conditions of climate, geography, or harsh poverty, the fragility of lives there, its distance from the centers of the West, and the way people relate to each other give it a "mysterious air" which Westerners from the very start struggle to understand, and which brings the feeling of *hüzün* closer to the associations of what in Lévi-Strauss's sense is meant by tristesse. It cannot be seen as a disorder in one person's perspective; *hüzün,* just like tristesse, is a very appropriate word for speaking of a culture, an environment and a feeling experienced by millions.[18]

Istanbul differs, the narrator claims, from poorer world cities like Delhi and São Paolo, as well as richer European cities, in the proximity of the "glories of the past and the history and ruins of civilizations."[19] This weak claim for the singularity of Istanbul's historical ruins is made in the face of obvious contradictions in order to buttress the strict division between inside and outside in which *hüzün* is a lesson to be learned by the West. That lesson is embodied in the memory of loss, in the post-Ottoman subject, as the knowledge of future loss of today's Western empire. Above all else, the inscrutability of *hüzün* is then linked to the loss of empire, which the Euro-Atlantic world certainly shares (if asynchronously)—and its force then really falls on the Anglophone United States reader, a countryman of the "American teacher" with whom these Turkish students had their untranslatable fun, as the subject of an empire yet to fall. As knowledge of future loss, we might say, *hüzün* is the postmodern pathos of imperial U.S. modernity, an essay within its nostalgic totality of fragments.

All this, of course, might be understood to sanction the functional monolingualism of world literature paradigms now being imported into the self-study of one of *hüzün*'s objects, as I have read it here: the United States. But this would undercalculate or discount the incomplete and uneven translation history of Pamuk's work, to which real incommensurabilities sometimes accrue in ways that make that work less easily appropriable by or for a global perspective than may seem, even if it does seem to be offered *to* it. Unlike a younger fellow expatriate such as the novelist Elif Şafak, Pamuk continues to write his original work exclusively in Turkish, and this limits and marks his access to such a so-called world audience, the scholarly portion of which, at least (for reasons of "rigor" in scholarship, among others), still experiences the linguistic difference between "original" and translation with a healthy degree of inhibition. If that inhibition ought not to be hypostasized, either, into sanctioned ignorance, we will have to consider modalities of reading, recirculating, and commenting on such works that bend fully neither to pragmatic comradeship nor, perhaps, to the erotic terror of unchallengeable, indeed sometimes sadistic, expertise. Which stand somewhere, that is to say, between the disseminating global exchange of translation and the perfect secrecy of a round and full local world. For if Pamuk's narrator deploys the word *hüzün* as a lesson in incommensurability, he does so knowing, in a sense, that the lesson *cannot* be learned: that the lesson would be (and perhaps should be) abject terror; but of which, as in so much institutional life in an apparently permanently disenchanted world, symbolic manipulation—by which I mean, of course, not only literature, but literary criticism itself—provides a salutary or unsalutary virtual experience.

TĘSKNOTA: A NEW AMERICA

Where the virtuality of Pamuk's Istanbul, postimperially haunted by the United States, is re-presented to a world openly facing the *crisis* of globalization, in the work of Eva Hoffman, that virtuality describes the immigrant's experience of "America" itself from a perspective in which is preserved something of the triumphalist decade from 1989/91 to 2001.[20] If that is the case, then perhaps these two memoirs, very pointedly deploying individual "foreign words" from minor languages in the reading faces of monolingual implied U.S. readers, stand at something of a crossroads in U.S. imperial critical power, in which some of the voices that are in fact speaking very determinedly *to* the United States are, however, no longer bothering to do so (but did they ever?) in its own language. The jump cut narrative of Hoffman's memoir *Lost in Translation: A Life in a New Language* moves from Cracow to Vancouver to Houston and Cambridge, Massachusetts, ending (nonincidentally) in New York, and turning on a series of episodes in the trauma of permanent and irrevocable transition from the narrator's native Polish to the acquired everyday and literary English in which she composed the manuscript. Much of the lyric and narrative power of these episodes turns on the Polish word *tę sknota* at the center of many of them—and which appears repeatedly, on the memoir's pages, in italicized Polish. Like Pamuk's *hüzün*, a Turkish word fated to remain untranslated in its English-destined text, *tęsknota* is here "lost" in translation insofar as for the romantic Polish national marooned in the unsentimental North American New World, it "adds to nostalgia," Hoffman's narrator tells us, "the tonalities of sadness and longing."[21] Like *hüzün* a more substantive and collective form of melancholy than anything a culturally individualized North American might experience, *tęsknota* in *Lost in Translation* appears at and marks moments of substantive linguistic crisis in the personal and intellectual life of the narrator. We might say, in fact, that the burden given this single alien Polish word—in what is after all a global market-friendly English-language literary text—is to gather, concentrate in itself, and contain and dissipate for the work's reader, in its typographic interpolation into the discrete space of globalization that is the *book page*, the sublime alienation of what Hoffman's narrator calls "cultural passage":

> Resourceful Lila has organized English lessons for our passage, so that, as she puts it, we don't seem like "dumb peasants" when we arrive. She has a textbook, and each day tries to take us through a few sentences.... Usually, I would absorb this stuff easily, eager to pick up some new tidbits of knowledge. But now I can't concentrate; I don't want to let the sounds in. "I don't think I like English," I tell them miserably, and Janek says, "Barbarian. Primitive." ... When the sun comes out, throwing a midday glitter over the waves, I turn toward the sea hypnotically, full of a discomfiting, longing feeling. *Tęsknota*.[22]

Tęsknota, the categorically unique signifier, stands for precisely that incommensurability of language-worlds that splits the self, unleashing *Bildung* as dissemination, not as consolidation—while *tęsknota* the italicized foreign word "lost in translation" restores that consolidation in the proper name. Nostalgia, in this narrative, is not merely the nostalgia of a European emigrant for the old country and its putatively native language: it is also a nostalgia for the Euro-Atlantic fantasy of New World innocence, which declines and then falls away during the narrator's North American assimilation. An episode turning on the anglicization of the narrator's and her sister's names is, in this respect, at once an earnest retailing of Ellis Island apocrypha of nominal trauma, and a kind of performance of that trauma as, for all its symbolic brutality, (always) already overcome. "Our Polish names," Hoffman's narrator writes, "didn't refer to us; they were as surely us as our eyes or hands. These new appellations, which we ourselves can't yet pronounce, are not us. They are identification tags, disembodied signs pointing to objects that happen to be my sister and myself."[23]

This memoir of dissemination, of the nominalization of the proper name, is a remembered story of the experience of lack, of the fall from presence in language: "I'm not filled with language anymore, and I have only a memory of fullness to anguish me with the knowledge that, in this dark and empty state, I don't really exist."[24] And it is this threat of "not really existing" here that is the very pretext of *Lost in Translation,* the published book: which tells us the story, once it has been overcome, of its overcoming. In *Lost in Translation,* this mandate, to identify an experience of de-identification, is declared in a conflation of writing—"I can't write"—with being: "I don't really exist." For it is in the security of publication (and of publication in English), that this loss of the subject in and "as" Polish is narrated: in other words, from its recovery, the reconsolidating operations of which Hoffman's narrator both sensitively and ambivalently undermeasures. Contrasting herself with the eager cultural convert Mary Antin, Hoffman's narrator points to the ineradicable pain of being "consciously of two worlds" and of knowing "the other story behind the story of triumphant progress." But the new postmodern "America" in which Hoffman's narrator finds herself, dividing her selfhood where the unproblematically assimilated Antin remained whole, may be closer to the New World colonial fantasy of Antin's Old Europe than she wants to believe: it is a fantasy of freedom in deterritorialization, which empties the ground of the social landscape in order to fix a renovated figure of itself there. "I have come to a different America, and instead of a central ethos, I have been given the blessings and the terrors of multiplicity. Once I step off that airplane in Houston, I step into a culture that splinters, fragments, and re-forms itself as if it were a jigsaw puzzle dancing in a quantum space. . . . Perhaps a successful immigrant is an exaggerated version of the native. From now on, I'll be made, like a mosaic, of fragments—and my consciousness of them."[25]

As projected by the European emigrant, the New World mentality of American life "in a culture which is still young, and in which the codes and conventions are still up for grabs" takes the place of the Polish language as a myth of innocence, a sacred origin, which the narrator goes to such lengths to disclaim. To the extermination of "old" North American cultures (and their original languages) to make way for this playfully childlike new America, the narrator seems sometimes willfully blind, in a complicated performance that makes *Lost in Translation*, like *Istanbul: Memories and City*, something of a contemporary world literary allegory. Perhaps nothing in the book is so rich in this respect as its closing paragraphs, which claim the existential privileges of the multiplied self while simultaneously resolving its plurilingualism under one voice. "Each language modifies the other," Hoffman's narrator writes, "crossbreeds with it, fertilizes it. Each language makes the other relative. Like everybody, I am the sum of my languages . . . though perhaps I tend to be more aware than most of the fractures between them."[26] The immigrant's colonial counterposition of Old with New worlds, of native with acquired language, yields to the global citizen's postcolonial cosmopolitanism, and with it bilingualism to plurilingualism: "New York, Warsaw, Tehran, Tokyo, Kabul—they all make claims on our imaginations, all remind us that in a decentered world we are always simultaneously in the center and on the periphery, that every competing center makes us marginal."[27]

Arguably, what ought to, and in fact *do* make such claims on our imagination are not solely the "alternate" world cities—in which in this "contemporary world," at least, English speakers, and readers of books translated from English, can always be found—but the alternate worlds themselves, which these capitals stand for. "Warsaw," "Tehran," "Tokyo," "Kabul" here are little more than metonyms for New York, the name at the head of this analphabetic list and the only place here where *Lost in Translation* itself could be published, and from which it could be disseminated. Like Pamuk's *hüzün, tęsknota* is a translated untranslatable word from a language configured by a premise of genre as unknown—unknowable—to a reader who is not expected to know it—and who in fact may be understood to be *expected not to know* it. Where *hüzün* condenses onto Istanbul, we might say, the memory of future loss, in the lesson that one cannot know *hüzün* without knowing the loss of empire—and thus, in a sense, without doing something we might call "learning Turkish"[28]—*Lost in Translation*, more sensibly, more pragmatically—but also, perhaps, more realistically, by which I mean, with a keener ear for critical silence—issues no such invitation to "learn Polish." The translation is done, the world of *tęsknota* lost irredeemably. The future that Pamuk's narrator imagines for his "world" reader—that of a U.S. empire of the Euro-Atlantic "West" forced to face what the young Lukács called "the profound melancholy of the historical process"—is for Hoffman's narrator the present of the end of history.

LANGUAGE MEMOIR AND THE LAW OF GENRE

In this book, I have argued that the living-death "living on" of the archive of plurilingual experience is not itself a research object, but is rather a structural border marking a space where plurilingual experience, including plurilingual writing, meets (or more often, fails to meet) material book publication, and thus the *constitution* of a research object. To write *on* this border zone is certainly difficult, inasmuch as it mandates self-reflexivity in a critical enterprise itself subject to (indeed, demanding!) publication—and so equally bound to, and by, its effects. Always, at such moments of enlightenment within a long-sanctioned ignorance, we are presented with a disciplinary fork in the path. I want to suggest that these are moments of the radically unexpected and unknown, as well as (or instead of) moments of acquisition, in a way that the material "impossibility" of a radically plurilingual literature illuminates for us: and that our "choice," if we make a choice, need not be, or be only, the customary one—to download as much content as possible into the gap (or, more realistically, to hire a representative specialist to embody and thus defer it for us). We might say that many of even the most progressive recent formulations of a "new comparative literature," as much as those of a "new American studies," fail entirely to come to grips with the contrast always already implicit between the scholar's genre of the article in which such formulations are presented, and the literary or nonliterary genres with which literary studies is otherwise presumably directly concerned[29]—a contrast to which the demi-academic "creative" texts of lapsed, independent, or merely *writerly* scholars (such as Ilan Stavans's, Alice Kaplan's, Eva Hoffman's, and Orhan Pamuk's own memoir-narrators) are often less blind. Many artifacts in the critically burgeoning genre of "language memoir," by contrast, engage in a quite excruciating form of comparison of the mode of academic reception they imagine with the mode of presentation they engage. To the extent that many such "autocritographies" stand as "personal" or "creative" works by scholars in disciplinary transition or revolt,[30] I have suggested, they force us to ask the question of how scholars create the knowledge they trade—and whether the discipline producing knowledge includes forms of its destruction as well.

It is this unraveling, so to speak, of critical discipline that I have marked as "untranslation." Even an argument for the inhumanity or nonhumanity of language itself, as medium of memory, can be constructed in forms of discourse—for example, the idiom of reification and discovery at work in much properly trained scholarly prose—that positivize as the content of memory what is only comprehensible in and as memory's forming constitution. Nonfiction narrative accounts of language acquisition and bi- or plurilingualism, especially when combined with accounts of, and arguments for, untranslatability, are necessarily self-reflexive, we might say, insofar as published writing invokes the synchronic against the diachronic, the structure of a national language allegory against the personal story "lost in translation." It is in this sense, I will suggest, that we can think of the published book page as a discrete space of globalization: a field in which multilingual apposition in time (the time of the typographic line) and juxtaposition in space (the "field" of the page) must compete. To be heard, "I am many" must be said in the voice of one: that is the law of genre and of authorship itself.

What, following Kaplan, I have been calling "language memoirs" are, in a nontrivial sense, stories *in*, as much as they are stories *about* language. Their publication, then, is trivially noncongruent with their "writing," understood as a *medium* of the production of "works" and "books," not as its delivery vehicle. But if language is thus the very *medium of the writing* of language memoir—a both profound and banal observation—it remains that language memoir itself, as embedded in a discourse on a body of works, is no less an archive of books, which as such—in other words, in order to have been published—have to have contained and constrained that writing in specific, disciplinary ways.

I have already suggested that many such works develop a form of internal commentary on this predicament, which ranges from variations on what I have called the "proliferation thesis"—the "textualist" canard that any single given language is always already internally displaced, deterritorialized, and multiplied in itself—to the overtly confrontational culturalist stances of border culture literary production. The textualist position finds expression in the pragmatic monolingualism of language memoirs by contemporary multiethnic U.S.-based writers like Stavans and like Gini Alhadeff, for whom it gives pragmatic license to translate: "This book should be in several languages, all the ones spoken by the different members of my family; but I will translate for them as I go along."[31]

Then there is the culturalist challenge made to editors and scholars by writers like Cherríe Moraga, Gloria Anzaldúa, and Susana Chávez-Silverman, who demand that their readers "meet them halfway."[32] Within what Adorno would call the *Kraftfeld* structured by these antipodes, late twentieth- and early twenty-first-century diasporic "comparative" literature has already organized, in a way, a response to its critical readers. Enacted in typography and the negotiations of its conventions and norms, interlinguistic strategies of writing and publication imagine spaces and gradients of cultural globalization, reflected or produced in the gap in the law of genre and the interlinear "white" space of translation.

"Fear and Trembling before Language"

Organized by images of psychic splitting and originary repetition in the constitution of the subject in multiple languages, Alice Kaplan's own *French Lessons* is a rich source of such figuration. Here, too, in the imagination on the page of a divided medial–textual plurilingual language-world, we find an interrogation of the double movement through which the constitutive power of the plurilingual writing subject is visibly deferred, as something of a fait accompli, in and by the published material artifact of the book itself.

From the start, the narrator of *French Lessons* describes her pursuit of French-language fluency as an "existential" experience, remaking her in another language and thus liberating her from the provincial midwestern determinations of her U.S. identity. "I'm not writing only about French anymore," she tells us. "French is the mark of something that happened to me."[33] That "something," so extremely figurative as to take on literal density or weight, is a being divided into two language-selves living two phenomenologically quite separate lives. Early in the reminiscences of the narrator of *French Lessons,* this split is staged as a split in the narrator's proper name itself. Waiting for mail call in her dormitory at the Collège du Léman in Geneva, where she studies on a school year abroad, she is introduced to something of a new self embodied in "my name pronounced French style with the accent on the second syllable, ah-LEASE."[34] When she returns to Minnesota—now an alien and alienatingly U.S. American "landscape," rather than her former home—it is as someone marked bodily by the linguistic habitus of life outside the United States, who can feel French "sticking in my throat" and for whom speaking English again brings a sensation of disembodiment.[35] This contamination of the body by language difference is literalized by an attack of herpes simplex on one of the narrator's ears, an event she rereads through the logic of fracture, "as if half of my face had been at war."[36]

Throughout Kaplan's language memoir, the pure self-renovation of French, which works on the tabula rasa of the narrator's archetypal midwestern "Americanness," is counterposed to her maternal grandmother's Yiddish, an artifact of linguistic sedimentation she finds uncanny: "[Yiddish speakers] disturbed me: they were familiar, although I couldn't understand a word."[37] As the grandmother becomes senile and paranoid, in an exhaustion the narrator links to the historical breakdown of signification in Euro-Atlantic modernity and holocaust, she "cedes" her English to a Babelian mixture of the childhood languages (Lithuanian Russian, Yiddish, and synagogue Hebrew) she had avoided all her adult life in the United States. For the narrator, this "mad" speech is a kind of paradoxically pure plurilingualism, embodied in the traumatic *Augenblick* of the seam between language-worlds: at the limit of sentient degeneration, the grandmother no longer produces speech, nor language in any other productive form, but interlinguistic difference itself—that which, as Derrida put it in one of his most memorable nonformulations, *is not:*[38] "the change from one language to another," the narrator observes, "was all the communication she could produce."[39] It is in the hidden centrality, in *French Lessons,* of this figure of living death that what Kaplan calls "language memoir" most powerfully weighs the death of a radically plurilingual life in the artifactual record of a structurally monolingual published book. In losing her mind, after all, the grandmother loses the serial translative mode through which her childhood languages are suspended in United States English, the language of her adult life and the language in which her granddaughter, *French*

Lessons's narrator, composes her memoir. Where the grandmother, in her senility a victim of translation's breakdown, thus stands for the disseminating madness of plurilingualism, the narrator, as the agent *composing* its story, is bound to administer that madness, reintegrating it into signification.

When sentences in French fly into the narrator's head for no apparent reason (by which she means for no *communicative* reason), she is disturbed by the glimpse it affords of dark, dynamic need and desire, in place of the skillful technical accomplishment of proficiency; but that disturbance must be repelled, and repelled insistently, in order to continue writing. One is aware that by necessity, the very dynamic that the narrator brings onto the page of *French Lessons,* and which she strives to bring to its consequence, cannot have been permitted its play, by virtue of its own transmission, in the book's very *material* presence to the reader's hand. This is the "law of genre," the apparently "textual" law, seen at the point where it meets the laws of publication, and it perhaps explains why virtually nowhere, in an English-language memoir about the liminal *passion* of learning French, is the French language permitted, in any substantive sense, to take the page. "Language is not a machine," the narrator declares: "it is a function of the whole person."[40] Yet the narrator's motivation or ability to circumvent the mechanization of *publication,* which alone provides for the discursive afterlife of the narrator's *book*—and which structurally *contains* the subjective deconstitution at the center of her *text*—is necessarily (one might even say, unfortunately) contained.

Its most nuanced reflection, we might say, is found in the narrator's elegant meditation on the subjunctive mood where "most of life takes place . . . [a] realm of doubt, desire, fear and trembling before language."[41] Suspending the temporal segmentation and discretion of the *passé composé* within the "endless present" of the imperfect, it is the subjunctive, the narrator suggests, that gives us the gathering of "word" within "world" of extra- or unpublishable, "impossible" life: the life of writing in death, in a *book* in which the narrator, and finally also the author whom she displaces here, can only ever be a *character.*

But this is perhaps only the dynamic of all literature, so to speak, in an age of mechanically reproduced print-languages and an epistemic order of things sectioned by research periods, fields, and areas and defined by national languages: a division of labor, in literary studies, ensuring deeply incompatible ranges of specialization but bound as a whole by and in the material limit of the *book*. As I have already suggested, such containment is not a dynamic exclusively of Anglophone and Anglo-American domination of global book publishing—though that is its outer limit, today—but is reproducible in regional transnational and national contexts defined by other dominant languages, as well. The title of Emine Sevgi Özdamar's "Mutterzunge," the first short fiction in a celebrated volume of the same title, is a German word "foreignized" by Turkish, in a specific and determined *manipulation* the narrator is at pains to make clear straightaway. "In meiner Sprache," the narrator tells the German-speaking reader, who is assumed to know no Turkish, "heißt Zunge: Sprache" ("In my language, 'tongue' means 'language'").[42]

Passing a prison in Stuttgart and hearing the speech of Turkish prisoners inside, the narrator translates their Turkish into German, "teaching" the German-speaking reader the Turkish verb *görmek,* to see. Other Turkish words "taught" either explicitly, as here, or indirectly, include *işçi* (worker), *bahşiş* (tip), *hoca* (teacher), and the locution *İnşallah* ("God willing"). Another story, entitled "Großvaterzunge," explores the "repressed" Arabic vocabulary of neologistic modern Turkish, purified by secular modernization, in vivid illustration of how much closer Turkish Islam looks to Arab Islamic culture from the vantage point of exile in Germany. "Großvaterzunge" contains lists of Arabic loan words used in Turkish, along with German translations and lengthy dialogue sequences in which the narrator and her Arabic-language teacher, Ibni Abdullah, trade a common vocabulary mediated by German translation.

Elsewhere in *Mutterzunge,* however, in paragraphs of typographically unmarked code-switching dialogue between Turkish guest workers, the narrator refuses this didactic translation for German-speaking readers, producing passages that are impossible to fully comprehend without some knowledge of Turkish. Turkish agglutinative suffixes are added to German words, and the grammar of each language is interwoven with that of the other, lending the guest workers an existential and poetic voice that cannot be appropriated as native information.[43] This mode of *refusing* translation—closer to the effect achieved in the work of writers like Feridun Zaimoğlu (even when, as in Zaimoğlu's case, they have no patience with the politics of Turkish cultural exceptionalism)[44]—places greater pressure, we might say, on the artifactual form of the book in which it must circulate:

Gastarbeiter sprach:
"Sonra Dolmetscher geldi. Meisterle konustu. Bu Lohn steuer kaybetmis dedi. Finanzamt cok fena dedi. Lohnsteuer yok. Bombok. Kindergeld falan alamazsin. Yok. Aufenthalt da yok. Fremdpolizei vermiyor. Wohnungsamt da yok diyor. Arbeitsamt da Erlaubnis vermedi. Ben oglani Berufsschule ye gönderiyorum. Cok Scheiße bu. Sen krankami ciktin."[45]

This strong plurilingualism, which genuinely and aggressively blocks translation, at once conceals some of the affective content of the guest workers' speech, and (since it is a mixture of German and Turkish, not simply Turkish) leaves the door open, we might say, to the German language and to German speakers with no knowledge of Turkish—to *learning* Turkish, that is to say, in the reciprocative step toward what Zafer Şenocak called a "third language" in Germany.[46]

Where it is refused, of course, strong plurilingualism's invitation to language learning, as I have read it here, registers simply as noise, with all that it implies for the market optimization of reading. We might say that compromise with the profit-seeking of the book industry is written on the entire spectrum of contemporary literature, where it forces us to consider the *future* of our literary archives, not only their past—and where the strength of a work's plurilingualism often correlates with diminished visibility (publication by nonprofit "independent" publishing houses, or any of a scale of smaller units down to hand-printed limited editions) and either increased self-assertion as avant-gardism, or a kind of refusal of self-assertion altogether. Even, for example, in the second-wave recovery of work neglected by projects for U.S. ethnic studies focused initially on representations of identity,[47] patterns of selectivity in the analysis of formal, textual strategies are clearly visible—the containable or recuperable internal displacements of "broken English," for example, drawing the bulk of some scholars' attention, at the expense of interlinguistic displacements (in a mark, perhaps, of the scholar's own negotiations of interlingual and plurilingual training and competence).

To take a now classic example: editions of Theresa Hak Kyung Cha's *Dictée*, published by small independent presses in New York (Tanam) and Berkeley (Third Woman) before being reissued by the University of California Press in 2001, include a wealth of interpolated realia including photographs, film stills, reproduced handwritten and typescript letters, anatomical diagrams, Chinese characters, and images of Korean hangul, as well as long passages of broken and lineated prose in French.[48] In the arrangement of material, French-language passages are generally followed by English versions of the same text, either in succession or in facing-page arrangement (an exception is the sequence "Aller/Retour," which grafts them together, yet still does not leave much French without an English equivalent). The Korean appearing on the book's first page, on the other hand, goes untransliterated and untranslated, as do some of the Chinese characters. And the dictation lessons enstructured or dissolved in the work's French-language passages do seem (to judge from the habits of Cha scholarship, which either engage, or neglect or avoid *Dictée*'s plurilingualism[49]) to require bilingual reading, to the extent that the conventions of the dictation exercise itself and their violation (the transcription of punctuation words meant to be produced, rather than transcribed) invite one to monitor compliance.

Less has been published, thus far, on Karen Tei Yamashita's *The Circle K Cycles* (2001), an intergeneric work focused on the culture of dekasegi (Brazilians of Japanese descent who came to Japan as migrant laborers during the 1990s), which moves from English into the "Japanese English" of the retail market, Brazilian Portuguese, and Japanese, with one entire chapter in Portuguese and one in Japanese, followed by English versions. In a way, *The Circle K Cycles* manages to combine what at first appears to be the radical incommensurability of language-worlds—in the demand for trilingual English–Brazilian Portuguese–Japanese fluency—with a partial attenuation of that incommensurability, in appositive translation at a structural extreme (the appending of entire chapters in multiple versions). It is in fact by radicalizing the redundancy of appositive translation that *The Circle K Cycles* creates a text, and a book, whose material structure and attendant horizons of expectation stand oddly and interestingly between "strong" or constructive and "weak" or containing appositive plurilingualism. On the one hand, the wholesale interpolation of ten- to twenty-page blocks of continuous Portuguese or Japanese marks out large zones of potentially total opacity for the simultaneously monocultural and monolingual reader implied by the "Dekasegi Starter Dictionary" on *The Circle K Cycles*'s very first page; this impulse, we might say, is primarily constructive or productive of difference. As Kandice Chuh observes,

> In *Circle K Cycles*, generic hybridity structurally enables [Yamashita] to place variegated worldviews side by side. . . . [T]he interpretive flexibility required by the nonequivalence of *Circle K Cycles*'s constitutive pieces is a textual iteration of traveling through difference. Comparisons are drawn not toward synthesis of differences or in an easy celebration; rather they are left open to signification. This space of comparison is the space between the ability to read and the ability to understand a language; it marks the differential knowledge necessary to move into the realm of fluency, of access to worldview.
>
> Yamashita's structuring of *Circle K Cycles*, in other words, both prompts and models the movement into difference that hemispheric studies in one sense represents. . . . The likely monolingual U.S. readers for whom Yamashita is writing can acknowledge the presence of the Portuguese but cannot render it intelligible: now you see me, now you don't.[50]

And yet the mass-scale redundancy in the duplication of entire chapters in two or three languages seems mainly that: a purposefully massive redundancy that breaks *programmatically* with the conserving or containing drive of mainstream (trade) market-oriented and cost-conscious editorial practice. While its Portuguese and Japanese chapters remain, so to speak, luxuriously "useless" to the monolingual Anglophone reader of *The Circle K Cycles*, they do not appear constructed to conceal information from that reader, either. We must conclude, rather, that they serve as a kind of incentive and figure for language acquisition as a practice, without demanding it as a precondition for "understanding" the work—or at least the *entire* work. Again, Chuh:

> This doubled iteration structurally performs not only the difference that different languages make to representation but also the possibility of the incorporation of radical difference without its eradication. The interpretation

of the polyglot reader fluent in English, Portuguese, and Japanese is not prioritized in this scheme. Rather, it evokes conversation; it requires the forming of relations across differences to produce greater collective knowledge. Here, again, the relevance of Yamashita's work to conceptualizing hemispheric studies emerges: the internal structures of the text reproduce this representation of a unified field of differences in a way that approximates the idea of a nonassimilative hemispheric studies. . . . Yamashita's structuring of *Circle K Cycles* and the ways in which she thematizes cultural differences in its constitutive pieces compellingly and simultaneously illuminate the value of multilingual facility and insist that being monolingual need not be a definitive barrier to cross-cultural knowledge. She echoes in this way Gayatri Spivak's reminder that comprehension of difference does not require complete fluency. Rather, what is important is the effort to become fluent—to move into another's (or an other's) worldview by moving into another language.[51]

I quote directly from the work of another critic at such length here to return focus from the given critical object (the literary work) to the critical procedures that construct and manipulate it. In so doing, I want to make a point, in closing, about the interpenetration or interenfolding of critical desire, in literary studies today, with its designated objects. Since the collapse of the theoretical self-reflection that peaked in the 1980s, U.S. literary and cultural studies might be said to have confined its metacommentary to carefully circumscribed zones: defined "occasions" consisting of special sessions at major national conferences, or special issues of major journals, or "state of the profession" features such as those published in the Modern Language Association's journals *PMLA* and *Profession*. Let me suggest that this managed containment of self-reflection, in the discipline's new modes of reproducing itself, so to speak, "after theory," is no such small thing as a merely fashionable exhaustion by and of other mere fashions (high theory, "postmodernism," antiliterary cultural studies), but the restoration of nativist power over a "foreign" speech and writing for which the difference of languages itself—and the dangerously paradoxical or antinomian translative localization enacted by it—is a more than fair analogue.

In a U.S. context, it is arguably the strong plurilingual tendency within a certain subgrouping of Latina/o, and especially Chicana/o primary literary production, which we might say still poses a posteriori the most determined challenge today both to literary book publication itself and to the scholarship strongly dependent on book publication—and which perhaps consequently remains marginalized even in its very absorption by that scholarship. Taking as one of its important themes the marginalization of radical feminist and lesbian or queer Chicana writing in early academic formations of ethnic studies, the scholarship and personal writings of Cherríe Moraga and Gloria Anzaldúa focused insistently on the problem of bi- and plurilingualism *in publication*.[52] From her widely cited invitation to U.S., Mexican, and Latina/o readers "to be met halfway" in U.S. Spanish, with its echoes of Césaire's "Accommodez-vous de moi. . . . Je ne m'accommode pas de vous!"[53] to her denunciations of the racism of Anglo literary and cultural critics who cherry-pick the more inclusive meditations (and monolingual Anglophone passages) in *Borderlands/ La Frontera: The New Mestiza*,[54] to her critiques of literary and cultural critics of color "contributing to the invisibility of our sister-writers,"[55] Anzaldúa consistently pushed back against *translative* publication with a determination that even mainstream academic ethnic literary studies, invested as it must be in the continuity and stability of ethnic literary production, is bound to find indecorous.

In its afterlife in a U.S. studies newly self-conscious, again, Anzaldúa's major work is thus a form of hesitation between the incommensurability of lesbian feminist Chicana difference and the refusal to *translate* that difference (embodied in the radicalized code-switching of *Borderlands/ La Frontera*), on the one hand, and a dedication to intercultural communication demanding worthwhile compromise, on the other. This is, we might say, still the strongest case *visible*, on the U.S. academic literary studies scene today, for intercultural contact as *strong* contact, or collision. For Anzaldúa, everything turned on the visibility accorded by book publication, a visibility determined by language acquisition *as a practice* and a "state" of pluralized identity rather than as a means to an end in translation: "Because white eyes do not want to know us, they do not bother to learn our language, the language which reflects us, our culture, our spirit."[56] Indeed, there is reason to read what Henry Staten terms the "Aztlanism" of Chicana/o writing as this provocation of *strong* contact, rather than the recidivist, regressivist or separatist identarian essentialism Staten ascribes to it (and which moves against his own consent to Gayatri Chakravorty Spivak's stress on "inaccessibility *under the most favorable conditions*").[57]

Like the essays and poems in Moraga's *Loving in the War Years: Lo que nunca pasó por sus labios,* the prose and prose-poetry sequences in *Borderlands/La Frontera: The New Mestiza* interpolated paragraphs, stanzas, and entire poems and sections of nonfiction prose in variants of what can only be *printed* as Spanish, without providing (what would also clearly be) English equivalents. Where this limited the critical audience for *Borderlands/La Frontera* and works like it, by literally and symbolically repelling the scholarly reader without the cultural and linguistic competence to "work" on the book, it carved niches within fields and subfields from comparative literature, U.S. studies, and ethnic studies down to Chicana/o studies itself, placing pressure simultaneously on the micrological identarianism of field studies and the macrological struggle of an incipiently "global" field to live up to its name.[58] That that pressure today can no longer be contained *or* relieved by euphoric discourses of hybridization placing a premium on *translative* mixture is one argument implicit, perhaps, in the sharp contrast Paul Allatson draws between Spanglish and the Spanish/English of Susana Chávez-Silverman's *Killer Crónicas: Bilingual Memories/Memorias Bilingües* (2004). Distinguishing between the bilingual code-switching of the line of Chicana writing represented by Moraga and Anzaldúa and the idiomatic inflection of English by Spanish in the aesthetic promoted in Ilan Stavans's *Spanglish: The Making of a New American Language* (2004),[59] Allatson observes: "[D]eparting from Stavans's unabashed enthusiasm for Spanglish, it must be emphasized that Susana Chávez-Silverman's chronicles do not necessarily represent a coming to literary fruition of Spanglish. The power and inventiveness of *Killer Crónicas* lies, more precisely, in the author's adept code-switching between English and Spanish. While the chronicles provide ample evidence of neologistic wordplay in both English and Spanish, one that might indeed be regarded as a literary form of Spanglish, their narrative momentums are firmly anchored in an unequivocal at-homeness in both tongues."[60] It is precisely this double- (or triple-, or quadruple-) voiced publicity in code-switching, its bypassing of the *literarity* of idiom, that I want to suggest offers another form of value on the critical scene of comparative literary studies today— and which, so as both to warn of its literary or literarist incorporation *and* to honor Stavans's own refusal of avant-garde silence, I will suggest we think in Stavans's (finally positive and affirmative) terms, as *kitsch*. As conceivable space, in other words, for nonrelation. Not the private nonrelation of avant-garde autonomy, moving from idiom to nonsense to silence, seeking escape from appropriation. Rather, a *public* nonrelation—in which we find precisely not, or not *only* hybrid or syncretic language, but also, as Juliana Spahr suggests in her work on Pacific Basin literatures, "multilingual dialogue in multilingual situations."[61]

Perhaps only electronic publication, making use of multilingual character set encoding standards (such as the imperfect, but interesting Unicode), could permit the publication—the *chance* of publication—of a radically, anarchically plurilingual literature, and the literary criticism that might follow it: making more than mere talk of our mandates for a renovated and radically plurilingual "new American studies," a "new comparative literature," and so on. In the very tenuousness of their lives in print, such works of twentieth- and twenty-first-century literature that have already pushed toward this condition figure a kind of impossibility in and for print-capitalist literary culture itself, an impossibility that makes them avant-garde in truly the least silly sense of that term. I mean their ability to index for us, in all the fullness of its contradictions, the mixed modernity of what Harry Harootunian calls "noncontemporaneous contemporaneity":[62] a *Zeitgeist* for an age with neither time nor spirit to spare.

Afterword

Unicode and Totality

By way of an afterword, I want here to offer a brief history—and in a way, a political economy—of Unicode, the character set encoding standard that today mediates much, or perhaps all, of a contemporary scholar's *writing*, depending on how extensively she or he uses a personal computer.

It is a fascinating history, replete with correspondences to the tropological realm in which many of us in the literary culture feel at home. Whether we find it liberating or constraining (or both), most younger scholars today, I would venture, have long since accustomed themselves to the idea that the accumulating life's work on our computer hard drives only exists, in any material sense, as patterns of magnetized spaces, "on" and "off" states set and unset by electrical pulses. It is not an image of the letter "A," for example, that is written to the surface of the hard disk when I press the key marked with that letter, writing these words. What is "written," rather, is one such pattern of magnetized spaces, representing a binary number assigned to the letter "A" in an internal code table. It is this binary encoding that allows us to "process" words with the word processing software we use to write: to rapidly search, sort, and modify text, as well as to transmit it.

Much, or perhaps all of our writing as contemporary scholars—depending, again, on how extensively or exclusively one uses a personal computer—is mediated by character set encoding. It is, in other words, digital—and if one composes first or exclusively on the computer, "born" that way. Our work is always already, if one wants to put it this way, "in code," or encoded. I do not mean this to be taken as a presentist or futurist demand to "get with the program"—a fatuous gesture all too common in new media studies, at least as a subfield of a perhaps generally anachronistic literary studies—but rather as an observation about the conditions of scholarly knowledge production today, as conditioned by a system that, not incidentally, has a cultural politics already hidden in it. For character encoding has a technical history as marked by cultural language politics as the history of machine translation.

Here is why. The local storage and retrieval of data that I perform by pressing the key marked with the letter "A" is, straightforwardly, an encoding and decoding operation. So, equally straightforwardly, is the remote transmission over a telecommunications link, which I perform by sending electronic mail, uploading or downloading my document files, and so on. For patterns of bits or "binary digits"—those series of magnetized spaces on the hard drive, or of pulses sent through a telecommunication channel—to be represented as alphabetic letters, both transmitting and receiving hardware must share a standard code table. The historical development of these code tables, I want to suggest, is effectively a technical allegory of postwar development—in which one might also, if inclined, find something of the language politics of U.S. American studies, comparative literature, and multicultural, multiethnic, and global or world literature studies arrayed in line. There is a postwar "American" moment, in which U.S. industries set the standard for the rest of the redeveloping and developing world. That moment is followed by an initial, Euro-Atlantic period of internationalization, during the 1960s and '70s, comprising individual nationalization projects and the creation of a European community, as well as the growth of Japan. What followed subsequently—in the politically, if not necessarily technically significant year 1991—might be taken as a moment in what we now call globalization, in which U.S. industries incorporated European and East Asian redevelopment into a "global" framework again legislated by U.S. needs.

The first code standard for data processing in the English language was created in 1963 by the nonprofit American Standards Association (now the American National Standards Institute) to encourage the voluntary compliance of manufacturers of computing equipment in building inter-operative systems. ASCII, or American Standard Code for Information Interchange, which encoded ninety-five characters used in U.S. English typography, quickly became the international standard, since U.S. computer manufacturers dominated the industry. ASCII was "international-ized" in 1967, when the International Organization for Standardization (ISO) in Geneva published an expanded code standard adding to ASCII those Roman characters used in writing Western European languages. At the same time, various projects oriented to the needs of individual national languages were begun. Expanded ASCII standards for Central and Eastern European languages, as well as Turkish and the Greek and Cyrillic alpha-bets followed, while a Japanese Industrial Standard incorporating ASCII appeared in the early 1970s. To the extent that these code standards sup-plemented ASCII with characters needed for data processing in a specific national language other than English, they can be regarded as enterprises of translation, necessarily bilingual and *serial* in nature. And this is an era, then, of the successful assertion of written language "rights" against an ini-tially monolingual "international" code standard.

With the transnational integration of telecommunications networks came a perceived need for multilingual data processing, and thus for the global integration of such language rights. In 1991 a U.S. rival to the Euro-pean ISO standard emerged. Researchers from the Xerox Corporation formed the Unicode Consortium in 1991 and published their first ver-sion of a standard for "unique, universal, and uniform" code providing number assignments for all characters in all languages in use in the world. If the internationalization of the ASCII standard, between 1963 and the late 1980s, was in many ways essentially *serial* and *translative* in its expansion from one national language standard to the next, Unicode (backed by Apple, Microsoft, IBM, and Hewlett-Packard, among others), embodies a vision of the parallel or simultaneous processing of data on a global scale: a vision of global linguistic integration. Where the historical development of ASCII and ISO produced numerous individual national variations, Unicode, one might say, aims to "freeze" that development in a totality.

Unsurprisingly, Unicode is controversial. It has been criticized for a market-oriented strategy that produced messy revisions of the first standard, as estimates of the number of world language characters exceeded estimates designed into the standard. Unicode was criticized as well for relying on representative committees speaking for entire language cultures, and for failing to accommodate a vast number of infrequently used characters that are indispensable for the digitizing of public records, such as those used for personal and place names in Japanese. By far the most controversial aspect of Unicode is its abstraction of character, or standard form (a unit of text), from glyph, or variant form (a graphic unit) in East Asian languages. Those critical of the Unicode project accuse it of attempting to consolidate the Chinese character set used in China, Japan, and Korea by eliminating so-called "redundant" or "superfluous" variants (and here, as I think you can see, we return to the question of "optimization" with which I began). Unicode's defenders, meanwhile, describe resistance to this process of abstraction as, in one linguist's words, "an unfortunate flaw in Eastern attitudes."[1]

As a trope in the simple sense of that term (a theme or motif), I want to suggest, Unicode merges literature's twin twentieth-century foils, the universal and code. As a technical protocol, it is haunted by the literary inefficiency of writing, in the claims that variants make on standards. In fact it is haunted, we could say, by a logic of excess, of superfluity and waste, within its logic of conservation: by the need for the standard to accommodate legacy (older, partial standards of expanded ASCII), so as to encourage timely commercial adoption. As a system defining universally efficient transmission, it must emit redundant waste in the form of merely local variation, precisely to claim its place *as* system.

As in the history of machine translation, literature is frequently and explicitly made a limit case. Thus one technical critic of Unicode imagines its character-optimizing strategies applied to English-language vocabulary, concluding that the elimination of superfluous variants "would be the end of both the Bible and Shakespeare."[2] Defenders, meanwhile, point to Unicode's dedication to scholarly use, in the incorporation of historic and extinct scripts, and its tolerance for the idea of fictional languages (proposals to include Klingon, as well as Elvish scripts invented by J. R. R. Tolkein remain under consideration). This persistence of technical reference to literary language as the human and inhuman other of code should put another face, I would think, on the contemporary crisis of the humanities.

My suggestion in this book has been that, like any other disciplinary emergent, "world literature" lives on a *scene:* a word I use in its colloquial sense in U.S. English, where it connotes novelty and elective affinity, an exclusiveness neither barring entry nor prohibiting exit—and which stands, more than anything else, for the institutional moment. It is a term I draw from the liminal register of the demimonde, for reasons I have already indicated, and which expose a personal concern both with the cost (to literature) of literary-critical vanguardism driven by scientized research paradigms, and for the practical fate of the literary avant-garde—such as it is. To speak of a cultural "scene," I want to say, is to impute a certain level of organization, of pattern, to previously undetected activity—and to mark the start of its incorporation into official culture, as well. Likewise, to speak of the scene of literature is merely to emphasize the institutional optic already implied by the research field.

The economies of book publishing and the entertainment media, which produce what many of us interested in debates around world literature still use as primary research material—I mean new *works* of literature— are today highly and especially *exclusive.* I use the intensifier "highly" to acknowledge that *any* economy is necessarily exclusive—while insisting that the contemporary scene is a special case, defined by the transnational integration, during the last fifteen to twenty years, of the Anglo-American and Anglo-global book publishing industries into media conglomerates. This transformation has destroyed the economy of literary publishing in the United States and the United Kingdom, eliminating smaller and midsized houses and raising profit expectations from the single digit traditional to the industry to the double digits demanded from other media— with a predictably homogenizing effect. Observing this, Francesca Orsini suggests that "the global cultural market now subverts Bourdieu's description of the field as an 'economic world reversed,' in which commercial success is a bar to symbolic recognition."[3]

As a technical protocol, the Unicode project aims to produce and to maintain in perpetuity a single unified code map containing all characters in all the languages in the world. And as a trope, then (again, in the simplest sense of that term), Unicode recapitulates what Umberto Eco called *la ricerca della lingua perfetta,* the search for the perfect language.[4] That is to say, an entire history of projects for a universal mathematical, and later, an international auxiliary language, in the *creation* of a global system of communication. As such a world-system in miniature, Unicode has the advantage of remaining plainly *created:* an aspect bearing not at all on its (hotly debated) suitability as a protocol, yet heavily on its usefulness as a trope, where it reminds us that a world-system, where it exists, is created rather than found. This emphasis, which is nothing if not integral to world-system theory in the work of Immanuel Wallerstein and others, is attenuated, for some reason, when the model is "ported" (to use a software programming term) to literature.

Still, one thing should be clear. Character set encoding is not concerned with the translation of one human language into another. Nor does it involve replacing one human language with another, human or technical. Rather, it is a system—a publishing system—representing a totality of human languages, *in their difference,* in a single matrix. In that respect, it shares the spirit, but literally not the letter, of the international auxiliary language projects of the nineteenth century and the first, monolingual wave of research in machine translation.

As a system of representation, of course, Unicode must necessarily lag behind new emergents—an abstraction that the constant invention of new Chinese and Japanese characters merely literalizes. As always, the question is how much value this lag must acquire. And while the world-system models of some current literary-critical methodology may leave it too little, I do want to guard here against loading it down with too much in compensation. This is a real danger. We might say that already, today, professional discourse networks focused on commensurable translation are shifting to focus on incommensurable untranslatability, with a dishearteningly predictable emphasis on the foreign languages of Islam. That this emphasis is also an appropriation, and as such, entirely in line with new mandates for U.S. imperial national defense, is beyond question. Yet our task here, as I suggested in this book's introduction, is perhaps not to account for, or to apostrophize, diamantine nodes of the local, utterly invulnerable to appropriation. The task, if there is a task, is rather to think plurilingualism, the plurilingualism of any "world literature" today, within existing and possible models of the world, the globe, the planet. Unicode is, after all, not a system of babble, of "imperfect or inarticulate" mixed speech. Rather, it is paradoxically a system of Babel, of dispersion into difference. As such, it is a "kitsch" figure, in the sense lent that term by the narrator of Stavans's *On Borrowed Words*, of plurilingualism in translation: of plurilingualism in a global public sphere.

To think world literature as kitsch, I'm suggesting, is to disarticulate the *literary* in "world literature" from the *world* in "world-system." It is a disarticulation, I have already suggested, that maintains two drives—the statist and the anarchist drives, as it were, of literary studies—in tension. If, in a political–economic context finally oriented to action, the thought of totality (as heuristic, rather than as algorithmic)[5] is progressive—and I think it is—then arguably, in a literary context oriented to thought as a *complement* to, rather than a replacement for action, it is regressive—not least in the conformation that the map demands from the mapped world. If one struggle, that is to say, with which we can all join is the struggle to make sense of real, distant causes bearing on us, and of the possibility that we *may* be closed in totality, then the other, I'll suggest—and this is where literature matters—is to prevent that closure from blinding us: to *open* totality and put it to work.

Notes

1. Ross Chambers, *Mélancolie et opposition: Les débuts du modernisme en France* (Paris: Librarie José Corti, 1987); Ross Chambers, *The Writing of Melancholy: Modes of Opposition in Early French Modernism* (Chicago: University of Chicago Press, 1993).

2. Chambers, *The Writing of Melancholy*, xi; Chambers, *Mélancolie et opposition*, 11.

3. Friedrich Nietzsche, "Vom Nutzen und Nachteil der Historie für das Leben," in *Sämtliche Werke, Kritische Studienausgabe I: Die Geburt der Tragödie, Unzeitgemässe Betrachtungen I–IV, Nachgelassene Schriften 1870–1873*, ed. Giorgio Colli and Mazzino Montinari (Munich: Deutscher Taschenbuch Verlag; Berlin: de Gruyter, 1988), 268; Friedrich Nietzsche, "On the Utility and Liability of History for Life," in *Unfashionable Observations*, trans. Richard T. Gray (Stanford, Calif.: Stanford University Press, 1995), 105. (Gray gives it as "mania to collect.")

4. James Livingston presses this point fruitfully. "The cultural function of the modern historian," Livingston writes, "is to teach us how to learn from people with whom we differ due to historical circumstances. . . . But these people with whom we differ, and from whom we must learn, are, to begin with, other historians; for there is no way to peek over the edges of our present as if they aren't there, standing between us and the archive, telling us how to approach it. . . . No one gets to the 'primary sources,' whether they are constituted as the historical record or as the literary canon, without going through the priests, scribes, librarians, professors, critics—the professionals— who created them in retrospect, in view of their own intellectual obligations and political purposes. In this sense, history is not the past as such, just as the canon is not literature as such; it is the ongoing argument between historians, among others, about what qualifies as an event, a document, an epoch." See Livingston, "On Richard Hofstadter and the Politics of 'Consensus History,'" *boundary 2* 34, no. 3 (2007): 34–35.

5. Against such a reflex—and in context of "the historicist idiom now dominating literary studies"—Ellen Rooney invokes Peggy Kamuf's useful tropism "historicality": "A literary work has a historical context, as we call it, but no more or less than any document or artifact produced in the past; but the work, if it is still read and studied when this 'context' will have subsided into archival compost, has a relation as well to a future, by which it remains always to some extent incomprehensible by any given present. This is the dimension of the work's *historicality*, which is therefore not to be simply confused or conflated with historical 'context.'" See Kamuf, *The Division of Literature; or, The University in Deconstruction* (Stanford, Calif.: Stanford University Press, 1997), 164; qtd. in Rooney, "The Idiom Doesn't Go Over," in "Forum: Conference Debates; Gayatri Chakravorty Spivak's Influences: Past, Present, Future; MLA Annual Convention, 28 December 2006, Philadelphia," *PMLA* 123, no. 1 (2008): 242.

6. Chambers, *The Writing of Melancholy*, xi; Chambers, *Mélancolie et opposition*, 11.

7. Chambers, *The Writing of Melancholy*, xi; Chambers, *Mélancolie et opposition*, 11.

8. "Verschmelzung von 'linker' Ethik und 'rechter' Erkenntnistheorie." See Georg Lukács, *Die Theorie des Romans: ein geschichtsphilosophischer Versuch über die Formen der grossen Epik*, Sammlung Luchterhand, 36 (Frankfurt am Main: Luchterhand, 1989), 15; Gyorgy Lukács, *The Theory of the Novel: A Historico-Philosophical Essay on the Forms of Great Epic Literature* (Cambridge, Mass.: MIT Press, 1971), 22.

9. See Martin Heidegger, "Die Zeit des Weltbildes," in *Holzwege* (Frankfurt am Main: Vittorio Klostermann, 1957), 69–104; Martin Heidegger, "The Age of the World Picture," in *Off the Beaten Track*, ed. and trans. Julian Young and Kenneth Haynes, 57–85 (Cambridge: Cambridge University Press, 2002).

10. "Working with Mary Trouille on an English version of *Mélancolie et opposition* has been an enriching experience. It has taught me something I was unable to acknowledge five years ago: that in the melancholy experience of writing about melancholic writing there was also an intense pleasure, derived in large part from devising critical texts whose own linguistic texture had something in common with the texts they were about" (Chambers, *The Writing of Melancholy*, xv).

11. Elizabeth Bruss, *Beautiful Theories: The Spectacle of Discourse in Contemporary Criticism* (Baltimore: Johns Hopkins University Press, 1982), 44, 47.

12. Chambers, *The Writing of Melancholy*, xi; Chambers, *Mélancolie et opposition*, 11.

13. See Chambers, *The Writing of Melancholy*, xiii; Chambers, *Mélancolie et opposition*, 13. Also see Ross Chambers, *Room for Maneuver: Reading (the) Oppositional (in) Narrative* (Chicago: University of Chicago Press, 1991), esp. xi–18; and Ross Chambers, *Story and Situation: Narrative Seduction and the Power of Fiction* (Minneapolis: University of Minnesota Press, 1984). Chambers's narratological concept of "opposition" rescues decadent modernist melancholy after 1848 (reread, as Chambers makes clear, through 1968) from the charge of ahistoricism, turning on the play of narrative and "textual" functions through which literary melancholy as duplicitous *énonciation* appeals to a reader prising open, or prised open by, an interval spacing the literary

work from its own (historical) context. As such, it draws explicitly on a Certeauian model of reading as a maneuver "between the possibility of disturbance in the system and the system's power to recuperate that disturbance," capable of creating "not radical, universal, or immediate change," but "only changes local and scattered" (*Room for Maneuver*, xi). My own concept of "opposition" is purposefully cruder, and closer to what Chambers discards as outmoded "resistance," marking the somewhat less graceful anticipatory (and sometimes mute) protest, by late twentieth-century multilingual narrators of texts, of the monolingualism of their material posterity in *books*— a protest, in other words, against the constraints of book publication itself, as a system, and the imagination of an oppositional space *outside* that system, rather than always already inside it (the latter a prime figure, as I see it, of Euro-Atlantic self-congratulation). Chambers's central assumption—that his chosen texts, in anticipating a reader, both record their own context of production and propose interpretive contexts that postdate it—may be vulgarized in my glossing of it here, where I read my *own* chosen text/books as proposing (though as often through denial as through affirmation) reading contexts outside the book medium itself.

14. It may be that the indisciplined choice of contemporary literature as one's "field" is also, implicitly or explicitly, an attempted evasion of the canonicity demanding interpretation, in the first place. In this sense, antiquarianism—in the peculiar pure existential form described by Walter Benjamin in "Ich packe meine Bibliothek aus," perhaps—can be understood as criticism's complement ("criticism" marking a mode tied to the present and future of literature), not its enemy. This, too, is worth reflection. As a topic of one's "work," in the horse-trading of competitive academic literary scholarship today, multilingual literature seems, like no other, to revive postmodernist variations on the modernist antiquarian drive—especially where it enters the pseudo-generalist domains of discourse in the U.S. literary public sphere, such as it is, and among scholars mixed by field and historical period (at large nonspecialized disciplinary conferences, for example, or job talks). One might ascribe this to the status of exotic oddities such works quite rightfully assume in their fundamentally liminal nature, which arouses the urges to collect, catalogue, and display; however one reads it, the topic seems to me unique in its ability to generate both pleasant and unpleasant disciplinary self-consciousness of the interpenetrative and interpellative materiality of the literary research objects *text* and *book,* in their coerced and elective affinities. Following a number of papers I have delivered on this subject, informal discussion has sometimes degenerated into reference-collecting and reference-trumping one-upmanship, in a dynamic that confronts the old consensualist literary-historiographic mode of documenting artifactual eccentricities with the newer, ostensibly theory-driven (but in fact no less positivist) normative interventionist mode of mobilizing them as inassimilable exceptions (to one or another paradigm or other hegemonic formation). It is because this critical behavior, as an index to procedural fault lines in the self-reproduction of literary humanist bureaucratic culture, interests me every bit as much as its objective pretexts (actually existing works of multilingual literature)—and to be sure, because I find such *Sammelwut* dispiritingly antiseptic—that I long ago

gave up the ambition to make *In Babel's Shadow* a panoramic study, even within one field or period. See Walter Benjamin, "Ich packe meine Bibliothek aus—Eine Rede über das Sammeln," in *Gesammelte Schriften*, vol. 4, part 1, ed. Tillman Rexroth, 388–96 (Frankfurt am Suhrkamp, 1991); Walter Benjamin, "Unpacking My Library: A Talk about Collecting," in *Selected Writings*, vol. 2: 1927–1934, ed. Michael W. Jennings, Howard Eiland, and Gary Smith, 486–93 (Cambridge, Mass.: Harvard University Press, 1999).

    15. "Discourse," in this sentence, is purposefully closer to common than to specialized usage; but that purpose is not to take a voluntarist position (either calculatedly or spontaneously) on the availability or distinction of more ordinary speech within the constrained framework I use here. To the pertinence here of Foucault's counterintuitional understanding of the "archive" (in *L'Archéologie du savoir*), and of the form of residuality (*rémanence*) that counterconstitutes it, should be added that of Gayatri Chakravorty Spivak's early critique of Foucault—specifically, on the critical consequences of abandoning ideology critique tout court. There, the Althusserian critic who, for Spivak, better speaks to what *cannot be said* is the Macherey of *Pour une théorie de la production littéraire*—who was every bit as perceptive as the archaeological Foucault regarding the "rarity" (*rareté*) of discourse, Spivak implies, but does not sacrifice ideology critique's heuristic planar schism to systemic enclosure, as Foucault perhaps must. See Gayatri Chakravorty Spivak, "Can the Subaltern Speak?" in *Marxism and the Interpretation of Culture*, ed. Cary Nelson and Lawrence Grossberg (Urbana: University of Illinois Press, 1988), 286. Any even casual reader of Spivak's work knows that what I have said here hardly goes to the depth of the problem at all. See also the reworking of "Can the Subaltern Speak?" in *A Critique of Postcolonial Reason: Toward a History of the Vanishing Present* (Cambridge, Mass.: Harvard University Press, 1999), 198ff., as well as Gayatri Chakravorty Spivak, "Foucault and Najibullah," in *Other Asias*, 132–60 (Malden, Mass.: Blackwell, 2008).

    16. In a Brazilian context, regarding vulgar Marxist "systematicity," Roberto Schwartz writes of the extraperipherality of those whom capital does not, in fact, want; see Eva Corredor and Roberto Schwartz, "Interview with Roberto Schwartz," in *Lukács after Communism: Interviews with Contemporary Intellectuals* (Durham, N.C.: Duke University Press, 1997), esp. 178, 186. In a related (if equally Eurocentrist) context, one might consult the exceptionally eloquent Paul Mann: "One is quite willing to accept the fact that for those inside a culture there is no outside; one is quite willing to drop the rebel, the outlaw, the exile, or any of the other stock figures under which most readers will subsume this refusal, and to take the critique of autonomy all the way. But that is not the same as acceding to the implication that lacking an ideal exteriority one can only play by the economy's rules, that one must continue to supply it with recuperative occasions. It is the arrogance of discourse to assume that all resistance must acknowledge it, that secrecy is surrender, that unless its enemy shows itself no enemy exists. We cannot judge what might occur in such privacy; we cannot know what gifts anonymity provides." See Mann, *The Theory-Death of the Avant-Garde* (Bloomington: Indiana University Press, 1991), 144.

17. See Haun Saussy, "Exquisite Cadavers Stitched from Fresh Nightmares: Of Memes, Hives, and Selfish Genes," in *Comparative Literature in an Age of Globalization,* ed. Haun Saussy (Baltimore: Johns Hopkins University Press, 2006), 3.

18. See Franco Moretti, *Graphs, Maps, Trees: Abstract Models for a Literary History* (London: Verso, 2005); Christopher Prendergast, *Debating World Literature* (London: Verso, 2004); Pascale Casanova, *La république mondiale des lettres* (Paris: Éditions du Seuil, 1999); Pascale Casanova, *The World Republic of Letters* (Cambridge, Mass.: Harvard University Press, 2004).

19. See Saussy, *Comparative Literature in an Age of Globalization;* Christopher Bush and Eric Hayot, eds., "Responding to *Death of a Discipline:* An ACLA Forum," special issue, *Comparative Literature* 57, no. 3 (2005); Djelal Kadir, ed., "Globalization and World Literature," special issue, *Comparative Literature Studies* 41, no. 4 (2004).

20. See David Damrosch, *What Is World Literature?* (Princeton, N.J.: Princeton University Press, 2003); Emily Apter, *The Translation Zone: A New Comparative Literature* (Princeton, N.J.: Princeton University Press, 2005); Rey Chow, *The Age of the World Target: Self-Referentiality in War, Theory, and Comparative Work* (Durham, N.C.: Duke University Press, 2006); Wai Chee Dimock, *Through Other Continents: American Literature across Deep Time* (Princeton, N.J.: Princeton University Press, 2006); Martin Puchner, *Poetry of the Revolution: Marx, Manifestos, and the Avant-Gardes* (Princeton, N.J.: Princeton University Press, 2006).

21. See Gayatri Chakravorty Spivak, *Death of a Discipline* (New York: Columbia University Press, 2003); Gayatri Chakravorty Spivak, *Imperative zur Neuerfindung des Planeten/ Imperatives to Re-imagine the Planet* (Vienna: Passagen, 1999).

22. Franco Moretti, "Conjectures on World Literature," *New Left Review,* no. 1 (January–February 2000): 55.

23. Stanley Cavell, "Foreword: An Audience for Philosophy," in *Must We Mean What We Say? A Book of Essays,* 2nd ed. (Cambridge: Cambridge University Press, 2002), xxxv.

24. See Juliana Spahr, "Connected Disconnection and Localized Globalism in Pacific Multilingual Literature," *boundary 2* 31, no. 3 (2004): 75–100; Emily Apter, "Global *Translatio:* The 'Invention' of Comparative Literature, Istanbul, 1933," *Critical Inquiry* 29, no. 2 (2003): 253–81; Apter, *The Translation Zone.*

INTRODUCTION

1. The Modern Language Association of America occupies a peculiar place in the United States intellectual public sphere, today: on the one hand, advocating such "cultural intelligence" to the U.S. public, as the last agent charged with protecting it (linguists aside—and leaving aside their employment in departments of language and literature—who in the managerial sector of the U.S. university are more likely to be plurilingual than literary humanists?); on the other hand, forced to advocate the very same thing internally, to its own constituency. Such double voicing is often a feature of the annual presidential address to the association, as a rhetorical occasion—and of the reports of the association's task forces on pedagogy and curriculum design, as well.

The U.S. Association of Departments of Foreign Languages, as might be expected, also takes a leading role in advocating cultural intelligence as embodied in language acquisition and plurilingualism. A selection of publications marking this intensification after 2001 might include Michael Geisler, "Global English—Global Freeze? The Cultural Expertise of Foreign Language Departments and the Future of Intellectual Diversity," *ADFL Bulletin* 33, no. 3 (2002): 6–12; Claire Kramsch, "Alien Wisdoms in English and Foreign Language Programs," *PMLA* 117, no. 5 (2002): 1245–46; Mary Louise Pratt, "Presidential Address 2003: Language, Liberties, Waves, and Webs—Engaging the Present," *PMLA* 119, no. 3 (2004): 417–28; Pratt, "Building a New Public Idea about Language," *Profession*, 2003, 110–19; Domna C. Stanton, "Working through the Crises: A Plan for Action," *Profession*, 2004, 32–41; Domna C. Stanton, "On Linguistic Human Rights and the United States Foreign Language Crisis," *Profession*, 2005, 64–79; Haun Saussy, "Language and Literature: A Pedagogical Continuum?" *Profession*, 2005, 113–21; Michael Geisler, "To Understand a Culture, Learn Its Language," *Chronicle of Higher Education* 52, no. 29 (2006): B11–12; Marjorie Perloff, "A Language Initiative for Faculty Members," *MLA Newsletter* 38, no. 2 (2006): 3–4; Domna C. Stanton, "Presidential Address 2005: On Rooted Cosmopolitanism," *PMLA* 121, no. 3 (2006): 627–40; Doug Steward, "The Foreign Language Requirement in English Doctoral Programs," *Profession*, 2006, 203–18; and the report of the MLA Ad Hoc Committee on Foreign Languages, entitled "Foreign Languages and Higher Education: New Structures for a Changed World," *Profession*, 2007, 234–45. Service branches of the U.S. armed forces have not made the massive investment in language training that one might (perhaps naïvely) have expected, after 2001— among other reasons, because proposals for the computerized automation of translation are often more attractive. Still, in October 2001, the Defense Language Institute Foreign Language Center in Monterey, California, was empowered to grant associate of arts degrees for the first time, while degree program changes as of early 2008 have removed time limits to the completion of degrees, permitted the award of multiple degrees, and expanded some curricular requirements.

2. See Gloria Anzaldúa, *Borderlands/La Frontera: The New Mestiza* (San Francisco: Aunt Lute Books, 1987): "[W]e Chicanos no longer feel that we need to beg entrance, that we need always to make the first overture—to translate to Anglos, Mexicans and Latinos. . . . Today we ask to be met halfway" (18).

3. The growth of Anglo-American academic Translation Studies (I capitalize the phrase here, in acceptance of its aggressively disciplinary self-assertion) since the collapse of the Soviet Union as a rival empire, culture of belief, and linguistic entity, is stunning. Though many would locate in the 1990s a "cultural turn" incorporating into translation studies (among other things) the fully developed perspectives of postcolonial criticism, one might as easily read that turn as a moment in the *institutionalization* of a postcolonial studies stripped of its critique of the academy itself (an observation now made somewhat routinely, and in its own way, bureaucratically, about the legacy of Edward W. Said)—and look to a "harder" turn imaginable for the present conjuncture, as Anglo-American scholars examine, again after 2001, their complicities in the

management of foreign culture. Susan Bassnett remains the most active and systematic periodizer of the practice–discipline of translation studies; see in particular her *Translation Studies* (London: Routledge, 2002); and Susan Bassnett and Harish Trivedi, *Postcolonial Translation: Theory and Practice* (London: Routledge, 1999); as well as Susan Bassnett, "Translating Terror," *Third World Quarterly* 26, no. 3 (2005): 393–403. Especially notable work that in one way or another engages the question of a "harder" turn includes Emily Apter, "Global *Translatio*," 253–81, and *The Translation Zone*; Timothy Brennan, "The Cuts of Language: The East/West of North/South," *Public Culture* 13, no. 1 (2001): 39–63; Timothy Brennan, *Wars of Position: The Cultural Politics of Left and Right* (New York: Columbia University Press, 2006); Spahr, "Connected Disconnection and Localized Globalism," 75–100. Rey Chow provides a useful critique of necessarily selective, Eurocentrist U.S.-based professional plurilingualism as a prerequisite for comparative work, aligning its assumption of parity with equally unuseful "current popular debates about translation." See Chow, *The Age of the World Target: Self-Referentiality in War, Theory, and Comparative Work* (Durham, N.C.: Duke University Press, 2006), 79n28. Spivak's *Death of a Discipline* is immensely provocative on translation as both necessary and necessarily difficult; as with the provocations of Said and Brennan (along with those of Djelal Kadir, and, as I will emphasize at points throughout this book, Gloria Anzaldúa), Spivak's interventions are often enough affirmed at second hand and rarely taken to heart. Finally, see also Stanley Corngold, "Comparative Literature: The Delay in Translation," in *Nation, Language, and the Ethics of Translation,* ed. Sandra Bermann and Michael Wood, 139–45 (Princeton, N.J.: Princeton University Press, 2005); Ciaran Ross, "Blasket Island Autobiographies: The Myth and Mystique of the Untranslated and the Untranslatable," *Translation and Literature* 12, no. 1 (2003): 114–43; Shireen K. Patell, "Untranslatable You," *Cardozo Law Review* 27, no. 2 (2005): 897–912. In addition, published in 2007 alone, see the issue of *Theatre Journal* (59, no. 3) devoted to "the stakes of theatrical translation" (see especially the editor's introduction by Jean Graham-Jones and articles by Laurence Senelick and Sarah Bay-Cheng); the collection *The Shock of the Other: Situating Alterities,* ed. Silke Horstkotte and Esther Peeren (Amsterdam: Rodopi, 2007), esp. Ananya Kabir, "A Language of One's Own? Linguistic Under-Representation in the Kashmir Valley," 139–48, and Nicole Côté, "The Braultian Path to the Other: Estrangement and Nontranslation," 161–69; David L. Clark, "Lost and Found in Translation: Romanticism and the Legacies of Jacques Derrida," *Studies in Romanticism* 46, no. 2 (2007): 161–82; Eleonora Federici, "The Translator's Intertextual Baggage," *Forum for Modern Language Studies* 43, no. 2 (2007): 147–60; Daryl R. Hague, "Fuzzy Memories: Why Narrators Forget They Translate for Animals," *Translation and Literature* 16, no. 2 (2007): 178–92; Julie Candler Hayes, "Unconditional Translation: Derrida's Enlightenment-to-Come," *Eighteenth-Century Studies* 40, no. 3 (2007): 443–55; Dorota Glowacka, "A Date, a Place, a Name: Jacques Derrida's Holocaust Translations," *CR · The New Centennial Review* 7, no. 2 (2007): 111–39. I hope no one will mistake my omission here of work published in other languages for an oversight.

4. See Edward W. Said, *The World, the Text, and the Critic* (Cambridge, Mass.: Harvard University Press, 1983), 5–9; Emily Apter, "Comparative Exile: Competing Margins in the History of Comparative Literature," in *Comparative Literature in the Age of Multiculturalism,* ed. Charles Bernheimer, 86–96 (Baltimore: Johns Hopkins University Press, 1995); David Damrosch, "Auerbach in Exile," *Comparative Literature* 47, no. 2 (1995): 97–117; Aamir Mufti, "Auerbach in Istanbul: Edward Said, Secular Criticism, and the Question of Minority Culture," *Critical Inquiry* 25, no. 1 (1998): 95–125; Apter, "Global *Translatio,*" and *The Translation Zone,* chap. 3; Nergis Ertürk, "Modernity and Its Fallen Languages: Tanpınar's *Hasret,* Benjamin's Melancholy," *PMLA* 123, no. 1 (2008): 41–56. See also Spivak, *Death of a Discipline,* 87, 87n19.

5. See Werner Sollors, introduction to *The Multilingual Anthology of American Literature: A Reader of Original Texts with English Translations,* ed. Marc Shell and Werner Sollors, 1–11 (New York: New York University Press, 2000), and Marc Shell, afterword to Shell and Sollors, *The Multilingual Anthology of American Literature,* 684–92; Marc Shell, ed., *American Babel: Literatures of the United States from Abnaki to Zuni* (Cambridge, Mass.: Harvard University Press, 2002); Werner Sollors, ed., *Multilingual America: Transnationalism, Ethnicity, and the Languages of American Literature* (New York: New York University Press, 1998).

6. See Moretti, "Conjectures on World Literature," 54–68; Jonathan Arac, "Anglo-Globalism," *New Left Review,* no. 16 (2002): 35–46; Jale Parla, "The Object of Comparison," *Comparative Literature Studies* 41, no. 1 (2004): 116–25; Harald Weinrich, "Chamisso, Chamisso Authors, and Globalization," trans. Marshall Brown and Jane K. Brown, *PMLA* 119, no. 5 (2004): 1336–46.

7. See Lawrence Venuti, *The Scandals of Translation: Towards an Ethics of Difference* (London: Routledge, 1998); and Lawrence Venuti, *The Translator's Invisibility* (London: Routledge, 1995).

8. Some of these words were first drafted during the period between 2003 and 2005, as the long-term impact of the events of 2001 on the U.S. intellectual scene was itself just coming into view. Since then, from a U.S. perspective, one wave of developments after another has suggested what one might choose to call forms of "relocalization" (the indisputably imperial globality of the "war on terror" notwithstanding). In the rise of rival new superpowers and the wobbly resurgence of old ones, threats to the U.S. dollar as a world reserve currency, newly centripetal pressure applied to suburban sprawl by inflated U.S. domestic energy prices and deflated home prices, an abrupt embrace of governmentality (in economic and housing policy, education, food safety, and health care) by a U.S. electorate supposedly hardened against it, one catches a glimpse of what some U.S. intellectual discourse network to come will presumably be calling the "end of globalization." I am not simply endorsing such an idea, of course, and I am perfectly well aware that from a systemist perspective, all these developments might as easily be read not as an end, but as a new and more intensive cycle of the stricture we call globalization. See, for example, Perry Anderson, "Editorial: Jottings on the Conjuncture," *New Left Review,* no. 48 (November–December 2007): 5–37.

9. See Gérard Genette, *Seuils* (Paris: Éditions du Seuil, 1987), 20ff., esp. 35ff. ("Composition, tirages"); Gérard Genette, *Paratexts: Thresholds of Interpretation*, trans. J. E. Lewin (Cambridge: Cambridge University Press, 1997), 16ff., esp. 33ff. ("Typesetting, printings"). Genette notes "le rôle de commentaire indirect que peuvent jouer les choix typographiques à l'égard des textes qu'ils affectent" (that "typographic choices may provide indirect commentary on the texts they affect"). Of the typesetting of the 1852 edition of Thackeray's *The History of Henry Esmond*, he observes, "au moins faut-il admettre qu'il en existe deux versions: l'une où le propos mimétique est étendu au paratexte typographique (et orthographique), l'autre où il est restreint aux thèmes et au style" ("It must at least be admitted that two versions of that book exist: one in which the imitative intention is extended to the typographical [and orthographical] paratext, the other in which the imitative intention is limited to theme and style"). See Genette, *Seuils*, 35–36; Genette, *Paratexts*, 34.

10. See Genette, *Seuils*, 316ff. ("L'épitexte public") and 341ff. ("L'épitexte privé"); Genette, *Paratexts*, 344ff. ("The public epitext") and 371ff. ("The private epitext").

11. On the complex history of a historically *belletristic* demand for "clarity," see John Guillory, "The Memo and Modernity," *Critical Inquiry* 31, no. 1 (2004): 108–32.

12. This "seduction discourse" through which publication brokers communicate with literary authors today structures the reading transaction as a contest of erotic technique ("The author really drew me in"; "In the end, I wasn't entirely satisfied"), sometimes displaced onto exchange ("I don't buy it").

13. See Paul Mann, *Masocriticism* (Albany: State University of New York Press, 1999), x, xii: "Every manifesto, every exhibition, every review, every monograph, every attempt to take up or tear down the banner of the avant-gardes in the critical arena, every attempt to advance the avant-garde's claims or to put them to rest: no matter what their ideological strategy or stakes, all end up serving the 'white economy' of cultural production. It is, finally, circulation alone that matters. . . . What if there were an avant-garde that was no longer committed to throwing itself on the spears of its enemies but operated in utter secrecy? What if the very history of cultural recuperation led us to imagine that some segment of what had once been the avant-garde must finally have learned from its mistakes and extended its trajectory into silence and invisibility? It might be necessary then to turn that silence and invisibility back against the critical project; it might be necessary to inflict that silence on one's own discourse and suffer it as a kind of wound." See also Paul Mann, *The Theory-Death of the Avant-Garde*, 143: "If the death of the avant-garde is its complete representation within the white economy, then one must assume that other projects have realized this and decided to disappear. In the end it is the theoretical condition of this disappearance that poses the greatest challenge." Mann must be the most abjectly self-conscious U.S.-based literary critic still working within the dominant Euro-Atlantic dispensations of the discipline. As the penultimate "masocritic," he stands, perhaps, for the spectacular blowout of Eurocentrist First Worldism: a self-immolation still utterly limited by that geoepistemological horizon (as is my own project in this book). On the one hand, Mann is just another jaded theorist of the enclosure of capitalist modernity, of its incorporation, in

advance, of any ideological "resistance," or positing of exteriority. On the other hand, he retains the *imagination* of an exteriority: the mark of hope—an intellectual's singular responsibility. While it remains blind, perhaps, to the *substantive* extraperipherality of those whom capital does *not* want, Mann's "masocriticism" is an important and, for my purposes here, indispensable hesitation before the complacent productivity of what remains of U.S. critical theory today.

14. Jacques Derrida, "Living On/Border Lines," in *Deconstruction and Criticism*, trans. James Hulbert (New York: Continuum, 1979), 95.

15. Even merely within the literary humanities, the literature on what has for some time now been called "globalization" is immense. In place of the futile attempt to offer a set of definitive placemarks, I will offer, with the usual caveats, a database-driven illustration of how credulously this phrase is traded. At this writing (September 2008), Google Books lists 813 volumes of relatively specialized writing published in English since 1990, across disciplines, containing the phrase "increasing globalization"; the same search run on Google Scholar (which includes books, journal articles, and reviews) yields "about 7,080" (Google's language) relatively discrete citations.

16. Another way to ask this: how is it that in the United States today, even literary humanists—even, sometimes, in fields defined by comparative methodology—must resort to inveigling a certain type of (usually U.S.-born) graduate student, and even to inveigling each other, to learn foreign languages? (The cluster of commentary cited in note 1, above, brims with such well-meant cajolery.) What democratic or antidemocratic structural conditions eliminate intensive language training from the reproduction of the profession, even as such exhortation becomes a treasured rhetorical imperative? U.S.-born monoglots who fantasize about "existentially" polyglot Europeans (a forgivable delusion) are perhaps only deferring critical inquiry. Étienne Balibar suggests that as a facility that *becomes* a critical object, "translation" (and the condition of that facility, plurilingualism) is dynamically unevenly developed: a facility of intellectuals and writers who develop translation "studies" on the one hand, and of anonymous migrants—Balibar's phrase—on the other. At the intermediary levels of the division of labor, Balibar writes, "this virtually universal competence [in translation] is prevented, blocked by the almost uniformly monolingual national education systems." See Balibar, *We, the People of Europe? Reflections on Transnational Citizenship* (Princeton, N.J.: Princeton University Press, 2004), 178.

17. Susan Bassnett-McGuire, *Translation Studies* (London: Methuen, 1980), 5.

18. Ibid., 14.

19. See Roman Jakobson, "On Linguistic Aspects of Translation" (1959), in *The Translation Studies Reader*, ed. Lawrence Venuti, 113–18 (London: Routledge, 2000). On Whorfism as the "repressed" of contemporary linguistic science, see Deborah Cameron, "Linguistic Relativity: Benjamin Lee Whorf and the Return of the Repressed," *Critical Quarterly* 41, no. 2 (1999): 153–56.

20. See especially André Lefevere, *Translation, Rewriting, and the Manipulation of Literary Fame* (New York: Routledge, 1992); and Itamar Even-Zohar, *Polysystem Studies,* a monograph published as vol. 11, no. 1 (1990) of the journal *Poetics Today*.

21. See Djelal Kadir, "To World, to Globalize—Comparative Literature's Cross-roads," *Comparative Literature Studies* 41, no. 1 (2004): 1–9.

22. I have borrowed this distinction from Jeffrey T. Nealon's discussion of what he calls "the *differend* between Foucault's work and Derrida's." See Nealon, *Alterity Politics: Ethics and Performative Subjectivity* (Durham, N.C.: Duke University Press, 1998), 17ff. On the "diachrony of synchrony" in antisystemic utopian thought, and the un-representability, as a historical transition, of its temporal paradox, see Fredric Jameson, "The Barrier of Time," in *Archaeologies of the Future: The Desire Called Utopia and Other Science Fictions* (New York: Verso, 2005), esp. 86–90.

23. On U.S. independent publishing as a social movement, and as clearly distin-guishable from corporate and university press publishing, see Jerome Gold, *Publishing Lives: Interviews with Independent Book Publishers in the Pacific* (Seattle: Black Heron Press, 1995), 13–14. On self-publishing in North America after the consolidation of the publishing industry in the 1990s, see Juris Dilevko and Keren Dali, "The Self-Publishing Phenomenon and Libraries," *Library and Information Science Research* 28, no. 2 (2006): 208–34. On the effects of conglomeration on children's book publish-ing, with specific attention to Spanish–English bilingualism, translation, and the rela-tionship between national U.S. and independent presses in the U.S. Southwest, see Marie Ann Parker, "The Contributions of Small Presses to the Field of Multicultural Children's Books" (PhD diss., University of Arizona, 2006). On independent publish-ing in an Anglo-American context, see John Hampson and Paul Richardson, *Kitchen Table to Laptop: Independent Publishing in England* (London: Arts Council England, 2005). In an international context, and in connection with artist's books and the visual arts generally, see Maria Fusco, ed., *Put About: A Critical Anthology on Independent Publishing* (London: BookWorks, 2004).

24. Major New York trade houses have created imprints that publish books in Spanish, such as Vintage Español (Random House/Vintage), Rayo (HarperCollins), and Atria (Simon and Schuster); at least at present, however, such imprints publish significant amounts of material in translation to Spanish from English, as well as publishing original Spanish editions of works whose canonization arguably required English translation (for example, *One Hundred Years of Solitude*). New original writing in U.S. Spanish composes a minor to negligible share of their output. It is uncertain, at present, if the creation of such imprints is best understood as a response to, or a pro-duction of, consumer demand for their products, and to what extent they will (as either response *or* production) provide mass publication opportunities for new origi-nal literary writing in U.S. Spanish, and thus for awareness, at what must pass for the public level, of an "indigenous" Spanish-language U.S. American literature. Beyond that, of course, are the unfashionable question of what kind of literature that will be, and the unanswerable question of what *unfielded* groups of cultural producers already producing a vital literature in Spanish, but invisible to a literary studies bound to "teachable" texts (meaning first, works in mass-distributable print), will think of it.

25. See Venuti, *The Scandals of Translation*, 167ff. By some counts, one quarter of the world's books are published in English originals or translations, while fully half are

translated *from* English. For journalistic approaches citing statistics without attribution, see Natasha Wimmer, "The U.S. Translation Blues," *Publishers Weekly,* May 21, 2001, 71; Margo Jefferson, "The Fortress of Monoglot Nation," *New York Times,* October 26, 2003; John O'Brien and Tim Wilkinson, ". . . And More on Translations," *Context: A Forum for Literary Arts and Culture* 15 (2004): http://www.dalkeyarchive.com /article/show/222 (accessed December 20, 2009). As of October 2008, UNESCO's Index Translationum, a bibliographic database of books translated and published in 100 UNESCO member states since 1979, lists English as the top source language, with 984,545 records (up from 813,739 in 2004, and out of a total of more than 1.5 million) to 183,465 for the second-ranked language, French (up from 154,507 in 2004). English is the fourth-ranked target language, after German, Spanish, and French, in a sequence with much smaller rank differentials (269,887 records for German, 206,537 for Spanish, 199,363 for French, and 113,070 for English). Germany's Bertelsmann AG is now a major player in what one might call "Anglo-global" publishing, but this hardly qualifies my point here: see Pierre Lepape's report on the 2004 Frankfurt Book Fair, entitled "Lost without Translation: English-Language Books Dominate World Publishing," *Le Monde diplomatique,* May 5, 2004, and, for its counterpart held during a U.S. election cycle dominated by talk of the end of empire, Motoko Rich, "Wheeling and Dealing and Finding Books to Translate into Dutch," *New York Times,* October 20, 2008.

26. This is the source of that popular canard of U.S. cultural cosmopolitanism, the biographical note that one's writings have been translated into seven (or nine, or twelve) languages—a symptomal source of pride, perhaps, for writers the majority of whom would never dream of writing in a language foreign to them.

27. The sense of "worlding" here is Djelal Kadir's; see Kadir, "To World, to Globalize." Increasingly marginalized in U.S. popular media, book criticism continues to engage the question of the distribution of resources for publication—a question that necessarily entails judgment on deserts to publication, in a consolidated industry forced to create profit margins comparable to entertainment media (and thus driven to quickly produce, and discard, hyped literary "stars"). About the only solace to be taken from this is that the critical function, which U.S. scholarship in literary studies today largely refuses, grows more rather than less dynamic as pressure builds in the system. On polemics in contemporary book criticism in U.S. popular media, see Heidi Julavits, "Rejoice! Believe! Be Strong and Read Hard! The Snarky, Dumbed-Down World of Book Reviewing," *The Believer,* March 2003, 3–15; Sven Birkerts, "Critical Condition: Reading, Writing and Reviewing: An Old-Schooler Looks Back," *Bookforum,* Spring 2004, 8–12; Brian Lennon, "Sentimental Education," *Bookforum,* Summer 2004, 31–34; Gail Pool, *Faint Praise: The Plight of Book Reviewing in America* (Columbia: University of Missouri Press, 2007).

28. It must be said that observations of the opportunity cost of *choosing* critical visibility, by writing in the imperial literary standard, are often met with a certain panic— dismissed as vanguardist or ultraleftist, hopelessly pessimistic, mystical, theocratic, or even terroristic, when they may as well be straightforwardly materialist observations

of the structures of exclusion through which a bureaucratic apparatus maintains itself—and simple requests for scholarly self-understanding on that count. That every writer worth writing about is *free* to write and to be read is, after all, a convenient position for scholars needing ever greater quantities of critical raw materials: first of all, *visible*—in contemporary literary studies, *published* (and therefore publish*able*)—work. But one must keep both shores in sight, here; as Gayatri Chakravorty Spivak has put it apropos of linguistic postcoloniality as "enabling violation" (here, in the Indian context): "In order for there to be an all-India voice, we have had to dehegemonize English as one of the Indian languages. Yet it must be said that, as a literary medium, it is in the hands of people who are enough at home in standard English as to be able to use Indian English only as the medium of protest, as mockery or teratology; and sometimes as no more than local color, necessarily from above." See Spivak, "Bonding in Difference: Interview with Alfred Arteaga," in *The Spivak Reader: Selected Works of Gayatri Chakravorty Spivak,* ed. Donna Landry and Gerald MacLean (New York: Routledge, 1996), 19.

29. In all but its most recidivist modes, U.S. literary and cultural studies scholarship today operates by identifying the exception and rebinding it to the rule. It is in this (banal) sense that the canon-shattering procedures of academic cultural studies repeat canon formation—with radically different intent, to be sure, as well as effect.

30. Ilan Stavans, *On Borrowed Words: A Memoir of Language* (New York: Viking, 2001), 249–50.

31. Ibid., 122.

32. The phrase that ostensibly appeared on title pages of Yiddish translations of Shakespeare's plays is "fartaytsht un farbesert" (or "ibergezetst un farbesert"), usually rendered as "translated and improved." "Fartunkeld" ("obscured"; as "fartunkeln," also "darkened," and as a comparative, "more/better than") is apparently negative here, in relation to the relative neutrality of "translated"; "farveserd"—not to be found in a Yiddish dictionary—might be a solecism for "farbesert." (Entirely fancifully, but in keeping with the spirit of this passage, it might be permitted to evoke the German *verwesen,* to corrupt or rot.)

33. See Benjamin, "Ich packe meine Bibliothek aus," 388–96; Benjamin, "Unpacking My Library," 486–93.

34. Stavans, *On Borrowed Words,* 11.

35. Ibid., 30.

36. Ibid., 88.

37. The question of Rodriguez's reception is a difficult one, and his positions have evolved in time, beginning with his second book, *Days of Obligation: An Argument with My Mexican Father* (1992). See Rafael Pérez-Torres's reconsideration (in conversation with the work of Josefina Saldaña) of the meaningful persistence, in Chicana/o studies, of contrasts between the conservative reception of the Rodriguez who vaulted onto the national stage in the mid-1980s, and the work of Gloria Anzaldúa, in Pérez-Torres, *Mestizaje: Critical Uses of Race in Chicano Culture* (Minneapolis: University of Minnesota Press, 2006), 13ff. For my purpose here, what is important is the drift of

those contrasts into the wide-angle view of U.S. studies more generally, where they "survive," in Jacques Derrida's sense, in metadisciplinary self-reflection after "9/11." Derrida translates Walter Benjamin's locution "fortleben" (from the 1921 essay "Die Aufgabe des Übersetzers" ["The Task of the Translator"]) as "sur-vivre" in Derrida, "Des Tours de Babel," in *Difference in Translation,* ed. and trans. Joseph Graham, 165–248 (Ithaca, N.Y.: Cornell University Press, 1985); the French original appeared subsequently in Derrida, *Psyché: Inventions de l'autre* (Paris: Galilée, 1987), 203–33.

38. The National Language Act of 2008, introduced March 5, 2008, by Republican senator James Inhofe (Oklahoma) "to declare English as the national language of the Government of the United States, and for other purposes." See also HR 5759, English as the Official Language Act of 2008, introduced by Paul Broun (R-Ga.) in the U.S. House of Representatives April 10, 2008.

39. See "White House Says Bush Doesn't Speak Spanish All That Well," Associated Press Worldstream, May 4, 2006.

40. Richard Rodriguez, *Hunger of Memory: The Education of Richard Rodriguez: An Autobiography* (New York: Bantam, 1983), 138.

41. Ibid., 32.

42. Ibid., 114–15.

43. See Christine Brooke-Rose, *The Christine Brooke-Rose Omnibus* (Manchester: Carcanet, 1986).

44. On the page, English is the language of the narrator's speech to the hairdresser, as well as of the narrator's interior monologue. French is used initially by the hairdresser in replying to the narrator; following that, there is a brief exchange in mixed Turkish and French ("Oui, merci, teşekkür ederim. Lutfen madame"). German, in turn, appears in the narrator's voiced entries from a Turkish-to-German dictionary (the narrator is looking up an overheard—and misheard—Turkish word).

45. Brooke-Rose, *Between,* in *The Christine Brooke-Rose Omnibus,* 466–67.

46. "Serbo-Croatian" here is a historical descriptor, designating one of the official languages of Yugoslavia until 1991.

47. Claire Kramsch, "The Multilingual Experience: Insights from Language Memoirs," *Transit* 1, no. 1 (2005): http://escholarship.org/uc/item/9h79g172 (accessed December 20, 2009).

48. In "The Multilingual Experience," Kramsch describes *Between* as a "language memoir."

49. I have borrowed this distinction from the vocabulary of computation, as Friedrich A. Kittler appropriates it in his rhetorical histories of technology. See especially Friedrich A. Kittler, *Aufschreibesysteme 1800/1900* (Munich: Wilhelm Fink Verlag, 1985); Friedrich A. Kittler, *Discourse Networks 1800/1900,* trans. Michael Metteer with Chris Cullens (Stanford, Calif.: Stanford University Press, 1990). For Kittler, the invention of the phonograph enables verbal language to be transcribed at far greater speeds than was possible using either handwriting or the typewriter. In Kittler's analysis (which is not strictly historiographic), two effects follow from this new possibility of recording what people say. First, the normative pedagogy of advanced literacy—of

which national language standardization is one element—yields to the empirical study of "spontaneous" structured usage. Second, insofar as it is bound to that normativity, the prestige of the symbolic registrations of bourgeois art and literature is threatened. Writing, as data storage, is now no longer serial, read or written one piece at a time; rather, it is parallel, read or written in multiple simultaneous processes. Modernist literature, in Kittler's analysis, is a kind of reformation undertaken in order to compete with new media; Kittler sees the historical avant-gardes, as extremist forms of such competition, adopting a new aural paradigm of noise (in Morgenstern's sound poems, for example) or visually materializing language (for example, in the experimental typography of Russian and Italian Futurism). While I am not simply following Kittler into the McLuhanite determinism for which he is (justly or unjustly) maligned, I *do* think it is useful to consider what I am calling *strong* plurilingual literature as straining to "express" the existential parallelism of a life lived simultaneously in multiple language-worlds, within a print medium (the book) that imposes seriality (including the seriality of "communication") on it.

50. See Moretti, *Graphs, Maps, Trees;* Casanova, *La république mondiale des lettres;* Casanova, *The World Republic of Letters.*

51. Pascale Casanova, "Literature as a World," *New Left Review,* no. 31 (February 2005): 90.

52. See Christopher Prendergast, "Negotiating World Literature," *New Left Review,* no. 8 (March–April 2001): 100–121, esp. 108n4 and 118ff. This is an irony, Prendergast points out, as the "Republic of Letters" in late seventeenth and early eighteenth century Europe was a network of partly private communications (*literally* letters).

53. See Immanuel Wallerstein, "New Revolts against the System," *New Left Review,* no. 18 (December 2002): 29–39.

54. Wai Chee Dimock, "Genre as World System: Epic and Novel on Four Continents," *Narrative* 14, no. 1 (2006): 90. See also Wai Chee Dimock, *Through Other Continents: American Literature across Deep Time* (Princeton, N.J.: Princeton University Press, 2006), esp. 73ff.

55. I read Stavans's narrator as neither simply lamenting, nor simply affirming the kitsch of the "interstices" between language contexts; on the question of value here, the narrator remains productively confused (or productively confuses the question). It seems clear, however, that the narrator does *choose* kitsch, just as one might "choose" translation, faced with the alternative (never being heard in one's "own voice"). This is a vexed topic; one cluster of positions in contemporary critical discourse working through translation studies, today, is staked on the idea that translation is inevitable, that it makes no sense to speak of "choosing" it. The critical First Worldism of such a position—by which I mean simply the presumption of speech (or writing) and the privilege of being heard (or read)—should be noted.

56. Yoko Tawada, "Das Fremde aus der Dose," in *Talisman: Literarische Essays* (Tübingen: Konkursbuch Verlag, 1996), 42; Yoko Tawada, "Canned Foreign," in *Where Europe Begins,* trans. Susan Bernofsky and Yumi Selden (New York: New Directions, 2002), 86–88, translation modified.

57. Nonexhaustively, we might speak here of other "MigrantInnenliteratur" writers in Germany (Libuse Moníková, Wladimir Kaminer, Rafik Schami, Emine Sevgi Özdamar), as well as South Asian writers in the United Kingdom, "Arab" writers in France, and Chicana/o writers in the United States—all contexts in which "immigrant" nonnative or assimilated "ethnic" speakers of a constitutional or structural national language draw the attention, first, of a native-language media industry, then of the criticism and scholarship that assembles them into literary-historical trends.

58. The classic position, and one First Worldist in the extreme, is that of Peter Bürger, whose analysis is nevertheless searching and nuanced. See Peter Bürger, *Theorie der Avantgarde* (Frankfurt: Suhrkamp Verlag, 1974); Peter Bürger, *Theory of the Avant-Garde,* trans. Michael Shaw (Minneapolis: University of Minnesota Press, 1984). Needless to say, Bürger has many fatuous imitators (and opponents).

59. Casanova, *La république mondiale des lettres,* 241; Casanova, *The World Republic of Letters,* 175.

60. Mann, *The Theory-Death of the Avant-Garde.*

61. Damrosch, *What Is World Literature?* 289.

62. In application to Joyce, the term "fascicular" is taken from the work of Deleuze and Guattari. See Gilles Deleuze and Félix Guattari, *A Thousand Plateaus: Capitalism and Schizophrenia,* trans. Brian Massumi (Minneapolis: University of Minnesota Press, 1987), 5: "Joyce's words, accurately described as having 'multiple roots,' shatter the linear unity of the word, even of language, only to posit a cyclic unity of the sentence, text, or knowledge." I take up the contrast of Joycean with Steinian literary modes in the essay composing chapter 3. It goes without saying here that this leaves unexamined the role that African American Anglophone literary traditions, just for example, have or have not played in generating the Joyce–Stein prose-literary "system" that partly organizes the self-understanding of U.S. postmodernism. On this topic, see Aldon Nielsen, *Black Chant: Languages of African-American Postmodernism* (Cambridge: Cambridge University Press, 1997); Aldon Nielsen, *Integral Music: Languages of African American Innovation* (Tuscaloosa: University of Alabama Press, 2004).

63. See Shell and Sollors, *The Multilingual Anthology of American Literature.* See also Jena Osman and Juliana Spahr, eds., "Translucinación," special issue, *Chain* 10 (Summer 2003). See also Juliana Spahr and Jena Osman, eds., "Different Languages," special issue, *Chain* 5 (1998).

64. Jena Osman and Juliana Spahr, "Editors' Notes," *Chain* 10 (Summer 2003): iii.

65. Shell, afterword, 690–91.

66. See, for example, Apter, "Global *Translatio*": "Looking again more closely at the table of contents of the Istanbul literary review [*Publications de la faculté des lettres de l'Université d'Istanbul,* 1937], we see a paradigm of *translatio* emerge that emphasizes the critical role of multilingualism within transnational humanism. The juxtaposition of Turkish, German, and French attests to a policy of *nontranslation* adopted without apology. [Leo] Spitzer's own contributions are exemplary here; in each individual essay one hears a cacophony of untranslated languages. And as a literary critic in command of French, German, Hebrew, Hungarian, Latin, Greek, Italian, English,

Provençal, Spanish, Portuguese, Catalan, Rumanian, Gothic, Anglo-Saxon, Sanskrit, Lithuanian, Old Church Slavonic, Albanian, Neo-Greek (and now, we ascertain, Turkish as well), he had many languages to choose from. It was, of course, a common practice among highly educated European literary scholars to leave passages and phrases free-standing in a naked state of untranslation; but for Spitzer nontranslation was a hallowed principle of his method" (277). One might argue persuasively that it is better to read something in translation than not to read it at all; but one might also consider the extent to which this way of framing the question saturates reading with comprehension—constructing a collectively and contractually, if not actually and individually monolingual reader (in the classroom, for example). The pedagogical bases for such constructions are practical to a fault: what students will do with any given text is fundamentally unpredictable. And teaching anecdotes, therefore, demonstrate nothing. Still, in teaching Gloria Anzaldúa's *Borderlands/La Frontera: The New Mestiza,* for example, as a nonexpert in Chicana/o and Latina/o studies, in courses focused on migration and language acquisition across national and ethnic categories, to overwhelmingly monolingual Anglophone and virtually monoethnic undergraduates at a rural public U.S. university, I find that those students without even the most rudimentary knowledge of Spanish (easily half or more of any given enrollment) are more curious about, and less reflexively hostile to, the book's strong plurilingualism than one might condescendingly expect.

67. See Alice Kaplan, "On Language Memoir," in *Displacements: Cultural Identities in Question,* ed. Angelika Bammer, 59–70 (Bloomington: Indiana University Press, 1994); and Peter Cowley, "Lost and Found: The Language of Exile," *Mots Pluriels,* no. 23 (2003): http://www.arts.uwa.edu.au/MotsPluriels/MP2303pc.html (accessed January 7, 2010).

68. On the one hand, one might understand such "masocriticism" as itself an eminently self-congratulatory mode of Euro-Atlantic modernity. On the other hand, it may be that the metropolitan critique of the academy that forms such a vital critical substrate of postcolonial studies, for example, has been most effectively contained and negated by the ethnographic focus on the colony itself as a research object. For this argument, see Susie Tharu's contribution to Patricia Yaeger, "Editor's Column: The End of Postcolonial Theory? A Roundtable with Sunil Agnani, Fernando Coronil, Gaurav Desai, Mamadou Diouf, Simon Gikandi, Susie Tharu, and Jennifer Wenzel," *PMLA* 122, no. 3 (2007): 642–45.

1. LANGUAGE AS CAPITAL

1. The Canadian Constitution recognizes English and French; the Swiss Constitution, German, French, Italian, and Romansh; the Constitution of India, eighteen languages, including Bengali, Gujarati, Hindi, Kannada, Kashmiri, Punjabi, Sanskrit, Sindhi, Tamil, and Urdu; the 1996 Constitution of South Africa, eleven official languages plus eight "nonofficial" national languages. The United Kingdom has no official language, but English is the only language spoken by as much as 95 percent of its population. The Australian Constitution recognizes only English. New Zealand has

no written constitution, but recognizes English and Maori as official languages. No official language is recognized in the Constitution of the United States, but twenty-seven states have passed laws making English their single official language, and variations on an English language amendment have been introduced periodically since 1981.

   2. See these works by Alastair Pennycook: *Global Englishes and Transcultural Flows* (London: Routledge, 2007); "Language Education as Translingual Activism," *Asia Pacific Journal of Education* 26, no. 1 (2006): 111–14; (with Sohail Karmani), "Islam, English, and 9/11," *Journal of Language, Identity, and Education* 4, no. 2 (2005): 157–72; "Language Policy and the Ecological Turn," *Language Policy* 3, no. 3 (2004): 213–39; "Mother Tongues, Governmentality, and Protectionism," *International Journal of the Sociology of Language* 154, no. 1 (2002): 11–28; *English and the Discourses of Colonialism* (London: Routledge, 1998); "The Right to Language: Towards a Situated Ethics of Language Possibilities," *Language Sciences* 20, no. 1 (1998): 73–87; "English and Capital: Some Thoughts," *The Language Teacher* 27, no. 10 (1997): http://www.jalt-publications.org/tlt/files/97/oct/pennycook.html (accessed December 21, 2009); and *The Cultural Politics of English as an International Language* (London: Longman, 1994).

   3. Pennycook, "English and Capital."

   4. Casanova, "Literature as a World," 71–90.

   5. A "literary field," for Bourdieu, is a space defined by the social positions of actors in a world of cultural capital: between the lionized writer and the avant-garde challenger, for example: an antagonism around which Casanova builds her entire "république mondiale des lettres." See Casanova, *La république mondiale des lettres;* Casanova, *The World Republic of Letters.*

   6. It is for this reason, perhaps, that "fluent in X languages"—where X is a number between 3 and say, 6—is a surprisingly and suspiciously common claim in U.S. business biographies, when such fluency in the "existential" sense connoted by *bilingual, trilingual, multilingual, plurilingual* is in fact relatively rare, especially in the United States.

   7. Leonard Forster, *The Poet's Tongues: Multilingualism in Literature* (Cambridge: Cambridge University Press, 1970), 2.

   8. See in particular these works by Pierre Bourdieu: "The Forms of Capital," in *Handbook of Theory and Research for the Sociology of Education,* ed. J. G. Richardson, 241–58 (New York: Greenwood Press, 1986); *Language and Symbolic Power* (Oxford: Polity Press, 1991); *Distinction: A Social Critique of the Judgement of Taste* (Cambridge, Mass.: Harvard University Press, 1984); and *La distinction critique sociale du jugement* (Paris: Éditions de Minuit, 1979).

   9. George Steiner understood "global English" precisely this way—as successor to and improvement on Latin, both in imperial reach *and* in innate comprehensiveness and powers of incorporation. For Steiner, English is perceived by its nonnative speakers as easier to acquire than any other second language, which speaks to its nature as well as to its provenance—this, among other reasons, is why the international auxiliary

language Esperanto failed to replace it. (Writing in 1975, Steiner elided the distinction between British and U.S. varieties of English, which has become more significant in the intervening quarter century.) As he celebrates the internationalization of English, Steiner also laments it: the autonomy of other language cultures is thereby eroded, destroying linguistic diversity; meanwhile, English loses the cultural specificity that created a unique "English literature." See Steiner, *After Babel: Aspects of Language and Translation*, 3rd ed. (New York: Oxford University Press, 1998), 468ff.

10. What one might, glossing the work of Lawrence Venuti, call the "proliferation thesis" on English-language hegemony in fact has no single source, of course, and its motive might certainly be said to be cultural survival in one instance, and professional opportunism in the next. It is perhaps easiest to mark in the kind of appropriations of Foucault's late work (as a vehicle for power-resistant free creative subjectivity) critiqued by Jeffrey T. Nealon in *Foucault beyond Foucault: Power and Its Intensifications since 1984* (Stanford, Calif.: Stanford University Press, 2008), or in equally instrumentalizing North American readings of the work of Deleuze and Guattari, or Michel de Certeau, or Derrida understood as a "deconstructionist." But—and insofar as such redactive appropriations suggest an anxiously positional and productivity-driven attenuation of (time for) reading—any such "thesis" is perhaps better understood as produced by and in, rather than strictly motivating, the way we argue now, as Gayatri Chakravorty Spivak analyzed it in an early essay. Discussing the instrumentalized utterance "Because the text deconstructs itself, the author is not responsible for what the text seems to say," Spivak comments at length on "the conservatism that has developed out of these potentially radical [deconstructive] positions—the unexamined use of the argument that great texts deconstruct themselves, and thus that the canon might be preserved after all." (With this observation, of course, Spivak also notes the vast structure of incitement to such "mistakes," noting with compassion that both the scholar making this reductive argument, and her opponent, were "confronting tenure-decisions at the time.") See Spivak, "Finding Feminist Readings: Dante-Yeats," in *In Other Worlds: Essays in Cultural Politics* (New York: Routledge Classics, 2006), 21–25. It goes without saying that any substantive debate of the relation of administrative to administered languages in decolonization will be rooted in the specifics of historical context, without sacrificing the illumination comparison brings. The work of Braj Kachru stands in useful counterpoint with that of Pennycook in this respect; see Kachru's *Asian Englishes: Beyond the Canon* (Hong Kong: Hong Kong University Press, 2004); *The Alchemy of English: The Spread, Functions, and Models of Non-Native Englishes* (Oxford: Pergamon, 1986); and *The Indianization of English: The English Language in India* (Delhi: Oxford University Press, 1983). Another (classic) heuristic includes the positions of Edward Kamau Brathwaite and Ngũgĩ wa Thiong'o (grounded, of course, in quite different specific histories). See, for example, Kamau Brathwaite, *History of the Voice: The Development of Nation Language in Anglophone Caribbean Poetry* (London: New Beacon Books, 1984); and Ngũgĩ wa Thiong'o, *Decolonising the Mind: The Politics of Language in African Literature* (London: J. Currey; Portsmouth, N.H.: Heinemann, 1986). In arguing for the "proliferation of variables"

within the global hegemony of English, Lawrence Venuti has made extensive use of the work of Deleuze and Guattari, particularly their concept terms "assemblage" and "to minoritize"; while Venuti's work is indisputably of immense value, here, such *implementations* of the anti-arborescence of works such as *Mille plateaux* might be said to have absorbed too little of Deleuze and Guattari's own hesitation before Joycean "fascicular" unities that contain and recuperate, rather than proliferate variables. See Venuti, *The Scandals of Translation*, esp. 9–13. By Gilles Deleuze and Félix Guattari, see *Capitalisme et schizophrénie: L'Anti-Oedipe* (Paris: Éditions de Minuit, 1972); *Capitalisme et schizophrénie 2: Mille plateaux* (Paris: Éditions de Minuit, 1980); *Kafka: Pour une littérature mineure* (Paris: Éditions de Minuit, 1975); *Anti-Oedipus: Capitalism and Schizophrenia*, trans. Robert Hurley, Mark Seem, and Helen R. Lane (Minneapolis: University of Minnesota Press, 1983); *A Thousand Plateaus: Capitalism and Schizophrenia*, trans. Brian Massumi (Minneapolis: University of Minnesota Press, 1987); and *Kafka: Toward a Minor Literature*, trans. Dana Polan (Minneapolis: University of Minnesota Press, 1986).

11. Ralph Waldo Emerson, "English Traits," in Ralph Waldo Emerson et al., *English Traits*, vol. 5 of *The Collected Works of Ralph Waldo Emerson* (Cambridge, Mass.: Harvard University Press, 1994), 171.

12. Ibid., 27.

13. Ibid., 19.

14. Ralph Waldo Emerson, Ronald A. Bosco, and Douglas Emory Wilson, *Society and Solitude*, vol. 7 of *The Collected Works of Ralph Waldo Emerson* (Cambridge, Mass.: Harvard University Press, 2007), 103.

15. In the United States and United Kingdom, this system includes the "undifferentiated patronage" of chain bookstores, entertainment conglomerates, and Hollywood film, linked in a network that André Lefevere described as mimicking royal or modern totalitarian patronage—dispensing ideology, economic benefit, and social status simultaneously. See Lefevere, *Translation, Rewriting, and the Manipulation of Literary Fame*, 14–19.

16. Venuti, *The Scandals of Translation*, 159.

17. Ibid., 9.

18. Forster, *The Poet's Tongues*, 3.

19. An assumption that the work of Braj Kachru, for example, forcefully counters.

20. Robert Crawford, *Devolving English Literature* (Edinburgh: Edinburgh University Press, 2000), 5.

21. Ibid., 269.

22. Ibid., 300–301.

23. For treatments of the dialectic of common language more specifically sensitive to Derrida's insights on this topic than Crawford permits himself to be, one might turn to a wealth of recent anthropological and ethnographic research and writing integrating the insights of poststructuralist literary theory and focused predominantly on Southeast Asia. In addition to the work of Benedict Anderson, especially useful in this context are James T. Siegel, *Fetish, Recognition, Revolution* (Princeton, N.J.: Princeton

University Press, 1997); Rosalind C. Morris, *In the Place of Origins: Modernity and Its Mediums in Northern Thailand* (Durham, N.C.: Duke University Press, 2000); and Vicente L. Rafael, *The Promise of the Foreign: Nationalism and the Technics of Translation in the Spanish Philippines* (Durham, N.C.: Duke University Press, 2005). Siegel, for example, has demonstrated how translations into Melayu (Bahasa Indonesia), the Indonesian lingua franca, effectively enculturated a hitherto market-restricted and thus "weightless" language, creating a kind of subject-not-a-subject, a living language with no ancestor, incapable of being either foreign *or* domestic. One acquired this language, in Siegel's analysis, by "mutual imitation," that is, by repetition, not by transmission. Inherently, therefore, the lingua franca is without authority or heritage, without difference as marked by posited properties or proper names. In place of an "I" in a world, the lingua franca provides a series of temporarily inhabited subject positions neither authentic nor inauthentic, neither translatable nor untranslatable; in place of mutual incommensurability between natural languages (as, for example, in French Algeria) it offers the infinite *artificial* convertibility of a chain of self-substituting signifiers, anchored neither by life (origin) nor death. The "I" of the lingua franca is "incipient in dual form," an originary repetition that in repeating continually disavows origin. I mean here only to caution, of course, against conflating *any* "common language" with a "world language" (especially when that world language is a hegemonic language) for the purpose of locating and *retrieving* subversive variation in English, for example—which necessarily requires its own frame of analysis. Siegel's both rigorous and innovative analysis of the displacement of colonial Dutch by Melayu cannot, in other words, serve as a model for the analysis of the internal variation of English, or be pointed to as proof that all expanding languages are always already and automatically deterritorialized. (Siegel himself makes no such generalized claim; in fact, his larger argument explicitly resists it.)

24. See Franco Moretti's "Conjectures on World Literature," 54–68; "More Conjectures," *New Left Review*, no. 20 (April 2003): 73–81; "Graphs, Maps, Trees: Abstract Models for Literary History, 1," *New Left Review*, no. 24 (December 2003): 67–93; *Graphs, Maps, Trees*. In addition, see Casanova's *La république mondiale des lettres, The World Republic of Letters,* and "Literature as a World." Especially persuasive to me have been Christopher Prendergast's critical reviews of *La république mondiale des lettres* and of Moretti's essays in their published form in *New Left Review*, as well as Gayatri Chakravorty Spivak's remarks on world-system theory and literature and, in a different context, Lawrence Venuti's challenge to André Lefevere. See Prendergast, "Negotiating World Literature," 100–121; and Christopher Prendergast, "Evolution and Literary History," *New Left Review*, no. 34 (August 2005): 40–62; Spivak, *Death of a Discipline*, 107ff.; Venuti, *The Translator's Invisibility*, 117–18. Djelal Kadir's positions in related debates have influenced my thinking as well—as has, in yet another direction, Christopher Newfield's response to John Guillory in an exchange on the disciplinary legacy of the Sokal hoax. See Djelal Kadir, "To World, to Globalize," 1–9; Djelal Kadir, "Comparative Literature in an Age of Terrorism," in Saussy, *Comparative Literature in an Age of Globalization*, 68–77; Christopher Newfield, "Critical Response I: The Value of Nonscience," *Critical Inquiry* 29 (Spring 2003): 508–25.

25. See Immanuel Wallerstein, *The Modern World System,* vol. 1, *Capitalist Agriculture and the Origins of the European World-Economy in the Sixteenth Century* (New York: Academic Press, 1974); Giovanni Arrighi, *The Long Twentieth Century: Money, Power, and the Origins of Our Times* (New York: Verso, 1994); Anthony Giddens, *The Consequences of Modernity* (Stanford, Calif.: Stanford University Press, 1990).

26. See Lefevere, *Translation, Rewriting, and the Manipulation of Literary Fame,* 100ff.

27. After Adalbert von Chamisso, who took up writing in German in exile from postrevolutionary France. See Weinrich, "Chamisso, Chamisso Authors, and Globalization," 1336–46.

28. Ibid., 1345.

29. Casanova, *La république mondiale des lettres,* 37

30. Casanova, *The World Republic of Letters,* 21.

31. This is a later modification of Casanova's arguments in *La république mondiale des lettres,* responding in part to Prendergast's review essay on its French edition. See Prendergast, "Negotiating World Literature," and Casanova, "Literature as a World."

32. Casanova, "Literature as a World," 82.

33. Wallerstein allows that both popular social movements (socialist parties, trade unionism) and popular national movements (in the unification of European nation-states and in decolonization) divided along state-oriented and autonomist lines, in the intensity of the fight for survival. "Many early versions of these movements," Wallerstein notes, "were totally destroyed. . . . [O]ver the last three decades of the nineteenth century both types of movement went through a parallel series of great debates over strategy. . . . For the social movement, this was the debate between the Marxists and the anarchists; for the national movement, that between political and cultural nationalists. What happened historically in these debates . . . was that those holding the 'state-oriented' position won out. The decisive argument in each case was that the immediate source of real power was located in the state apparatus and that any attempt to ignore its political centrality was doomed to failure, since the state would successfully suppress any thrust towards anarchism or cultural nationalism." See Wallerstein, "New Revolts against the System," 30.

34. Weinrich, "Chamisso, Chamisso Authors, and Globalization," 1343.

35. Anthony Burgess, introduction to G. V. Desani, *All about H. Hatterr* (New York: Farrar, Straus, and Giroux, 1970), 7.

36. Ibid.

37. Ibid., 8.

38. Burgess reminds us of the novel's explosive success on its first publication in 1948, citing without irony the back-handed praise of Eliot, who wrote, "It is amazing that anyone should be able to sustain a piece of work in this style and tempo at such length" (ibid.).

39. Ibid., 9.

40. Ibid., 10.

41. Burgess's formulation here stresses linguistic, ethnic, generic, and institutional syncretism, as well as invoking the cosmopolitan explicitly. "Whole language" was a

pragmatic method of reading instruction developed in the late 1960s as an alternative to the top–down schemata of phonics.

42. Salman Rushdie, "The Empire Writes Back with a Vengeance," *Times of London*, July 3, 1982, 8.

43. An inversion echoed by writers like Mulk Raj Anand, who construed "Indian English" as at once a distinct national variety of English, pressing for recognition against the global normativity of the metropolitan centers, and an important component of English as a global language and of a democratic world culture. Anand set Indian English against the "cosmopolises" of London and New York, defined by a "closed literary language" and a standard English. For Anand, Indian English is to be understood as a vital part of "the pool of the world democracy," "literature as a means of communication," "a one world culture." See Anand, "Variety of Ways: Is There a Shared Tradition in Commonwealth Literature?" in *Awakened Conscience: Studies in Commonwealth Literature*, ed. C. D. Narasimhaiah, 441–46 (New Delhi: Sterling Publishers, 1978).

44. Burgess, introduction, 9.

45. Kachru distinguishes between *deviation* and *mistake* in Indian variations of English. For Kachru, certain classes of "Indianisms" in English are primarily literary, appearing only in written works and never in spontaneous spoken language. The primary function of such "author-specific" Indianisms is, Kachru says, "to recreate a native speech event in a second language." See Kachru, *The Indianization of English*, 10ff.

46. Uma Parameswaran claimed Mulk Raj Anand as the first Indian writer in English to explore the defamiliarizing effect of vernacular idiom translated literally. See Uma Parameswaran, "Salman Rushdie in Indo-English Literature," *Journal of Indian Writing in English* 12 (1984): 15–25.

47. Bilingual, bicultural speakers of English may, to be sure, be "alienated" (or entertained) by the untranslatability of idiom across languages; the effect surely registers more strongly for the speaker with no knowledge of the source language whatsoever. This is also something of the comedy of machine translation, where what is funny is the computer's inhuman lack of access to mediating cultural knowledge.

48. Desani, *All about H. Hatterr*, 143.

49. Ibid., 180.

50. Ibid., 197.

51. Ibid., 54.

52. Ibid., 67. Cf. Rudyard Kipling, *Kim* (London: Penguin Books, 1992): "'And now we have walked a weary way,' said Kim. 'Surely we shall soon come to a parao [a resting-place]'" (111); "'Huh! It is only a pahari' [a hillman], said Kim over his shoulder" (114).

53. Desani, *All about H. Hatterr*, 70.

54. Ibid., 144.

55. See M. K. Naik, *Studies in English Literature* (New Delhi: Sterling Publishers, 1987), 19.

56. Desani, *All about H. Hatterr*, 120.

57. Desani's authorial "intentions" are nondecisive, in a system (ours) that disseminates and archives literature in published book, not original manuscript, form. That Hatterr—like the other novelistic and autobiographical subject positions of works considered in this book—reflects aloud on the constraints of material book publication is a constitutive, not reflective, condition, suggesting that one can have no *separate* "intention" in writing a text (especially a plurilingual text) once one has decided to write and attempt to publish a *book.* As elsewhere in this book, my argument here is that plurilingual writing *is* plurilingual publication—that the national-language constraints of book publishing volatilize the border between literary composition and editing for publication, to the point that it cannot sensibly be taken for granted.

58. I rely here on the typology of *Hatterr's* devices compiled by Naik.

59. Bill Ashcroft, Gareth Griffiths, and Helen Tiffin, *The Empire Writes Back: Theory and Practice in Post-Colonial Literatures* (New York: Routledge, 2002), 32.

60. Monika Fludernik, "What Is Hybridity (And Why Are They Saying Such Terrible Things About It)?" in *Hybridity and Postcolonialism: Twentieth-Century Indian Literature,* ed. Monika Fludernik (Tübingen: Stauffenberg Verlag, 1998), 11.

61. Cecil Nelson argued that the relatively minor syntactic variations of English in Raja Rao's *Kanthapura* (1938) produce an English still very "familiar," in weak contrast with the devices employed in Russell Hoban's *Riddley Walker* (1980); but this contrast might strike one as underreading the former novel and overreading the latter. See Cecil Nelson, "Syntactic Creativity and Intelligibility," *Journal of Indian Writing in English,* no. 12 (1984): 1–14; Raja Rao, *Kanthapura* (London: G. Allen and Unwin, 1938); Russell Hoban, *Riddley Walker* (New York: Summit Books, 1980).

62. See Tawada, "Das Fremde aus der Dose," 39–44; Tawada, "Canned Foreign," 85–90.

63. See Amos Tutuola, *The Palm-Wine Drinkard and His Dead Palm-Wine Tapster in the Dead's Town* (London: Faber and Faber, 1952).

64. Dylan Thomas, "Blythe Spirits," *The Observer,* July 6, 1952, 7.

65. See Ngũgĩ wa Thiong'o, *Decolonising the Mind,* 5ff.

66. See S. C. Harrex, "The Novel as Gesture," in *Awakened Conscience: Studies in Commonwealth Literature,* ed. C. D. Narasimhaiah, 73–85 (New Delhi: Sterling Publishers, 1978).

67. Gerhard Stilz, "'Truth? Hell, you will get contrast, and no mistake!' Sanitizing the Intercultural Polylemma in G. V. Desani's All about H. Hatterr (1948/72)," in *Hybridity and Postcolonialism: Twentieth-Century Indian Literature,* ed. Monika Fludernik (Tübingen: Stauffenberg Verlag, 1998), 80.

68. Ibid., 95.

69. G. V. Desani, "Difficulties of Communicating an Oriental to a Western Audience," in Narasimhaiah, *Awakened Conscience,* 403.

70. See Haydn M. Williams, "G. V. Desani's *All about H. Hatterr* and the Météque Tradition," in *Essays on Poetry and Fiction: V. A. Shahane Commemorative Volume,* 153–64 (Delhi: Doaba House, 1988).

71. Salman Rushdie, "Damme, This Is the Oriental Scene for You," *New Yorker*, June 23, 1997, 50–61.

72. Thanks to Ben Conisbee Baer for this thought. On this point (in a more determinedly Eurocentrist context) see also Jacques Rancière, "Althusser, Don Quixote, and the Stage of the Text," in *The Flesh of Words: The Politics of Writing*, 129–45 (Stanford, Calif.: Stanford University Press, 1994); Jacques Rancière, *La Chair des mots: Politiques de l'écriture* (Paris: Galilée, 1998).

73. See William Melvin Kelley, *Dunfords Travels Everywheres* (Garden City, N.Y.: Doubleday, 1970): "Sosssspread dPoelms o'yHands on d'circulbar Tabletop n feel dBubbarhymble o'dBreathers o'a'free Airtime. Withdrawninwinwithin Chiarlyle Donelow, Buttlerbattler, n do a'expluraltory kultur Surch in what mightcall hSelf dIntomate-Posture, n findhat aMass o'Movengmumbleng vpile dPast on dOreillely-Pressent" (190).

74. See Hoban, *Riddley Walker*: "On my naming day when I come 12 I gone front spear and kilt a wyld boar he parbly ben the las wyld pig on the Bundel Downs any how there hadnt ben none for a long time befor him nor I aint looking to see none agen" (1).

75. The results count for *Dunfords* is unchanged since 2004, when I first drafted this passage; that for *Riddley Walker*, meanwhile, is up from twenty-one. On the inflection of *Dunfords*'s literary-critical posterity by the novel's linguistic obscurity, see Aldon Nielsen, *Black Chant: Languages of African-American Postmodernism* (Cambridge: Cambridge University Press, 1997), 6ff.

76. Carter V. Findley, "Sir James W. Redhouse (1811–1892): The Making of a Perfect Orientalist?" *Journal of the American Oriental Society* 99, no. 4 (1979): 586–87. The question that forms Findley's subtitle is profoundly interrogative.

77. Ibid., 587.

78. While Derrida elsewhere stresses the escape of *Ulysses*'s English from its own authorization, including the authorized translation supervised by Joyce himself, he recognizes the novel's imbrication in a structural literary industry, as well as that industry's operation. "Il resterait à savoir," he writes of an imagined supercomputer of Joyce studies, "si la langue fondamentale de cet ordinateur serait l'anglais et si son brevet (sa 'patent') serait américain, en raison de l'écrasante et signifiante majorité des Américains dans le trust de la fondation Joyce" ("It would remain to be seen if the fundamental language of this computer would be English and if its patent would be American, in light of the overwhelming and significant majority of Americans on the board of the Joyce Foundation"). See Jacques Derrida, *Ulysse gramophone: Deux mots pour Joyce* (Paris: Éditions Galilée, 1987), 107; Jacques Derrida, "Ulysses Gramophone: Hear Say Yes in Joyce," in *Acts of Literature*, ed. Derek Attridge (New York: Routledge, 1992), 286.

79. James Joyce and John Bishop, *Finnegans Wake* (New York: Penguin Classics, 1999), 485.

80. Casanova, *La république mondiale des lettres*, 446.

2. Translation Being Between

1. Forster, *The Poet's Tongues*, 26.

2. Joachim du Bellay (c. 1522–60) and Jan van der Noot (c. 1540–95), among others, practiced what Forster calls "auto-translation."

3. Benedict Anderson, *Imagined Communities*, rev. ed. (London: Verso, 1991), 44.

4. "Nothing is said here, that has not been said before.—Terence. / We ought to imitate bees, so they say, for they wander and turn lovely flowers into honey. / So then, they arrange what to bring in, and they distribute it into honeycombs. Seneca, Epist. 84. / Just as bees take all things away in flower-bearing leaps, / So too do we consume all golden sayings, / O golden and ever-worthy life. Lucretius, / To read and not select is to neglect. / To read and note nothing is foolishness. / Of no avail has your work then been, / When you read and do not take note. / Reading is null. . . ." See Francis Daniel Pastorius, "Francis Daniel Pastorius, His Hive, Melliotrophium Alvear or, Rusca Apium: Begun Anno Do[mi]ni or, in the Year of Christian Account 1696," microfilm reproduction in Rare Books and Manuscripts, Special Collections Library, Paterno Library, Pennsylvania State University, University Park, Pa. Quoted and translated in Francis Daniel Pastorius, "Bee-Hive," in Shell and Sollors, *The Multilingual Anthology of American Literature*, 23, 36–37. The epigraph at the beginning of this chapter adopts the format of the transcription in *The Multilingual Anthology of American Literature*, which integrates the lines from Lucretius (in Pastorius's handwritten manuscript, they are placed in a marginal paragraph).

5. This is entirely unremarkable, as is the fact that the curiosity sparked by the selection included in *The Multilingual Anthology of American Literature*, a mass-distributed purchasable book, propelled me to the physical archive housing the non-circulating microfilm reproduction of the handwritten manuscript book artifact; it would be disingenuous of me either to obscure the real order of succession here, in the dissemination of knowledge of my research objects, or to suggest that there is anything truly lamentable in it.

6. As a commonplace book composed for private use, and not for publication, the "Beehive" cannot be said to have been created in one iteration, as one might speak of major drafts and then editions of a book manuscript composed for publication (for example, Gloria Anzaldúa's *Borderlands/La Frontera: The New Mestiza*, mentioned later in this essay). This is another interesting way in which Pastorius's text, and its particular afterlife in *The Multilingual Anthology of American Literature*, differs from its companion texts.

7. Shell and Sollors themselves, I want to be clear, make no such claims—neither in *The Multilingual Anthology of American Literature* and the other projects of the Longfellow Institute at Harvard, nor in their individual bodies of work. It would be neither just nor edifying for me to cite specific examples, here; suffice it to say that much, if certainly not all, recent U.S.-based work on contemporary plurilingual literature strikes me as too easily constrained to celebrate its chosen emergent. Often as not, as I see it, the mandate to celebrate (and promote) requires a strategic bracketing of literary print culture's material constraints on the ideal forms of pluralization being

celebrated. One might say, in this connection, that in re-rejecting the disciplinary self-reflexivity that came with "theory," literary studies seems to have lost the ethnographic self-consciousness animating the most searching work in the U.S. humanities today—in a newly but commitedly literarist anthropology.

8. Luigi Donato Ventura, *Peppino* (New York: William R. Jenkins, 1885).

9. A clear majority of the second half to second two-thirds of the manuscript book is composed in English, which is also the language in which Pastorius most often addresses his imagined reader (though he does so also in German). Nevertheless, many closely written individual leaves of the "Bee-hive" are almost entirely composed of dense transcriptions and quotations from texts in languages other than English, and his prefatory texts frequently switch languages as he "honeycombs" them with commonplaces. In one of these prefatory inscriptions (the book contains several, introducing the several versions of the entire collection that were successively composed in a single copybook), Pastorius describes it as a volume collecting the "Best out of English (or Englished) Books . . . Excepted never the less some few lines out of . . ." (this is followed by a lengthy paragraph listing Pastorius's reading in other languages). His first intention for the "Bee-hive," he continues elsewhere, was to collect proverbs and sayings for his two sons; but considering "the Copiousness of Words Phrases & Expressions in the English," he added the indexes of (English) terms with definitions and illustrations (in English, but also Latin and other languages) and the concordances found in the volume. The language spoken in England and the English colonies, he observes, is a "Mingle-mangle of Latin, Dutch, French: Relicks or Remains of the Roman, Saxon & Norman Conquests. . . . And besides those there are also Hebrew, Arabick, Greek, Italian, Spanish, Danish and Welch words in the said English Tongue." English, he writes, encompasses "not only several of that primitive Language formerly spoken in Paradise, but has abundance of almost all the rest that had their Original at Babel." Other reflections on, and embellishments of, the story of Babel are to be found elsewhere in the "Bee-hive," as are reflections on "peculiar phrases in all tongues, which can't be translated into others word by word."

10. Shell, afterword, 690–91.

11. Very frequently, when making this point (which redacts somewhat the Heidegger of "Die Zeit des Weltbildes," published in 1938), I have been challenged by another common U.S. literary-critical redaction of Heidegger's thinking, drawn from the 1954 essay "Die Frage nach der Technik" ("The Question Concerning Technology"). I mean not at all, of course, to hypostasize a spontaneist distinction between so-called "human language" and technical code; I *do* mean to suggest that this distinction operates unavoidably in U.S. literary humanities discourse, as a set of antipodes organizing us, whether or not we know, admit, or enjoy it, in the literary-humanistic disciplinarity that structures our production of knowledge—and that it is therefore *not* something we can write off with a philosophical insight. It operates also, as I hope my argument here makes clear, in the self-production of contemporary science, which is at times astonishingly obsessed with literature as a disavowable object of desire. My sense here, in other words, is that in an apparently totally administered world, the

value indeterminacy of literature and "literarity," as brute historical antecedents to the writing that is binary computer code, are still very much locked in competitive tension with the value determinacy of applied technical "systems," even *after* the functionalization of the structuring antipode (e.g., in Foucault) or its deconstruction (by Derrida, whose finally extrasystemic imagination makes him more literally useful to me, here). When I cannot win the argument any other way, I ask my humanist interlocutor to compare her professional resources to that of the campus engineers.

12. Newfield's article is a dissenting response to John Guillory's "The Sokal Affair and the History of Criticism." See Guillory, "The Sokal Affair and the History of Criticism," *Critical Inquiry*, no. 28 (2002): 470–508; and Christopher Newfield, "Critical Response I," 508–25. See also Christopher Newfield, *Ivy and Industry: Business and the Making of the American University, 1880–1980* (Durham, N.C.: Duke University Press, 2003); and Christopher Newfield, *Unmaking the Public University: The Forty-Year Assault on the Middle Class* (Cambridge, Mass.: Harvard University Press, 2008).

13. Newfield, "Critical Response I," 522.

14. Ibid., 509.

15. Ibid., 522. Obviously, this redaction of Newfield's own redaction of Lyotard's thought removes it twice from the very use to which I am putting it here. Insofar as my framing concern here (as elsewhere) is with the modalities of contemporary literary criticism itself, I think such interior duplication is not only acceptable, but useful. The relevant work is Jean-François Lyotard, *La condition postmoderne: Rapport sur le savoir* (Paris: Éditions de Minuit, 1979); Jean-François Lyotard, *The Postmodern Condition: A Report on Knowledge,* trans. Geoff Bennington and Brian Massumi (Minneapolis: University of Minnesota Press, 1984).

16. See Umberto Eco, *The Search for the Perfect Language,* trans. James Fentress (Oxford: Blackwell, 1995), 196–97: "[Kircher] celebrated polygraphy as 'all languages reduced to one' *(linguarum omnium ad unam reductio)."*

17. The definitive history is W. J. Hutchins, *Machine Translation: Past, Present, Future* (Chichester: Ellis Horwood Limited, 1986). For historical details of interwar and immediate postwar research in machine translation, extracts from archived correspondence, and some citations from journalism of the period, I rely here (as well as in chapter 3) on Hutchins's invaluable work. See also W. J. Hutchins, "From First Conception to First Demonstration: The Nascent Years of Machine Translation, 1947–1954. A Chronology," *Machine Translation,* no. 12 (1997): 195–252; and W. J. Hutchins and Evgenii Lovtskii, "Petr Petrovich Troyanskii (1854–1950): A Forgotten Pioneer of Mechanical Translation," *Machine Translation,* no. 15 (2000): 187–221. Since I first composed (in 2003) the essay that composes the current chapter, Rita Raley and N. Katherine Hayles have published valuable commentaries on several of the same anecdotes from machine translation research, as well as on the texts by Weaver discussed by Hutchins and retailed here. I have learned a great deal from Raley's and Hayles's readings, though the material here predates in composition my awareness of their work on this topic. See Rita Raley, "Machine Translation and Global English," *Yale Journal of Criticism,* no. 16 (2003): 291–314; N. Katherine

Hayles, *My Mother Was a Computer: Digital Subjects and Literary Texts* (Chicago: University of Chicago Press, 2005), 110ff.

18. Warren Weaver, "Translation," in *Machine Translation of Languages: Fourteen Essays*, ed. William N. Locke and A. Donald Booth (Cambridge, Mass.: MIT Press, 1955), 18. Also qtd. in Hutchins, "From First Conception to First Demonstration," 195.

19. "W. W." is Warren Weaver, referring to himself in the third person.

20. Weaver, "Translation," 18.

21. Ibid., 16.

22. Ibid.

23. Ibid., 22.

24. Warren Weaver, "Foreword: The New Tower," in Locke and Booth, *Machine Translation of Languages*, vii.

25. On the interwar migration of German scholars to Turkey, see Horst Widmann, *Exil und Bildungshilfe: Die deutschsprachige akademische Emigration in die Türkei nach 1933* (Bern: Herbert Lang; Frankfurt: Peter Lang, 1973); Horst Widmann, *Atatürk ve Üniversite Reformu*, trans. Aykut Kazancı and Serpil Bozkurt (Istanbul: Kabalcı Yayinevi, 2000); Bağış Erten and Atilla Lök, "1933 Reformu ve Yabancı Öğretim Üyeleri," in *Modern Türkiye'de Siyasi Düşünce Tarihi*, vol. 3, *Modernleşme ve Batıcılık*, ed. Uygur Kocabaşoğlu, 537–44 (Istanbul: Iletişim, 2002). On the disciplinary foundation of U.S. comparative literature in Istanbul (a story that includes the second migration of Auerbach and Spitzer to the United States), see Said, *The World, the Text, and the Critic*, 5–9; Apter, "Comparative Exile," 86–96; Damrosch, "Auerbach in Exile," 97–117; Mufti, "Auerbach in Istanbul," 95–125; Apter, "Global *Translatio*"; Apter, *The Translation Zone*, chap. 3; Ertürk, "Modernity and Its Fallen Languages," 41–56. See also Spivak, *Death of a Discipline*, 87, 87n19.

26. Weaver, "Translation," 17.

27. Ibid.

28. Said, *The World, the Text, and the Critic*, 8. See also Ertürk, "Modernity and Its Fallen Languages," 41–42.

29. On McLuhan and machine translation, see Brian Lennon, "Misunderstanding Media: The Bomb and Bad Translation," *Criticism* 47, no. 3 (2005): 287–88.

30. Weaver, "Foreword: The New Tower," vii.

31. Warren Weaver, "Some Recent Contributions to the Mathematical Theory of Communication," in Claude Shannon and Warren Weaver, *The Mathematical Theory of Communication* (Urbana: University of Illinois Press, 1964), 6.

32. Ibid., 25.

33. In the seven-bit ASCII system used by personal computers to encode the symbols on an English typewriter keyboard, for example, what is contained in computer memory or written to the hard drive is not an image of the letter "E," but a seven-digit binary number representing it in the ASCII code table. Each digit of the seven represents a binary (on/off) state that, when set in sequence, determines the subset of character codes generatable from that sequence as it exists thus far, with the seventh and

final bit narrowing that subset to a single character. Each state set thus affects the probability (diminishing it for some single characters, increasing it for others) of this sequence producing a particular character code.

34. Claude Shannon, "The Mathematical Theory of Communication," in Shannon and Weaver, *The Mathematical Theory of Communication*, 66.

35. The letter u, for example, might be omitted after the letter q beginning a word, since in a reasonably large selection of English words, no letter other than u follows q when q begins a word. At the level of syntax, both definite and indefinite articles might be omitted from an English sentence, since they invariably precede the nouns to which they refer. On the other hand, THE, in the sequence GOING TO THE TSREO, helps me to see that TSREO is likely a garbled common noun and not a place-name; this might be an example of controlled redundancy assisting in error correction.

36. Weaver, "Some Recent Contributions to the Mathematical Theory of Communication," 8.

37. Ibid., 26.

38. In an analogy straight out of the corporate culture of 1949, Weaver writes, "An engineering communication theory is just like a very proper and discreet girl accepting your telegram. She pays no attention to the meaning, whether it be sad, or joyous, or embarrassing. But she must be prepared to deal with all that come to her desk" (ibid., 27).

39. Ibid., 28.

40. Lawrence Venuti, "1940s–1950s," in Venuti, *The Translation Studies Reader*, 69.

41. See Walter Benjamin, "Die Aufgabe des Übersetzers," in *Gesammelte Schriften*, vol. 4 (Frankfurt am Main: Suhrkamp Verlag, 1972), 11–21; Walter Benjamin, "The Task of the Translator," in *Selected Writings*, vol. 1, 1913–1926, ed. Michael W. Jennings and Marcus Bullock, trans. Harry Zohn (Cambridge, Mass.: Belknap Press of Harvard University Press, 1996), 253–64; Carol Jacobs, "The Monstrosity of Translation," *Modern Language Notes*, no. 90 (1975): 755–66; Paul De Man, "Conclusions: Walter Benjamin's 'The Task of the Translator,'" in *The Resistance to Theory* (Minneapolis: University of Minnesota Press, 1997), 73–105; Jacques Derrida, "Living On/Border Lines," 75–176; Jacques Derrida, "Des Tours de Babel," 165–248; Jacques Derrida, *L'oreille de l'autre: Otobiographies, transferts, traductions*, ed. Claude Lévesque and Christie V. McDonald (Montreal: VLB Éditeur, 1982); Friedrich Schleiermacher, "On the Different Methods of Translating," in *Translation/History/Culture: A Sourcebook*, ed. André Lefevere, 141–66 (London: Routledge, 1992); Steiner, *After Babel*; Venuti, *The Translator's Invisibility*; Venuti, *The Scandals of Translation*.

42. Steiner, *After Babel*, 28.

43. Ibid., 323.

44. Ibid., 309.

45. Ibid., 108.

46. Venuti, *The Translator's Invisibility*, 5.

47. Ibid., 20.

48. Franco Moretti, "The Novel: History and Theory," *New Left Review,* no. 52 (August 2008): 114.

49. See Derrida, "Des Tours de Babel" (English and French); José Ortega y Gasset, "The Misery and Splendor of Translation," in Venuti, *The Translation Studies Reader,* 49–63; Venuti, *The Scandals of Translation.*

50. RAT, as Gayatri Chakravorty Spivak has put it. See Gayatri Chakravorty Spivak, "Questioned on Translation: Adrift," *Public Culture* 13, no. 1 (2001): 14.

51. Shell, afterword, 690.

52. See Derrida, "Des Tours de Babel" (French), 212–13; Derrida, "Des Tours de Babel" (English), 171: "*And he war,* lit-on dans *Finnegans Wake* . . . Le *He war* . . . se rend intraduisible en sa performance même, *au moins dans ce fait* qu'il s'énonce en plus d'une langue à la fois, au moins l'anglais et l'allemand. Se même une traduction infinie en épuisait le fonds sémantique, elle traduirait encore en *une* langue et perdrait la multiplicité du *he war.* . . . [N]otons une des limites des théories de la traduction: elles traitent trop souvent des passages d'une langue à l'autre et ne considèrent pas assez la possibilité pour des langues d'être impliquées *à plus de deux* dans un texte. Comment traduire un texte écrit en plusiers langues à la fois? Comment 'rendre' l'effet de pluralité? Et si l'on traduit par plusieurs langues à la fois, appellera-t-on cela traduire?" ("'And he war,' one reads in *Finnegans Wake.* . . . The 'he war' . . . *will have been* untranslatable in its very performance, *at least in the fact* that it is enunciated in more than one language at a time, at least English and German. Even if an infinite translation exhausted its semantic stock, it would still translate into *one* language and would lose the multiplicity of 'he war.' . . . [L]et us note one of the limits of theories of translation: all too often they treat the passing from one language to another and do not sufficiently consider the possibility for languages to be implicated *more than two in a text.* How to translate a text written in several languages at once? How is the effect of plurality to be 'rendered'? And if one translates with several languages at a time, will that be called translating?").

53. It is of course also the case that the monolingual text is, like its "monolanguage," also already a fiction: one language is, so to speak, "always already" contaminated by others. In one of Derrida's paradoxical formulations, "'donc, il n'y a pas de bilinguisme ou de plurilinguisme' . . . donc 'il n'y a que du plurilinguisme'" ("'therefore, there is no bilingualism or plurilingualism' . . . therefore 'there is only plurilingualism'"). See Jacques Derrida, *Le monolinguisme de l'autre ou la prothèse d'origine* (Paris: Éditions Galilée, 1996), 42; Jacques Derrida, *Monolingualism of the Other; or, The Prosthesis of Origin,* trans. Patrick Mensah (Stanford, Calif.: Stanford University Press, 1998), 21. My point here is merely to establish a generic difference, and not to deny that monolingual identities are, looked at more broadly, subjects of multiplicity.

54. If, as in Juan Goytisolo's *Makbara,* Spanish is the base or source language, and the text includes passages in French, English, and Darija, then the novel cannot be translated into English, French, or Darija without, as it were, "losing" that language. See Juan Goytisolo, *Makbara* (Barcelona: Editorial Seix Barral, 1980); Juan Goytisolo, *Makbara,* trans. Helen Lane (London: Serpent's Tail, 1993). For another example, see Ingeborg Bachmann, "Simultan," in *Simultan: Neue Erzählungen* (Munich: Piper

Verlag, 1972), 7–45; Ingeborg Bachmann, *Three Paths to the Lake: Stories*, trans. Mary Fran Gilbert (New York: Holmes and Meier, 1989). In both texts, passages in English in the original can only be "read" in the original. These texts can never be offered to native readers of English in translation for *them* without this loss. The "minor language" here can never assume the position of a base or source: if it does, it vanishes as a different language. Compare this with the primarily fictive, rather than textual (literal) plurilingualism of Milorad Pavić's *Dictionary of the Khazars*, which, by posing the question at the level of representation, removes its impediments to translation. David Damrosch observes that "To an unusual degree, Pavić's book openly anticipates its international circulation after publication. Pavić actually arranges matters so that his book needs to be translated in order to achieve a full expression of his themes. Intent upon breaking up linear ways of reading, Pavić stresses a consequence of the multilingualism of the 'lost' original: its entries would have been alphabetized differently in Greek, Arabic, and Hebrew, so that readers in each language would inevitably have been reading different books, arranged in a different order in each translation. Pavić's original novel can only describe the difference without embodying it, since he doesn't really want to limit his readership to the few people who could read those three languages, even assuming that he could write them all himself, which doesn't appear to be the case.... Only a fiction in the original novel, the multilingual mobility of the entries become a reality once the Dictionary was translated." See Damrosch, *What Is World Literature?* 265.

55. See Jacques Derrida, *Margins of Philosophy*, trans. Alan Bass (Chicago: University of Chicago Press, 1982), 6.

56. Weaver, "Translation," 17.

57. Venuti, *The Scandals of Translation*, 2.

58. Ibid., 10.

59. Ibid., 159.

60. Ibid., 171.

61. See Steiner, *After Babel*, 356ff.; Venuti, *The Translator's Invisibility*, 191ff.

62. Anderson, *Imagined Communities*, 43.

63. Ibid., 44.

64. Ibid., 46.

65. Venuti, *The Translator's Invisibility*, 20.

66. Theodor W. Adorno, "Wörter aus der Fremde," in *Gesammelte Schriften II: Noten zur Literatur*, ed. Rolf Tiedemann (1959; Frankfurt am Main: Suhrkamp Verlag, 1996), 225; Theodor W. Adorno, "Words from Abroad," in *Notes to Literature*, vol. 1, trans. Shierry Weber Nicholsen (New York: Columbia University Press, 1991), 192.

67. See Pierre Lepape, "Lost without Translation: English-Language Books Dominate World Publishing," *Le Monde diplomatique*, May 5, 2004; and Rich, "Wheeling and Dealing and Finding Books to Translate into Dutch."

68. Emine Sevgi Özdamar, *Mutterzunge: Erzählungen* (Berlin: Rotbuch Verlag, 1990), 10.

69. Emine Sevgi Özdamar, *Mother Tongue*, trans. Craig Thomas (Toronto: Coach House Press, 1994), 12, translation modified.

70. Both the original German edition and the Coach House Press English edition of *Mutterzunge* either phoneticize or simply omit Turkish roman letters (ç, ş, ğ, ı, and İ) absent from the German and English alphabets, and thus inconvenient to typeset.

71. Anzaldúa, *Borderlands/La Frontera*, 18.

72. My disemplacement of these two examples from the particulars of their respective social and historical contexts here is no more than a mimicry of the custodial editorship that permits these books to be published and circulated—and thus stripped from those contexts—in the first place. I accept and recast that disemplacement, here, in order to return emphasis to the conditions of contemporary literary production by which I myself, even in commenting on these texts and on that disemplacement itself, am still substantively bound.

73. Christine Brooke-Rose, *Invisible Author: Last Essays* (Columbus: Ohio State University Press, 2002). This "final publication" was followed by Brooke-Rose, *Life, End Of* (Manchester: Carcanet, 2006).

74. Brooke-Rose, *Invisible Author*, 3.

75. Ibid., 43.

76. Brooke-Rose, *The Christine Brooke-Rose Omnibus*, 446–47.

77. Ibid., 437.

78. Ibid., 418.

79. Ibid., 419.

80. Ibid., 395.

81. Ibid., 408.

82. Ibid., 428.

83. Ibid., 452.

84. The narrator recalls this phrase imperfectly, or invents it altogether. Its grammatically correct equivalent (using current orthography for the French loan word *savun*) would be "Lux sabununa hayranım."

85. Brooke-Rose, *The Christine Brooke-Rose Omnibus*, 449–50.

86. See Damrosch, *What Is World Literature?*: "There can be no more global work, conceptually speaking, than *Finnegans Wake*, yet its prose is so intricate and irreproducible that it becomes a sort of curiosity in translation. *Dubliners*, a far more localized work, has been much more widely translated and has had a far greater impact in other languages. Literary language is thus language that either gains or loses in translation, in contrast to nonliterary language, which typically does neither. The balance of credit and loss remains a distinguishing mark of national versus world literature: literature stays within its national or regional tradition when it usually loses in translation, whereas works become world literature when they gain on balance in translation" (289).

87. Hutchins, "From First Conception to First Demonstration," 238.

3. Containment

1. David O. Woodbury, "The Translating Machine," *Atlantic Monthly* 204, no. 2 (1959): 60.

2. Weaver, "Translation," 18. Also qtd. in Hutchins, "From First Conception to First Demonstration," 195.

3. See Hutchins and Lovtskii, "Petr Petrovich Troyanskii (1854–1950)," 187–221.

4. Hutchins, *Machine Translation*, 133.

5. Ibid., 59, 141.

6. See Paul N. Edwards, *The Closed World: Computers and the Politics of Discourse in Cold War America* (Cambridge, Mass.: MIT Press, 1996). Hawkins contrasted the "closed world" of dramatic space in Shakespearean tragedy, unified by place and defined by "siege" movements of invasion or escape, with Northrop Frye's pastoral "green world," permitting or encouraging "questing" flow between locations. See Sherman Hawkins, "The Two Worlds of Shakespearean Comedy," in *Shakespeare Studies*, vol. 3, ed. J. Leeds Barroll, 62–80 (Cincinnati: Center for Shakespeare Studies, 1968).

7. Marshall McLuhan, *Understanding Media: The Extensions of Man* (Cambridge, Mass.: MIT Press, 1994), 80.

8. Edwards, *The Closed World*, 14.

9. Convinced (against Shannon's own view) that the mathematical theory of communication was adequately generalizable to all existing sign systems, Weaver first emphasized a strictly cryptanalytic approach to machine translation. As Hutchins notes, this reduction of translation to cryptanalysis was almost immediately discredited (*Machine Translation*, 30). One may nevertheless think what we call "realpolitik" as an *ideologically* closed system that can and was the context for technically more "open" models of automated translation. Hutchins provides a detailed account of the "fall" of the ideal of fully automated MT in his chapter "Expectations and Criticisms: The Decade from 1956 to 1966" (in *Machine Translation*, 174–89).

10. Edwards, *The Closed World*, 3.

11. Hutchins, *Machine Translation*, 16.

12. Woodbury, "The Translating Machine," 64.

13. The ground of my argument here is, therefore, *criterial* rather than *evidential:* offering reasons to accept an interpretation, as Elizabeth Bruss put it, rather than evidence "for" it. See Bruss, *Beautiful Theories*, 44.

14. A cursory Web search turns up any number of "Nadsat glossaries" compiled by *Clockwork* enthusiasts (generally more enthusiastic about Stanley Kubrick's film adaptation than about Burgess's novel itself)—along with inventive extensions to the "language" and even Nadsat–English translating software.

15. "In the manner of Eastern Languages, Russian makes no distinction between leg and foot—*noga* for both, or hand and arm, which are alike *ruka*. This limitation would turn my horrible young narrator into a clockwork toy with inarticulate limbs." See Anthony Burgess, *You've Had Your Time* (London: Heinemann, 1990), 38.

16. Then there is the English slang—"rozz," for example, which might be a transformation of the Russian *rozha* (roughly, "ugly mug"), but which Burgess scholar Geoffrey Aggeler believes is from *rozzer,* for policeman. See Geoffrey Aggeler, *Anthony Burgess: The Artist as Novelist* (Tuscaloosa: University of Alabama Press, 1979), 172.

17. Anthony Burgess, *A Clockwork Orange* (New York: W. W. Norton, 1986), 49.

18. According to one account offered by Burgess, the novel's title is taken from a Cockney slang phrase that reminded him of Stephen Dedalus's image of the world (in *Ulysses*) as an "oblate orange"—something natural that on closer inspection turns out to be unnatural, artificial. The Cockney phrase, Burgess says, is "as queer as a clockwork orange." See Anthony Burgess, "Clockwork Marmalade," *The Listener*, February 17, 1972. In *Joysprick*, a study of Joyce's language first published one year later, Burgess implied that the phrase had evolved under the influence of Malay (in which he became fluent) on his English prose: "When I wrote a novel called *A Clockwork Orange*, no European reader saw that the Malay word for 'man'—orang—was contained in the title." See Burgess, *Joysprick: An Introduction to the Language of James Joyce* (New York: Harcourt Brace Jovanovich, 1975), 177. Thanks to Rosalind Morris for first calling this claim to my attention. On Joycean style, Russian borrowings, and Malay, see also Burgess, *Re Joyce* (New York: W. W. Norton, 1968), 187ff. Like *Clockwork*, editions of the novels of Burgess's "Malayan Trilogy" were published with glossaries keyed to the italicized Malay (and Arabic, Urdu, Tamil, and Chinese) words and phrasing interpolated into the text. See, for example, Anthony Burgess, *The Long Day Wanes* (New York: W. W. Norton, 1992). On Burgess's resistance and acquiescence to including such glossaries, see also Aggeler, *Anthony Burgess*, 37ff.

19. Aggeler calls these "loanshifts." See Aggeler, *Anthony Burgess*, 171.

20. Ibid., 170.

21. Ibid., 172.

22. Burgess, *A Clockwork Orange*, 33.

23. Burgess, "Clockwork Marmalade," 22. In *You've Had Your Time*, Burgess adds: "The novel was to be an exercise in linguistic programming, with the exoticisms gradually clarified by context: I would resist to the limit any publisher's demand that a glossary be provided. A glossary would disrupt the programming and nullify the brainwashing" (38).

24. Theodor W. Adorno, "Der Essay als Form," in *Gesammelte Schriften 11: Noten zur Literatur*, ed. Rolf Tiedemann (Frankfurt am Main: Suhrkamp Verlag, 1996), 21; Theodor W. Adorno, "The Essay as Form," in *Notes to Literature*, vol. 1, trans. Shierry Weber Nicholsen (New York: Columbia University Press, 1991), 13.

25. Burgess claimed that Alex and his gang were initially modeled on Britain's "teddy boys," then additionally, after a trip to the Soviet Union in 1961, on the *stilyagi*—"style boys"—roaming the Soviet cities of the early 1960s. See Anthony Burgess, *A Clockwork Orange: A Play with Music* (London: Hutchinson, 1987), v.

26. Robert O. Evans, "Nadsat: The Argot and Its Implications in Anthony Burgess's *A Clockwork Orange*," *Journal of Modern Literature* 1, no. 3 (1971): 406.

27. Burgess, *A Clockwork Orange*, 1.

28. Ibid., 2.

29. Ibid., 7.

30. Ibid., 27.

31. Ibid., 31.

32. Ibid., 32.

33. Ibid., 33.

34. Ibid., 143.

35. Ibid., 38.

36. Ibid., 52.

37. Ibid., 3, 26.

38. Even these strings of numerals might be read as voiced, their patterns of repetition (or iteration) and ordinal decline mimicking verbal rhythm and harmony. In speaking of the numerals as "disturbances" of vocalized language, I mean simply to mark the awkwardness of using seven- or nine-syllable "names" in conversation (especially in colloquial sentence fragments).

39. See Burgess, *A Clockwork Orange: A Play with Music:* "It struck me that it might be a good idea to create a kind of young hooligan who bestrode the iron curtain and spoke an argot compounded of the two most powerful political languages in the world—Anglo-American and Russian. The irony of the style would lie in the hero-narrator's being totally unpolitical" (vi).

40. Jean Baudrillard was one of the most adventurous post-1968 theorists of "deterrence" as a closed system, in this sense. See Jean Baudrillard, *Simulacres et simulation* (Paris: Galilée, 1981); Jean Baudrillard, *Simulations* (New York: Semiotext(e), 1983).

41. Kevin Windle has compared two 1991 Russian translations of *Clockwork:* one made by V. Boshniak, who retranslated and transliterated Burgess's Russian loan words, setting them in Latin script within the Cyrillic text for the sake of *ostranenie,* and one by Evgenii Sinel'shchikov, who adopted Burgess's own preferred method of "reversing" the languages, inserting English into the Russian text where Burgess had inserted Russian into his English. Boshniak, Windle reports, objected that the alienating effect that might have been possible in either language in 1962, when *Clockwork* was first published, had been attenuated by 1991, by which time many more educated Russians had acquired some knowledge of English, and (perhaps more importantly) English loan words had been adopted into Russian in large numbers. Boshniak's attempt at reproducing this effect by switching alphabets runs the risk, Windle observes, of reducing it to mere visuality: "This raises interesting questions in the psychology of reading, but it seems likely that in these instances a degree of *ostranenie* may be achieved in the first few pages, after which the reader might simply cease to notice the script, or would do if Boshniak's method comprised only accurate transliteration. The effect would then be purely visual, and the device, once familiar, would become transparent, before being rendered invisible, forcing one to wonder whether this method could offer even an approximate equivalent to the original in terms of its phonic (as opposed to visual) effects." See Kevin Windle, "Two Russian Translations of *A Clockwork Orange,* or The Homecoming of Nadsat," *Canadian Slavonic Papers/Revue Canadienne des Slavistes* 37, no. 1–2 (June 1995): 163–86. Windle makes a number of interesting observations on linguistic double entendres and Russian cultural references (in one case, Boshniak's allusion to Chekhov) introduced in the Russian translations where none exist in the English edition, as well as on the Russian translators' failure to see where Burgess is using a Russian loan word with an idiomatic English

meaning (for example: "I didn't so much kopat the later part of the book," where "kopat," the verb "to dig," is used in its 1960s slang sense, "to like"—but incorporated back into Russian with its *literal* meaning).

42. Robert A. Heinlein, *The Moon Is a Harsh Mistress* (New York: Tom Doherty Associates, 1966), 12.

43. Ibid.

44. Ibid., 19–20.

45. Ibid., 16.

46. Ibid., 17.

47. Ibid., 39.

48. Ibid., 30.

49. Hutchins, "From First Conception to First Demonstration," 195.

50. Adorno, "Wörter aus der Fremde," 112; Adorno, "Words from Abroad," 187.

51. Juliette Taylor considers *Ada* Nabokov's most multilingual novel. See Juliette Taylor, "'A distortive glass of our distorted glebe': Mistranslation in Nabokov's *Ada*," *Linguistica Antverpiensia*, n.s., no. 4 (2005): 265–78. Published in 1969, *Ada* is Nabokov's late work, produced after he had already decided (as Antonina Gove put it) to "moderate" his use of Russian in the fiction he composed and published in English. See Antonina Filonov Gove, "Multilingualism and Ranges of Tone in Nabokov's *Bend Sinister*," *Slavic Review* 32, no. 1 (1973): 79–90.

52. See Vladimir Nabokov, *Bend Sinister* (New York: Vintage, 1990), 42, 61, 11, 75. A typology of French and Russian words and phrasing in *Bend Sinister,* and in Nabokov's other works, can be found in Gove, "Multilingualism and Ranges of Tone in Nabokov's *Bend Sinister*."

53. French was, of course, the second language of the upper classes of prerevolutionary Russia, useful as both private language (which servants, for example, might be counted on to least often comprehend) and self-consciously public acquired language that linked its Russian speakers to the transimperial space of France. For a contrast of French as a distancing, impersonal language with Russian as "affective" and intimate in Nabokov's work, see Gove, "Multilingualism and Ranges of Tone in Nabokov's *Bend Sinister*."

54. Nabokov, *Bend Sinister,* 127.

55. Ibid., 225, text in brackets in the original.

56. In Russian *begonia* means begonia.

57. The truth or falsity of that "information" is, of course, another matter.

58. Casanova, *La république mondiale des lettres,* 270; Casanova, *The World Republic of Letters,* 272.

59. Nabokov, *Bend Sinister,* 17.

60. Ibid., 125.

61. Gove, "Multilingualism and Ranges of Tone in Nabokov's *Bend Sinister*," 89.

62. Ibid., 89–90.

63. See Marina Tsvetaeva, *Vivre dans le feu: Confessions,* trans. Nadine Dubourvieux (Paris: Robert Laffont, 2005).

64. The herculean efforts of John E. Woods, Schmidt's U.S. translator, to transpose the idiosyncrasies of Schmidt's German into U.S. English are remarkably successful, one might say, less in recreating Schmidt's German in U.S. English than in reproducing the plurilingual *problem* of Schmidt's works, as published in traditional book form, in the Anglophone sphere. See, by Arno Schmidt: *Evening Edged in Gold,* trans. John E. Woods (New York: Harcourt Brace Jovanovich, 1980); *Scenes from the Life of a Faun: A Short Novel,* trans. John E. Woods (London: M. Boyars, 1983); *Collected Novellas,* trans. John E. Woods (Normal, Ill.: Dalkey Archive Press, 1994); *Nobodaddy's Children,* trans. John E. Woods (Normal, Ill.: Dalkey Archive Press, 1995); *Collected Stories,* trans. John E. Woods (Normal, Ill.: Dalkey Archive Press, 1996); *Two Novels: The Stony Heart and B / Moondocks,* trans. John E. Woods (Normal, Ill.: Dalkey Archive Press, 1997); *School for Atheists: A Novella = Comedy in 6 Acts,* trans. John E. Woods (Los Angeles: Green Integer, 2001).

65. Like three other late novels, Schmidt's *Zettels Traum,* a 1,334-page metafiction, was composed on outsized paper for reproduction in facsimile. See Arno Schmidt, *Zettels Traum* (Karlsruhe: Stahlberg, 1970); for a recent study of this work in English, see Volker Max Langbehn, *Arno Schmidt's Zettel's Traum: An Analysis* (Rochester, N.Y.: Camden House, 2003).

66. Other novels often grouped with KAFF auch MARE CRISIUM include *Schwarze Spiegel* (1951), *Die Gelehrtenrepublik* (1957), and *Die Schule der Atheisten* (1972). For a brief overview of these works, see Ursula Heise, "The Intellectual after World War III: Arno Schmidt's Science Fiction," *Electronic Book Review* 7 (Summer 1998): http://www.altx.com/EBR/REVIEWS/rev7/r7hei.htm (accessed January 5, 2010).

67. Characteristically, "KAFF" also contains a play on the English "chaff," referring to the wealth of "realia" inserted into both twin narratives in the form of astronomical, agricultural and botanical data, biblical and historical citations, mathematical tables, and contemporaneous news.

68. See John E. Woods, "Translator's Introduction," in Schmidt, *Collected Stories,* xiii; and Langbehn, *Arno Schmidt's Zettel's Traum,* 67ff.

69. See, for example, the works of Friedhelm Rathjen, including *Inselwärts: Arno Schmidt und die Literaturen der britischen Inseln* (Scheeßel: Edition ReJoyce, 2008); *Westwaärts: Arno Schmidt und die amerikanische Literatur* (Scheeßel: Edition ReJoyce, 2007); *Dritte Wege: Kontexte für Arno Schmidt und James Joyce* (Scheeßel: Edition ReJoyce, 2005); *Dublin, Bargfeld: Von James Joyce zu Arno Schmidt* (Frankfurt am Main: Bangert and Metzler, 1987). For a critical overview of Schmidt criticism itself, see Robert Weninger, *Framing a Novelist: Arno Schmidt Criticism 1970–1994* (Columbia, S.C.: Camden House, 1995).

70. Arno Schmidt, KAFF auch MARE CRISIUM (Baden-Baden: Stahlberg Verlag, 1960), 16–17; Schmidt, *Two Novels,*165.

71. One such passage mixes plays on Hertha's "collages" (*Kollahschn*) and "decollages" (*Dee=Kollahschn*) with a French proverbial invocation of homosexuality ("Ventre affamé n'a pas d'oreilles?") and concludes with a Greco-Roman catalogue of

pederastic terms ("Lesbizein Labda Laikastria Oris stuprum andrizomai siphniazein phoinikizein keletezein"). See Schmidt, KAFF auch MARE CRISIUM, 51.

72. Schmidt, KAFF auch MARE CRISIUM, 18; Schmidt, *Two Novels*, 165–66.

73. Schmidt, KAFF auch MARE CRISIUM, 19.

74. Schmidt, *Two Novels*, 166.

75. Schmidt, KAFF auch MARE CRISIUM, 83–84.

76. Schmidt, *Two Novels*, 217.

77. Schmidt, KAFF auch MARE CRISIUM, 41.

78. Ibid., 89.

79. Schmidt, KAFF auch MARE CRISIUM, 224; Schmidt, *Two Novels*, 324.

4. Language Memoir and Language Death

1. See Derrida, "Living On/Border Lines," 75–176; Derrida, "Des Tours de Babel" (English), 165–248; Derrida, "Des Tours de Babel" (French), 203–33.

2. I make this distinction for several reasons. One is that I believe we owe to literary and cultural criticism and scholarship itself (and even to its adamantly personal iterations, such as Kaplan's "On Language Memoir") that caution, originally derived from rejection of the intentional fallacy, now more than routinely extended to works of literature: the recognition, in other words, that even rigorous scholars may not always intend what they mean (and that good scholarship, like any good writing, often means more than it intended to). Another reason is that Kaplan's essay is now very much part of our recent critical history, a critical history that is (only now) beginning to be taken up and advanced by other academic scholars, in a way that (as I will suggest) both preserves *and*, unavoidably, damages its "personal" spirit. As the undisputed point of origin of the critical phrase "language memoir"—the source one must cite in any responsibly capacious discussion—Kaplan is now a character in an academic critical story, the reception story of a (small) wave of critical attention, as well as a working writer and scholar. It is with all these things in mind, then, that I speak with critical distance of "Kaplan's narrator."

3. Kaplan, "On Language Memoir," 59.

4. Even taken merely on their own fundamentally sociological grounds, Kaplan implies, the identity-paradigms of existing scholarship are insufficiently capacious. National and national-ethnic identity, for example, is trivially noncongruent with group identity marked by native competence in a particular language or languages, while class identity can be compromised by "cultural capital" including language competence, or lack thereof, *as* culture. (The same can be said of some modifications of these paradigms, such as the inversion, in postcolonial studies, of nationality into exile: a figure erasing the violence of forced migration, even—or especially—of group extinction.) One would have to add also that race and gender, though excluded from Kaplan's narrator's typology of sociological reading "screens," can also be understood, within the framework Kaplan's narrator sets out, as reifying experience *in* language. One would have to add "also also," then, that like national and national-ethnic identity, class position, and geocultural displacement (that of migration as well as exile), race

and gender are factors that *need* to be read for, and which *nonexclusively* mark out a spectrum of possible, permutable readings.

5. Kaplan, "On Language Memoir," 59.

6. In addition to Kaplan, "On Language Memoir," see Aneta Pavlenko, "Language Learning Memoirs as a Gendered Genre," *Applied Linguistics* 22, no. 2 (2001): 213–40; Mary Besemeres and Maureen Perkins, "Translated Lives," special issue, *Mots Pluriels,* no. 23 (March 2003): http://motspluriels.arts.uwa.edu.au/; Cowley, "Lost and Found"; Kramsch, "The Multilingual Experience." Kaplan groups together Alfred Kazin, *A Walker in the City,* Nabokov, *Speak, Memory,* Richard Rodriguez, *Hunger of Memory,* Eva Hoffman, *Lost in Translation: A Life in a New Language,* and her own *French Lessons: A Memoir,* comparing them with works of postwar French literature including Sartre, *Les Mots,* Nathalie Sarraute, *Enfance,* Annie Ernaux, *La Place,* and Mehdi Charef, *Le Thé au Harem d'Archi Ahmed.* Pavlenko, who views contemporary language memoir as a U.S. literary development, adds Julia Alvarez, *Something to Declare,* Andrei Codrescu, *The Disappearance of the Outside,* Judith Ortiz Cofer, *Silent Dancing: A Partial Remembrance of a Puerto Rican Childhood,* Cathy Davidson, *Views of Mount Fuji: On Finding Myself in Japan,* Ariel Dorfman, *Heading South, Looking North: A Bilingual Journey,* Maxine Hong Kingston, *The Woman Warrior,* Natasha Lvovich, *The Multilingual Self: An Inquiry into Language Learning,* M. Elaine Mar, *Paper Daughter: A Memoir,* Kyoko Mori, *Polite Lies: On Being a Woman Caught between Cultures,* David Mura, *Turning Japanese: Memoirs of a Sansei,* Karen Ogulnick, *Onna Rashiku (Like a Woman): The Diary of a Language Learner in Japan,* Luc Sante, *The Factory of Facts,* and Richard A. Watson, *The Philosopher's Demise: Learning French.*

7. Kaplan, "On Language Memoir," 69.

8. Where "life writing" seems once to have stood in for *biography,* contemporary scholarship has repurposed the term as a substitute for *autopublication* itself. It is in this second, more radical sense, which posits a non- or semipublic practice of writing brought into visibility by publication—and which seems more common to ethnography, trauma and disability studies, and areas of rhetoric and composition than to literary studies as such—that I here counterpose "life writing" to "language memoir."

9. Kaplan, "On Language Memoir," 60.

10. This is a more or less deliberate echo of Jameson's either mistaken or misunderstood (and in either case duly maligned) thesis on "Third World national allegory." It shouldn't be necessary to revisit either "Third-World Literature in the Era of Multinational Capitalism"—published in 1986, it is now two micro-epochs behind us—or the corrections (Ahmad et al.) it provoked, which are now also part of our common sense. Suffice it to say that in resisting a vision of world literature stripped of the particularities of national origin, Jameson counterprivileged peripheral national writers visible on the (scholarly) world stage—just one problem here being, perhaps, that the totality of Third World national allegory was nowhere near total *enough,* structurally excluding the (subnational, untranslated, unpublished, unread) writer who fails in one way or another to make it to the (scholarly) world stage. This is, of course, as others have said more eloquently, to naturalize the position of a dominant ("published")

class within the dominated (literary?) Third World—a naturalization I am trying to resist here in dwelling on the (material) difference between writing and publication that is an "oversight" of *symptomal* scholarly reading practice. See Fredric Jameson, "Third-World Literature in the Era of Multinational Capitalism," *Social Text,* no. 15 (1986): 65–88; Aijaz Ahmad, "Jameson's Rhetoric of Otherness and the 'National Allegory,'" *Social Text,* no. 17 (Autumn 1987): 3–25.

11. Kaplan, "On Language Memoir," 59, 64.

12. Margaret K. Willard-Traub, "Rhetorics of Gender and Ethnicity in Scholarly Memoir: Notes on a Material Genre," *College English* 65, no. 5 (2003): 512. Besemeres and Perkins, by contrast, make explicit claims for language memoir as a new genre, claims to which the academic form of preface to a special issue of a journal is, of course, virtually bound; Kramsch, on the other hand, pointedly names language memoir "a fashionable genre in popular publishing"—then goes on (perhaps in an effort to undermine its popularity, or its fashionability) to extend the categorical momentum of language memoir to a work of fiction, Christine Brooke-Rose's *Between,* and an autobiographical work of philosophical writing, Derrida's *Le monolinguisme de l'autre (Monolingualism of the Other).* Arguing from sociolinguistics, meanwhile, Pavlenko's recognition of language memoir as a distinct genre is part of an intervention in her own discipline: an attempt to force attention to the formal attributes of literary texts, which social-science methodologies, she suggests, often fail to distinguish from "data." Here the taxonomic study of literary genre—a practice that the poststructuralists among us tend to regard, today, as "containing" literary indeterminacy—is a practice of structuration restoring literary qualities to the (a) text. See Besemeres and Perkins, "Translated Lives"; Kramsch, "The Multilingual Experience"; Pavlenko, "Language Learning Memoirs as a Gendered Genre."

13. Douglas Hesse, "The Recent Rise of Literary Nonfiction: A Cautionary Assay," *JAC: A Journal of Composition Theory* 11, no. 2 (1991): 323–33.

14. Paul De Man, "Autobiography as De-facement," *MLN* 94, no. 5 (1979): 921; Paul De Man, *The Rhetoric of Romanticism* (New York: Columbia University Press, 1984), 70.

15. Paraphrasing Ross Chambers, Thomas O. Beebee describes this as genre's generation of "noise." See Beebee, *The Ideology of Genre: A Comparative Study of Generic Instability* (University Park: Pennsylvania State University Press, 1994), 17.

16. David Crystal, *Language Death* (Cambridge: Cambridge University Press, 2000), ix.

17. I have in mind here, of course, Edward Said's indictment of "textualist" literary theory as invested in mystified, collusive silence. See Edward W. Said, *The World, the Text, and the Critic,* 3–4.

18. Instructive here is Jacques Rancière's critique of the intellectual paranoia, or "displacement of non-relation," that moves at all costs against literary "madness." See Rancière, "Althusser, Don Quixote, and the Stage of the Text"; Rancière, *La Chair des mots: Politiques de l'écriture.*

19. Daniel Heller-Roazen does just that in his *Echolalias: On the Forgetting of Language* (Cambridge, Mass.: MIT Press, 2005), a work whose form points in the other

direction, as it were, toward the practice of scholarship *as* writing in philosophical, rather than personal essayism. Thanks to Ben Conisbee Baer for pointing me to Heller-Roazen's essay on language death, setting off a chain of associations that (eventually) became the present essay.

20. Crystal, *Language Death*, 1.
21. Ibid.
22. Ibid., 2.
23. Ibid.
24. Jacques Derrida, *Mal d'Archive: une impression freudienne* (Paris: Éditions Galilée, 1995), 13; Jacques Derrida, *Archive Fever: A Freudian Impression,* trans. Eric Prenowitz (Chicago: University of Chicago Press, 1998), 3.
25. Derrida, *Mal d'Archive,* 27; Derrida, *Archive Fever,* 17.
26. Crystal, *Language Death*, 35.
27. Ibid.
28. Laura Wides-Munoz, "'Star-Spangled Banner' in Spanish Draws Protest," Associated Press, April 28, 2006. Of course, part of the furor concerned a yet-to-be-released remixed version that altered some of the lyrics to criticize U.S. immigration law. Still, most negative public reaction, including that of the April 28, 2006, public statement by President George W. Bush, focused strictly on the issue of (official) language difference. See Terence Hunt, "Sing It in English: Bush Opposes Hispanic National Anthem," Associated Press, April 28, 2006; and Terence Hunt, "Oh, Say, We Can't See US Anthem in Spanish: US Senators," Agence France Presse, May 2, 2006. The following week, outgoing White House press secretary Scott McClellan went out of his way to rebut claims that Bush himself had sung the anthem in Spanish during the 2000 electoral campaign, insisting several times that Bush's Spanish was too poor for such an accomplishment. See "White House Says Bush Doesn't Speak Spanish All That Well."
29. Crystal, *Language Death*, 37.
30. See Timothy Brennan, "The Cuts of Language: The East/West of North/South," *Public Culture* 13, no. 1 (2001): 39–63; and Timothy Brennan, *Wars of Position: The Cultural Politics of Left and Right* (New York: Columbia University Press, 2006).
31. Brennan, "The Cuts of Language," 56.

<h2 style="text-align:center">5. The Other Other Literature</h2>

1. Saussy, "Exquisite Cadavers," 3.
2. Gönül Pultar, "Ethnic Fatigue: Başçılar's Poetry as a Metaphor for the Other 'Other Literature'," in Shell and Sollors, *The Multilingual Anthology of American Literature,* 124–39.
3. "Transpiring through the verses and inextricably entwined," Pultar writes of Başçılar's poems, "are such compelling themes as loneliness, exile *(sürgün),* migration *(göç),* and *hüzün,* that untranslatable word connoting sadness and melancholy, a sort of *tristessa,* which, looked at from one angle, are all traditional motifs in Turkish

poetics. . . . What is this sense of 'weariness' that emerges from the sadness, the *tristessa* of the transplant, articulated with such melancholy during a moment of *défaillance* by a persona of poetry that seems to encompass the whole of the poetry, as one big cry in the desert? What does it symbolize/signify? I suggest that this 'ethnic fatigue,' as I would like to term it, is a syndrome, perhaps long in the making, now surfacing more compellingly than ever, that is an apt metaphor for the other 'other American litera-ture,' the non-Anglophone one." See Pultar, "Ethnic Fatigue," 128, 135.

4. See Harry Harootunian, "Remembering the Historical Present," *Critical Inquiry* 33, no. 3 (2007): 471–94.

5. For an extended argument of this point, conducted by bringing scholarly argumentation to meet its poiesis, see Susan Howe, *The Birth-mark: Unsettling the Wilderness in American Literary History* (Hanover, N.H.: Wesleyan University Press/ University Press of New England, 1993). "I am drawn toward the disciplines of his-tory and literary criticism," Howe writes, "but in the dawning distance a dark wall of rule supports the structure of every letter, record, transcript: every proof of authority and power. I know records are compiled by winners, and scholarship is in collusion with Civil Government. I know this and go on searching for some trace of love's in-folding through all the paper in all the libraries I come to" (4). For more on Howe's negotiation of such double reading, see Stephen Collis, "Archival Tactics and the Poet-Scholar: Susan Howe and Charles Olson," *West Coast Line* 36, no. 2 (2002): 60–76. Walter Benn Michaels's critique of Howe is worth consulting as well; see Walter Benn Michaels, *The Shape of the Signifier: 1967 to the End of History* (Princeton, N.J.: Prince-ton University Press, 2004), 1–18.

6. Diana Taylor, "Remapping Genre through Performance: From American to Hemispheric Studies," *PMLA* 122, no. 5 (2007): 1416–17. Taylor argues that an understanding of "America" as a performance forces scholars to "rethink not only their object of analysis but also, more important, their scholarly interactions." In this con-text—which invokes, among other things, the relationship between the "creative" writers of U.S. literature and its critical analysts—one might also think of what Fredric Jameson wrote, early in his career, of the deeply personal and essayistic work of Walter Benjamin, now enormously influential (if seldom imitated) in U.S. literary and cul-tural studies. The philosophy of modernity, Jameson suggests, is almost always resigned to modernity, accepting intellectual specialization as fate and displacing its hopes for re-enchantment onto someone else: the artist or writer. Benjamin is unique, Jameson says, in that, rejecting that resignation, he "wants to save his own life as well." See Fredric Jameson, *Marxism and Form: Twentieth-Century Dialectical Theories of Litera-ture* (Princeton, N.J.: Princeton University Press, 1972): 61–62.

7. See Orhan Pamuk, *İstanbul: Hatıralar ve Şehir* (Istanbul: YKY, 2003); Orhan Pamuk, *Istanbul: Memories and the City*, trans. Maureen Freely (New York: Vintage International, 2006). My citations from the Turkish original here are in my own trans-lation unless noted otherwise. Freely's English edition of the book is strongly editorial (in consultation with the author), omitting some material and explanatorily expand-ing other material for a U.S. readership; while I have consulted it with profit, when I

cite it directly here, I cite it more as a kind of intermediate, rather than primary source. *İstanbul: Hatıralar ve Şehir* appeared in Turkish in 2003, in Finnish translation in 2004, and in a U.S. English translation (from Knopf) in 2005, along with Greek and Dutch translations. German, Italian, Croatian, Russian, Spanish, Serbian, Portuguese, French, and Catalan versions followed in 2007. Where decisively less than hegemonic languages are concerned, of course, a translation is often produced today by translation from the English translation itself, rather than by translating from the original text (this is the case, for example, with the Swedish translation of *İstanbul*).

8. One chapter in *İstanbul* adopts the name of Conrad's 1911 novel *Under Western Eyes*. Much of the late action in Pamuk's 2002 novel *Kar (Snow)*, as a simulated revolution erupts in Kars in eastern Turkey, turns on the protagonist Ka's representation of himself as having connections to the *Frankfurter Rundschau*, which, it is hoped, might publish the declaration authored by a political group.

9. One might say with some justice that Pamuk, who has taken the stance of a Turkish and world public intellectual keeping the academy at a mildly anti-intellectual arm's length, is more interesting to read symptomatically than idiopathically (in this, the philosophical engagement with ethical quandaries in his work is somewhat weaker than that of, say, Assia Djebar, or J. M. Coetzee).

10. This attenuates somewhat the competitive authority of the translator, in her claim to a specially *practical* form of expertise (something on which Lawrence Venuti, for example, frequently insists, and which stands in productive tension, in his work, with his genuine allegiance to the implacably antinomian double reading of poststructuralism). I am not celebrating this dynamic, still less suggesting it is the best object of interest, as the otherwise searching new work of Rebecca Walkowitz, for example, sometimes appears to do; neither, on the other hand, am I simply deploring it. See Rebecca L. Walkowitz, "Unimaginable Largeness: Kazuo Ishiguro, Translation, and the New World Literature," *Novel* 40, no. 3 (2007): 216–41.

11. For a reading of this dynamic in Pamuk's earlier works, see Ian Almond, "Islam, Melancholy, and Sad, Concrete Minarets: The Futility of Narratives in Orhan Pamuk's *The Black Book*," *New Literary History* 34, no. 1 (2003): 75–90.

12. See Cecilia Enjuto Rangel, "Broken Presents: The Modern City in Ruins in Baudelaire, Cernuda, and Paz," *Comparative Literature* 59, no. 2 (2007): 140–57.

13. On Pamuk's "Ottomanesque" "mixed style" in Turkish, which makes "impressionistic use of Perso-Arabic, Turkish and pure Turkish *(öz Türkçe)* language registers" (Erdağ Göknar, "My Name is Re(a)d: Authoring Translation, Translating Authority," *Translation Review* 68 [2004]: 52), see Esim Erdim Payne, "The Visible Translator: The Transformation of a Literary Text from the Sublime to the Picturesque," in *In Memory of Richard B. Klein: Essays in Contemporary Philology*, ed. Felice A. Coles, 159–73 (University, Miss.: Romance Monographs, 2005); Göknar, "My Name is Re(a)d," 52–60; Güneli Gün, "Something Wrong with the Language: A Translator Responds to Her Critics," *Times Literary Supplement*, no. 5006 (1999): 14; Esim Erdim, "The 'Survival' of a Literary Text: The Transformation of Images from the Sublime to the Picturesque in Güneli Gün's Translation of Orhan Parmuk's 'Kara Kitap'" (PhD diss.,

Kent State University, 1999). One might describe both Göknar's and Gün's translation practices, in their own testimony (and in the interpretation of Payne, in the case of Gün's work), as broadly Poundian, in the manner of Pound's translations of Cavalcanti: they construct an English analogue for Pamuk's style by displacing the Arabic–Persian–Turkish lexis of the original into Latinate, Anglo-Saxon, and contemporary U.S. English registers, as well as through *comparable*, rather than reproductive syntactic effects. As practicing translators, both are understandably more invested in the (difficult, and hermeneutical) necessity than in the impossibility of translation (a feature of Lawrence Venuti's exposition of Pound's practice, as well)—though both dwell at some length on why "it [*sic*] so difficult for Turkish literature to survive out of its cultural context" (Göknar, "My Name is Re(a)d," 56), as well as the tokenizing effects of corporate publishing's "reduction of a literary heritage onto one major writer per generation" (ibid., 57). See also Ezra Pound, "Guido's Relations," in Venuti, *The Translation Studies Reader*, 26–33; and Venuti, *The Translator's Invisibility*, 34ff. Unsurprisingly, that which in Pamuk's work is flat-out untranslatable appears to be more interesting in its untranslatability to those who analyze existing translations, rather than perform (and assume authority for) them. Dilek Kantar and Yeşim Aksan, for example, look closely at the narratorial "cognitive barrier" of the Turkish grammatical evidentiality marker *-mIş* and the consequences of its direct nonreproducibility in English. Specifically, they remark on the nonreproducibility of the double voicing of the Venetian slave narrator's discourse in *Kara Kitap*, in a scene where the narrator declares his refusal to convert to Islam. Where in the Turkish original the repertive *-mIş* marker clearly distinguishes the pasha's speech from the slave narrator's in which it is reported, in English translation, Kantar and Aksan write, "It is not clear whether these words belong to the *pasha* or to the narrator. In the Turkish version, this hybrid has reportive function, where in the English rendition it blurs the lines of the Easterner's and the Westerner's attitude toward religious conversion." See Kantar and Aksan, "A Linguistic Cross between Form and Content in Fiction," in *Bridges and Barriers in Metalinguistic Discourse*, ed. Urszula Okulska, Polish Studies in English Language and Literature 17 (Frankfurt am Main: Peter Lang, 2006), 363–64. On what the authors call the "hybrid text" of untranslatable Turkish locutions embedded in the English translation of *Kara Kitap* and "burdened with associations that are unacceptable to the target reader" (237), see Klaus Gommlich and Esim Erdim, "Evolving Imagery in the Translation of Orhan Pamuk's Kara Kitap," *Across Languages and Cultures* 2, no. 2 (2001): 237–49. Of the untranslatable and untransposable culturally specific double meaning of the lexically hybrid phrase "apartman karanlığı," the authors note that "To the Turkish reader, the phrase has, at least, two meanings: a certain section of a building, thus a certain physical space, and a certain psychological space that this physical space is associated with. The pun is lost on a target culture reader. . . . Only a reader who has experienced 'westernisation' and 'economic growth' in the form of hideous apartment edifices will have the necessary cultural background to recognise the airshaft as a symbol of the extension of the Ottoman past into the present modern Republic of Turkey" (243–44).

14. Pamuk, *İstanbul*, 98.

15. Ibid., 290.

16. Ibid., 291. The phrases "You are pushed" and "Yes sir you are pushed" appear in English in the original Turkish edition; the English word "pushed" is homonymous with a derogatory Turkish colloquialism *(puşt)* for a male homosexual. There is much more to be said about this, of course—including about the appeal to homophobia through which one is invited to enjoy this anecdote.

17. Ibid., 298.

18. Ibid., 101.

19. Ibid., 102.

20. This presumes that we are willing to consider 2001 something of a "break" or cut in history. That of course is debatable. Arguably, it is a break or cut in critical *discourse*, at the very least.

21. Eva Hoffman, *Lost in Translation: A Life in a New Language* (New York: Penguin, 1989), 4.

22. Ibid., 91.

23. Ibid., 105.

24. Ibid., 108.

25. Ibid., 208–9.

26. Ibid., 273.

27. Ibid., 274–5.

28. See Emily Apter's commentary on Leo Spitzer's essay "Türkçeyi Öğrenirken" ("Learning Turkish" or "While Learning Turkish") in *The Translation Zone*, 27ff.

29. An important exception is David Damrosch; see especially his *We Scholars: Changing the Culture of the University* (Cambridge, Mass.: Harvard University Press, 1995). On this topic, see also Marshall Brown, "Multum in parvo; or, Comparison in Lilliput," in Saussy, *Comparative Literature in an Age of Globalization*, 249–58; and, for a related example, Kadir, "Comparative Literature in an Age of Terrorism," 68–77. Noting the disjunction between affirmations of the need for more "creative" comparative scholarship and *actions* taken to enable, encourage, and actually enact it, Brown observes, "Not much of Caryl Emerson's admiration for [Mikhail] Epstein's [anti-scholarly] whimsy and her recognition of the ludicrousness of self-importance survives in the contributions to [the 2004 report of the American Comparative Literature Association]" (256). If Brown's own prescription—for more "fun" in comparative literature—could only be made by someone with relative job security and seniority (like other anti-alarmist contributors to the report), that does not entirely obviate his point, which is that—to transpose Brown's Anglophile essayism into the continental version it resists—scholars ought not so tenaciously to deny themselves circulation in a "libidinal" economy.

30. See Marianna Torgovnick, "Experimental Critical Writing," *ADE Bulletin*, no. 96 (Fall 1990): 8–10; and, for a different perspective, Jeffrey Williams, "The New Belletrism," *Style* 33, no. 3 (1999): 414–42.

31. Gini Alhadeff, *The Sun at Midday: Tales of a Mediterranean Family* (New York: Pantheon Books, 1997), 17.

32. Anzaldúa, *Borderlands/La Frontera*, 18.

33. Alice Kaplan, *French Lessons: A Memoir* (Chicago: University of Chicago Press, 1993), 201.

34. Ibid., 52.

35. Ibid., 70.

36. Ibid., 40.

37. Ibid., 12.

38. See Derrida, *Margins of Philosophy*, 6.

39. Kaplan, *French Lessons*, 13.

40. Ibid., 98.

41. Ibid., 146.

42. Özdamar, *Mutterzunge*, 7; Özdamar, *Mother Tongue*, 9. In standard German, *die Zunge* (the physical organ of the tongue) does *not* also mean "language" (that word is *die Sprache*, and the word for "mother tongue," *die Muttersprache*) as it can in Turkish (and many other languages). *Dil*, the modern Turkish word for the physical organ, also means "language"; "mother tongue" is *anadil*, which Özdamar *transposes* here, rather than translates, into German as *Mutterzunge*. (Because the English "tongue" is a *metonym* for "language," *anadil* translates directly into standard English—in Thomas's English translation, for example—bypassing the "foreignized" German of *die Mutterzunge*.)

43. For an illuminating analysis of the contrast of Turkish "testimonial" speech with German documentary discourse in Max von der Grün's book *Leben im gelobten Land: Gastarbeiterporträts* (1975), see Arlene Akiko Teraoka, "Talking 'Turk': On Narrative Strategies and Cultural Stereotypes," *New German Critique*, no. 46 (Winter 1989): 104–28.

44. See Feridun Zaimoğlu, *Kanak Sprak: 24 Misstöne vom Rande der Gesellschaft* (Hamburg: Rotbuch Verlag, 1994); Feridun Zaimoğlu, *Koppstoff: Kanaka Sprak vom Rande der Gesellschaft* (Hamburg: Rotbuch, 1998).

45. Özdamar, *Mutterzunge*, 75; orthography as in original.

46. See Zafer Şenocak, "Dialog über die dritte Sprache: Deutsche, Türken und ihre Zukunft," in *Atlas des Tropischen Deutschland* (Berlin: Babel Verlag, 1992), 85–90.

47. For a survey of positions in such work, see Agnes Lugo-Ortiz et al., "Forum: Conference Debates," *PMLA* 122, no. 3 (2007): 805–14—the edited publication of papers delivered as part of a MLA 2006 annual convention session entitled "Ethnic Studies in the Age of Transnationalism."

48. Theresa Hak Kyung Cha, *Dictee* (Berkeley: University of California Press, 2001); Theresa Hak Kyung Cha, *Dictée* (Berkeley: Third Woman Press, 1993); Theresa Hak Kyung Cha, *Dictée* (New York: Tanam Press, 1982).

49. For scholarship on *Dictée* especially attentive to the work's plurilingualism, see Eric Hayot, "Immigrating Fictions: Unfailing Mediation in *Dictée* and *Becoming Madame Mao*," *Contemporary Literature* 47, no. 4 (2006): 601–35; Josephine Nock-Hee Park,

"'What of the Partition': *Dictée*'s Boundaries and the American Epic," *Contemporary Literature* 46, no. 2 (2005): 213–42; Sue J. Kim, "Apparatus: Theresa Hak Kyung Cha and the Politics of Form," *Journal of Asian American Studies* 8, no. 2 (2005): 143–69; Eun Kyung Min, "Reading the Figure of Dictation in Theresa Hak Kyung Cha's *Dictée*," in *Other Sisterhoods: Literary Theory and U.S. Women of Color*, ed. Sandra Kumamoto Stanley, 309–24 (Urbana: University of Illinois Press, 1998); Shelley Sunn Wong, "Unnaming the Same: Theresa Hak Kyung Cha's *Dictée*," in *Writing Self, Writing Nation*, ed. Elaine H. Kim and Norma Alarcón, 103–40 (Berkeley: Third Woman Press, 1994). Of interest, as well, is how Cha scholarship vacillates in the symbolic dilemma posed by the work's title: is it the French "dictée," replete with accent aigu, of the first two editions—or the typographically anglicized "dictee" under which the University of California Press also (and inconsistently) publishes and catalogues the book? Sue Breckenridge suggests to me that omission of the accent aigu may reflect typographic convention, for capitalized French titles, or typographic constraints in cover design and/or electronic cataloging (all of which seem plausible).

50. Kandice Chuh, "Of Hemispheres and Other Spheres: Navigating Karen Tei Yamashita's Literary World," *American Literary History* 18, no. 3 (2006): 631, 633.

51. Ibid., 633, 634.

52. See Cherríe Moraga, *Loving in the War Years: Lo que nunca pasó por sus labios* (Boston: South End Press, 1983); Cherríe Moraga and Gloria Anzaldúa, eds., *This Bridge Called My Back: Writings by Radical Women of Color*, 2nd ed. (Latham, N.Y.: Kitchen Table–Women of Color Press, 1984); Gloria Anzaldúa, "Speaking in Tongues: A Letter to Third World Women Writers," in Anzaldúa and Moraga, *This Bridge Called My Back*, 165–73; Anzaldúa, *Borderlands/La Frontera*; Cherríe Moraga, *The Last Generation* (Boston: South End Press, 1993); Cherríe Moraga, *Waiting in the Wings: Portrait of a Queer Motherhood* (Ithaca, N.Y.: Firebrand Books, 1997); Gloria Anzaldúa and AnaLouise Keating, *Interviews/Entrevistas* (New York: Routledge, 2000).

53. See Anzaldúa, *Borderlands/La Frontera*, 18; Aimé Césaire, *Cahier d'un retour au pays natal*, ed. Abiola Irele (Columbus: Ohio State University Press, 2000), 15. See also Anzaldúa, *Borderlands/La Frontera*, 81: "Until I am free to write bilingually and to switch codes without having always to translate, while I still have to speak English or Spanish when I would rather speak Spanglish, and as long as I have to accommodate the English speakers rather than having them accommodate me, my tongue will be illegitimate."

54. Anzaldúa, *Borderlands/La Frontera*, 232: "For example, they take the passages in which I talk about *mestizaje* and borderlands because they can more easily apply them to their own experiences. The angrier parts of *Borderlands*, however, are often ignored as they seem to be too threatening and too confrontational."

55. Anzaldúa, "Speaking in Tongues," 167.

56. Anzaldúa, *Borderlands/La Frontera*, 165.

57. Henry Staten, "Tracking the 'Native Informant': Cultural Translation as the Horizon of Literary Translation," in Bermann and Wood, *Nation, Language, and the Ethics of Translation*, 116.

58. Shelley Fisher Fishkin's 2004 presidential address to the American Studies Association, which begins and ends by invoking Anzaldúa's work, is a good introduction to this struggle in a U.S. studies now looking back at itself, as well as at its own first wave of disciplinary deprovincialization, over the intervening historical marker "9/11." See Shelley Fisher Fishkin, "Crossroads of Cultures: The Transnational Turn in American Studies (Presidential Address to the American Studies Association, November 12, 2004)," *American Quarterly* 57, no. 1 (2005): 17–57.

59. Any specialist will note that many other important groups of, and individual authors are omitted here—and indeed, elsewhere in this book, in which I might profitably have discussed the work of Louis Wolfson, for example, as well as the more recent work of writers like Giannina Braschi, Coco Fusco, Guillermo Gómez-Peña, Shirley Geok-lin Lim, and those writers whose enactments of and meditations on plurilingualism appear, for example, in Isabelle De Courtivron's and Steven G. Kellman's valuable sources of sources *Lives in Translation* and *Switching Languages,* volumes I have used with profit in my course "Language Memoirs." See Isabelle De Courtivron, ed., *Lives in Translation: Bilingual Writers on Identity and Creativity* (New York: Macmillan, 2003); and Steven G. Kellman, ed., *Switching Languages: Translingual Writers Reflect on Their Craft* (Lincoln: University of Nebraska Press, 2003). Too, I might have followed more explicitly in the footsteps of critics like Kellman, in his *The Translingual Imagination* (Lincoln: University of Nebraska Press, 2000), and Martha J. Cutter, in her *Lost and Found in Translation: Contemporary Ethnic American Writing and the Politics of Language Diversity* (Chapel Hill: University of North Carolina Press, 2005). (This may be a good time to reread this book's preface.) As elsewhere, however, it would be senseless for me to attempt a catalogue of such work, here—either to pretend to a comprehensiveness that is anyway impossible, given my *critical goal,* or to gratify gatekeepers in the many specialized subfields and sub-subfields that are tangent here. For one such comprehensive catalogue (which is in fact more inclusive than its title may imply), see Laura Callahan, *Spanish/English Codeswitching in a Written Corpus* (Amsterdam: John Benjamins, 2004). Where the archival work of W. J. Hutchins, as a historian of machine translation, has served as one material base for my reflections in this book, Callahan's work in the sociolinguistics of literature has (along with that of Aneta Pavlenko) served as another. The invaluable documentary meticulousness of all three researchers is irreproducible here, where my goal, as a collaborator extending the conclusions all three leave to afterthought, has been to reflect on the conditions of possibility of future iterations of the extant objects they compile with such confidence—that *positivism* being the only meaningful limitation, or indeed liability, of their work. Too late to acknowledge properly—let alone to do this book any good— I discovered the polemical sociological and sociolinguistic work on translation of Anthony Pym, which grapples with this problem and much more. See, for example, Anthony Pym, "On the Pragmatics of Translating Multilingual Texts," *JoSTrans: The Journal of Specialized Translation,* no. 1 (January 2004): 14–28; Pym, "Translation après coup: On Why Translation Studies Has a Specific Object" (2007): http://www.tinet .org/~apym/on-line/translation/2007_liege (accessed January 12, 2010); Pym,

"Humanizing Translation History" (2008): http://www.tinet.org/~apym/on-line/research_methods/2008_humanizing_history_hermes.pdf (accessed January 12, 2010).

60. Paul Allatson, foreword, to Susana Chávez-Silverman, *Killer Crónicas: Bilingual Memories/Memorias Bilingües* (Madison: University of Wisconsin Press, 2004), x.

61. Spahr, "Connected Disconnection and Localized Globalism," 90.

62. Harootunian, "Remembering the Historical Present," 475.

AFTERWORD

1. Ken Whistler, "Why Unicode Will Work on the Internet," posted by timothy, Slashdot, June 9, 2001, http://slashdot.org/features/01/06/06/0132203.shtml (accessed January 12, 2010). See also Steven J. Searle, "A Brief History of Character Codes in North America, Europe, and East Asia," TRON Web, 2004, http://tronweb.super-nova.co.jp/characcodehist.html (accessed January 12, 2010); Steven J. Searle, "Unicode Revisited," TRON Web, 2004, http://tronweb.super-nova.co.jp/unicode revisited.html (accessed January 12, 2010).

2. Norman Goundry, "Why Unicode Won't Work on the Internet," Hastings Research Internet Papers Index, June 4, 2001, http://www.hastingsresearch.com/net/04-unicode-limitations.shtml (accessed January 12, 2010).

3. Francesca Orsini, "India in the Mirror of World Fiction," *New Left Review*, no. 13 (January–February 2002), 87.

4. Umberto Eco, *La ricerca della lingua perfetta nella cultura europea* (Bari: Laterza, 1993); Umberto Eco, *The Search for the Perfect Language* (Oxford: Blackwell, 1995).

5. That is, as speculative and investigative, rather than rule-based or rule-limited.

Index

1968 (as politically significant year), xiv, 15, 17, 84, 176n.13, 210n.40
1991 (as politically significant year), 168, 169, 188n.46, 210n.41

academic profession: anticolonial critique of, 141; bureaucratic character of, xi, 7, 64, 147, 177n.14, 180n.3, 187n.28; careerism in, 7, 52–53, 141–42; circumscription of, xiv, 7, 10, 21, 34, 39, 134–35; culture wars in, 64; as determined by imperial cultural legacies, 144; discourse of, ix–x, 2–3, 81, 129; eccentricity in, 52–54; ideal formations, 53–54; marginal formations, 53–54; modes of discipline in, xv, 123, 153; theory wars in, 138
Achebe, Chinua, 43, 49
ACLA (American Comparative Literature Association), xv, 220n.29
Adorno, Theodor W., 112, 124, 155, 206n.66, 209n.24, 211n.50
African English, 48–49
Aggeler, Geoffrey, 103, 208n.16, 209nn.18–21

Ahmad, Aijaz, 214n.10
Aksan, Yeşim, 219n.13
Alhadeff, Gini, 155, 221n.31
Allatson, Paul, 164–65, 224n.60
allegory: historical, 100; linguistic, 96; national, 214n.10; national language, 109, 128, 154; technical, 168; world literary, 152, 168, 214n.10
Almond, Ian, 218n.11
Alvarez, Julia, 214n.6
American studies. See U.S. American studies
Anand, Mulk Raj, 197nn.43, 46
anarchism, 40, 173, 196n.33
Anderson, Benedict, 57, 79–80, 194n.23, 200n.3, 206n.62
anglicization, 24, 34, 82, 103, 109, 150, 222n.49
Anglocentrism, 2, 35, 110
anticolonial: critique of the academy, 141; language politics, 47–48
Antin, Mary, 151
antinomy: of literary-critical practice, 142; of plurilingualism in translation, xviii, 11, 24–25, 123, 127, 136;

225

Charef, Mehdi, 214n.6
Chávez-Silverman, Susana, 155, 164–65
Chicana/o literature, 162–64, 190n.57
Chicana/o studies, 164, 187n.37,
    191n.66
Chinese (language), 57, 66, 77, 99, 160,
    170, 172, 209n.18
Chomsky, Noam, 73
Chow, Rey, xv, 179n.20, 181n.3
Chuh, Kandace, 161, 222nn.50–51
circulation: in global travel, 86–87; of
    literary-critical concepts, 3, 183n.13,
    220n.29; of literary texts, xiv, 18, 19,
    23, 33–34, 35, 36, 42, 48, 52, 58, 74,
    91, 100, 143, 144, 145, 149, 207n.72
closed system, 97–98, 111, 130, 208n.9,
    210n.40
closed world, 96, 208n.6
code: binary digits, 69–70, 167–68,
    203n.33, 204n.35; difference of
    language from, 63, 170, 201n.11; as
    language, 69; as model for translation,
    6, 65–66, 72, 73, 96, 112, 208n.9; and
    poetry, 64; as translatable, 64
code mixing, 44
code-switching, xiv, 154, 163; literary, 5,
    56, 116, 164, 222n.53
Codrescu, Andrei, 214n.6
Coetzee, J. M., 218n.9
Cofer, Judith Ortiz, 214n.6
cold war, ix, 62, 93, 96–97, 99, 111–12;
    language politics, 107; literary
    plurilingualism, 100, 117; metaphors,
    96
colonial condition of language, 47, 50
colonialism, 29, 30, 33, 47, 50, 78
Common European Framework for
    Language Learning and Teaching, 10
Commonwealth literature, 49, 197n.43,
    198n.66
communication, 23, 53, 65, 66, 68, 73,
    75, 99, 123, 124, 127, 156, 157, 163,

189n.49, 197n.43; mathematical
    theory of, 65–72, 79, 95, 204n.38,
    208n.9
comparative literature, xv, xviii, 2, 5, 40,
    68, 124, 141, 145, 146, 153, 155, 164,
    168, 220n.29; foundation of, 2,
    203n.25; new, 153, 165
computation, 64, 66, 68, 74, 96, 98, 107,
    188n.49
computational linguistics, 67
Conrad, Joseph, 218n.8
constitution: of Australia, 191n.1; of
    Canada, 191n.1; of India, 191n.1; of
    South Africa, 191n.1; of Switzerland,
    191n.1; of the United States of
    America, 192n.1
consumer. *See* reader
contact: incommensurability as/in, 6,
    137, 138; linguistic, 5, 49, 109, 111,
    135; rigorous vs. casual, 137, 111,
    137, 163; strong vs. weak, 8, 163
containment: as cold war metaphor,
    96–97; editorial, of foreign languages,
    10, 44, 150, 158, 161; as textual
    politics of cold war U.S. literature,
    93–122; of writing by books as
    commodities, 12, 154, 157, 177n.13
contemporary literature, xiii, xiv, 2, 4,
    10, 58, 80, 126, 159; archive of, 59,
    74, 81, 84, 85, 153, 154, 159, 171,
    176n.5, 198n.57; criticism and
    scholarship of, 19, 39, 177n.14;
    teaching of, 24, 127
content, literary, xiv, 4, 5
conversion, religious, 137–39, 219n.13
core (diagrammatic concept), 17, 36–
    39, 41, 47, 67, 90, 144, 146
cosmopolitanism, xiv–xv, 23, 25, 37–38,
    79, 89, 90, 91, 110, 111, 112, 127,
    138, 152, 186n.26, 196n.41
Courtivron, Isabelle De, 223n.59
Cowley, Peter, 25, 191n.67, 214n.6

185n.25, 193n.10, 194nn.16–17,
195n.24, 204nn.40–41, 46–47,
205n.49, 206nn.57–61, 218n.10,
219n.13
Verfremdungseffekt, 133. *See also*
defamiliarization
vernacular, 18, 32, 44, 46, 47, 50, 56, 78,
80, 113, 197n.43
voice, 10, 14, 16, 43, 104–5, 158, 164,
189n.55, 210n.38, 219n.13

Walcott, Derek, 34, 35, 43
Walkowitz, Rebecca L., 218n.10
Wallerstein, Immanuel, 19, 36, 39, 172,
189n.52, 196nn.25, 33
Watson, Richard A., 214n.6
weak plurilingualism. *See under*
plurilingualism
Weaver, Warren, 65–72, 73, 77, 94, 95,
100, 111, 112, 203nn.18–24, 26–27,
30–32, 204nn.36–39, 206n.56,
208nn.2, 9
Weinrich, Harald, 36–37, 39, 182n.6,
196nn.27–28, 34
Welsh (language), 43, 136, 201n.9
Whorf, Benjamin Lee, 6, 126, 135,
184n.19
Wiener, Norbert, 65, 66, 112
Willard-Traub, Margaret K., 128–29,
215n.12

Williams, Jeffrey, 220n.30
Wolfson, Louis, 223n.59
Wong, Shelley Sunn, 222n.49
Woods, John E., 212n.64
world economy, 36
worlding, as critical act, 7, 10, 21,
34–35
world literary space, 36, 38
world literature: African writing in
English as, 48; allegory of, 152, 168,
214n.10; antinomy of, xvii, 136;
debates, xv, xvi, xviii, 171; at Euro-
Atlantic limit, 23, 146; Indian writing
in English as, 47; as kitsch, xvii; as
label, 37; models of, 19–20, 40, 172,
218n.10; paradigms, 148; as system
vs. scene, xvi–xvii, 171
world republic of letters, 19, 36,
189n.52
world-structure, 18, 35, 38–39
world-system, ix, xvi, 18, 19, 28, 35–36,
38, 40, 58, 67, 95, 144, 172, 173
Wright, Richard, 43

Yamashita, Karen Tei, 160–62
Yiddish (language), 11, 12, 13, 156,
187n.32
Yoruba (language), 49

Zaimoğlu, Feridun, 158, 221n.44

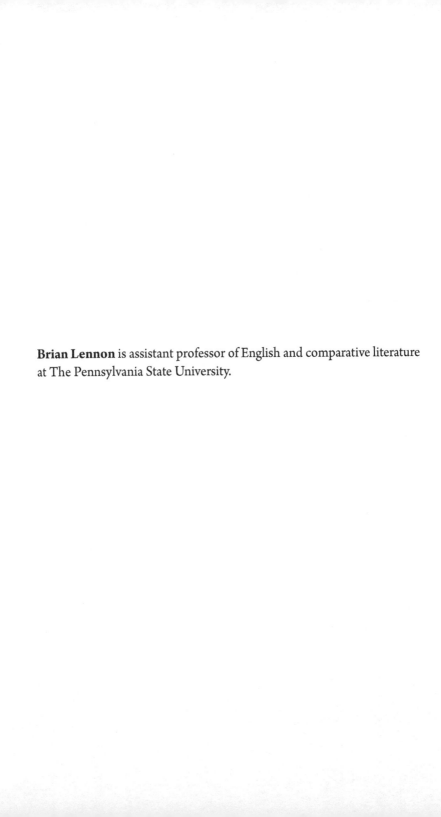

Brian Lennon is assistant professor of English and comparative literature at The Pennsylvania State University.

Lightning Source UK Ltd.
Milton Keynes UK
UKHW012154280220
359530UK00002B/138

9 780816 665020